The Vice Presidents

The Vice Presidents

*Biographies of the 45
Men Who Have Held the
Second Highest Office in
the United States*

by

Carole Chandler Waldrup

McFarland & Company, Inc., Publishers
Jefferson, North Carolina, and London

To my beloved granddaughter,
Allison M. Speagle

British Library Cataloguing-in-Publication data are available

Library of Congress Cataloguing-in-Publication Data

Waldrup, Carole Chandler, 1925–
    The vice presidents : biographies of the 45 men who have held the
second highest office in the United States / by Carole Chandler
Waldrup.
        p. cm.
    Includes bibliographical references and index.
    ISBN 0-7864-0179-6 (library binding : 50# alk. paper)   ∞
        1. Vice-Presidents — United States — Biography.   I. Title.
E176.49.W34   1996
973'.099 — dc20
    [B]   96-30538
                                                                                                    CIP

Manufactured in the United States of America

McFarland & Company, Inc., Publishers
    Box 611, Jefferson, North Carolina 28640

Table of Contents

Acknowledgments

No one writes a book without people helping in the background, and I want to take this opportunity to thank my son, Charles, for his assistance and advice on the research necessary to complete the book. My thanks go also to my daughter, Nancy Speagle, and my mother, Portia Chandler, for their unfailing encouragement and support and to my husband, Vester Waldrup, for his assistance with household chores and his willingness to endure scanty meals at times while the manuscript took shape.

Preface

Our vice presidents have been ridiculed and belittled from the time the office was first occupied, even by some of the occupants. The first vice president, John Adams, said, "My country has in its wisdom contrived for me the most insignificant office that ever the invention of man contrived or his imagination conceived."

The fault, if any, lies not with the men who have been vice presidents, but with the Constitution which assigns them only one duty — that of presiding over the Senate and casting tie-breaking votes.

It is time these men were recognized for their accomplishments in other areas of their lives, and in this book I tell about their achievements and abilities.

More than 30 percent of our vice presidents have ultimately become president, either by election in their own right or when the president died. Since the ratio is that high, it would behoove political party leaders to choose vice presidential candidates more for their character and abilities than for balancing the ticket geographically. Does the state in which a candidate lives really matter to most voters?

I hope the readers enjoy the book as much as I did when writing it. Researching is similar to solving a mystery, and I enjoy uncovering information I did not know before. I obtained most of my facts from reference books in the libraries at the University of North Carolina in Chapel Hill and in my local Pack Memorial Library in Asheville, North Carolina.

Carole C. Waldrup

1. John Adams

John Adams of Massachusetts had the distinction of being elected our first vice president, serving with President George Washington. Later Adams was elected our second president.

John Adams was born on October 20, 1735, in Braintree, now Quincy, Massachusetts. He was a great-great-grandson of pilgrims John and Priscilla Alden. John's father, for whom he was named, was a farmer and a craftsman of leather articles such as harnesses and shoes. He was a member of the local militia and served as constable, selectman, and tax collector in his township. His example contributed to his son's strong sense of obligation to serve his town.

John Adams's mother, whose maiden name was Susanna Boylston, had a much weaker inclination for public service. In fact, she resented her husband bringing home orphans and indigents for her to feed and provide with sleeping accommodations. After her husband's death, she remarried Lieutenant John Hall.

John Adams began his earliest education at home with his father as teacher, but as he later advanced, he went to Joseph Cleverly's Latin school. The boy hated both Cleverly and his school, preferring mathematics to Latin. The last school he attended was operated by Joseph Marsh, and in 1751, at age 16, young John Adams enrolled in Harvard College.

In 1755, Adams graduated with a bachelor of arts degree. He studied law with James Putnam of Worcester and was admitted to the bar in 1758.

Adams enjoyed reading, fishing, and hiking; he often hiked five miles a day. When reading, he made marginal notations in his books to express his opinions about various passages. He started smoking tobacco at age eight and never completely stopped.

John Adams also enjoyed the company of young women, especially in college, but according to his own statement, he remained celibate until his marriage to Abigail Smith on October 25, 1764.

Abigail had been a sickly child who never attended any formal school. She was tutored at home by her father, the Reverend William Smith, and she spent all the rest of her life reading in a quest for more knowledge. She was one of our most intelligent first ladies, and she held a firm belief that women were equal to men in worth.

John Adams. Reproduced from the collections of the Library of Congress.

Abigail and John Adams had five children born to them during their marriage; the eldest son, John Quincy, would be our sixth president.

John and Abigail had a good marriage. Abigail stayed home, caring for their five children and the family farm without complaining, while John worked diligently to help colonists achieve their dream of becoming an independent country with their own government. In his growing law practice, John met other patriots who shared the same goals.

When he was elected a member of the Continental Congress representing Massachusetts in 1774, John Adams saw an opportunity to enlist the aid of southern colonists in the struggle for freedom from British rule. Adams nominated George Washington from Virginia to be commander in chief of the newly organized Continental army, and Washington was chosen.

John Adams had a firm belief that the colonies must be united for the good of all. Regionalism would be fatal to a new democratic government in his view. Each state needed to furnish men to serve in the new army.

John Adams could not be a soldier himself because he was then in his forties and overweight. Instead he entered the diplomatic field while other colonists fought the Revolutionary War. The new country needed financial aid to succeed, and Adams went to France in 1778 and again in 1780 seeking aid.

Adams's diplomacy failed him in his contacts in France with Benjamin Franklin, who was serving as foreign minister to that country. Adams was appalled by Franklin's flirtations and romantic involvement with French women, and he threatened to report Franklin's behavior to officials in the colonies.

Upon failing to obtain French aid, Adams went on to Holland, and in 1782 he secured a large loan guarantee from Dutch officials. The next year he returned to France to sign the Treaty of Paris, in which the British government acknowledged the independence of the United States. Benjamin Franklin and John Jay also signed the document.

In 1785, John Adams was named the American minister to the Court of St. James. There he endured three frustrating years of constant snubs and refusals by British officials to establish diplomatic and commercial relationships with the United States.

Abigail had been shocked and disgusted with the citizens of France most of the time she lived in that country, and she welcomed the move to England. Their presentation to the Royal Court was cooly received, however. Ordinary English citizens also seemed to harbor resentment toward Americans, and Abigail felt bored and useless there while a large staff of servants ran her household. She decided she preferred to gain any further knowledge of Europe from history and geography books.

At last, John requested that he be recalled home. When they reached their Massachusetts home, John Adams learned that the formation of the new government for the United States was already underway. General George Washington was the apparent public favorite to be the first president, and John Adams was certain he deserved to be the first vice president.

When the election was held, George Washington received a unanimous vote from all 69 electors, while John Adams received only 34 votes. If John had aspired to the presidency, he would have been defeated. Both men were strong Federalists who believed in rule by a wide-ranging national government.

Adams had a passion for detail, and he wanted every part of the new government to be perfect. After he and General Washington took office, he agonized about how he should properly address President Washington. Should he be called "His Highness" or some other lofty title? Since John was himself both vice president and president of the Senate, did his duties overlap or did he leave one position while serving in the other?

Such queries only earned rude remarks and derisive names for Adams from other government officials. He was called "His Superfluous Excellency," "His Rotundity," and "Duke of Braintree."

In fact, John Adams had long been a student of political science and knew more about the theory of government than did George Washington. Both men made an honest effort, however, to do what was right for the country instead of taking actions which would insure their reelection. They were a good team.

John Adams was short in stature, somewhat roly-poly in appearance, plain in his dressing, and blunt in his speech. He was perceived as an honest man even by his enemies. He was a loyal supporter of President Washington through both his terms in office. When President Washington was elected for a second term, Adams received 77 electoral votes for vice president to 50 votes cast for Governor George Clinton of New York, the opposition candidate.

John Adams had mixed feelings about his job as vice president. He felt honored by being elected twice, but he said it was "the most insignificant office that ever the invention of man contrived or his imagination conceived." He said the office required severe duty, and it was not a kind of duty adapted to his character, being "too inactive and mechanical."

John Adams was not alone in finding his vice presidency irksome. The senators over whom he presided resented his condescending attitude toward them, as well as his instructions about their responsibilities and how they should vote on various issues.

Adams was convinced he was President Washington's logical successor. He endured two terms as vice president because he believed that was the best way to insure his election as president.

When President Washington decided two terms were enough in 1796, John Adams began campaigning for the top post. He was insulted when Samuel Adams, his patriot cousin, supported Thomas Jefferson in his bid to become the second president of the United States. Jefferson was a Democrat-Republican or anti-Federalist who espoused states rights over federal control.

John Adams became the nation's second president when he received 71 votes in the electoral college to Thomas Jefferson's 68. As was the custom at the time, as runner-up, Thomas Jefferson automatically became vice president. It was the first bipartisan election in the nation's history.

Adams hoped he and Jefferson could work together for the well-being of the country, as he and President Washington had done. Jefferson, however, resented both his defeat, and Adams's attitude toward France and its government. Adams had published articles before the election in which he compared the French government structure unfavorably with that of the United States. Thomas Jefferson admired France and its citizens greatly, and he called President Adams a monarchist.

President John Adams's intense dislike for France and her government caused a major crisis in the new government of the United States. France requested aid from the United States in her war with Britain that had recently begun. When aid was not forthcoming, French officials refused to meet with any agents of the United States government concerning France's imprisonment of American sailors who were working on British ships when France pirated the cargo of the ships.

President Adams sent three agents to talk to the French foreign minister, Talleyrand. The three agents sent by Adams were Elbridge Gerry, Charles Pinckney, and John Marshall. In official dispatches back to the United States, these agents referred to the French officials with whom they conferred as X, Y, and Z. These French officials demanded a bribe and a large loan from the United States government for the privilege of even negotiating with Talleyrand.

President Adams was so angry about the demands that he wanted to go to war with France, and he recalled George Washington to resume his former position as commander in chief of the armed services. The second effort to effect a political settlement was successful, however, and war was averted.

When President Adams signed the Naturalization, Alien, and Sedition Acts into law in 1798, the break with Vice President Thomas Jefferson was complete. The two men no longer spoke to each other. The acts gave President Adams and his government the right to imprison or expel any person considered dangerous to the United States government, and any native of any enemy country could also be imprisoned or expelled. Vice President Jefferson considered the laws to be insulting to French people currently in the United States.

The capital of the United States was located first in New York, then in Philadelphia, and finally at a permanent site on the Potomac River. On November 1, 1800, President John Adams slept for the first time in the new White House in Washington, District of Columbia, on the Potomac River. He was the first president to sleep in the White House.

Abigail was sick and did not arrive until a few days later. She found the White House incomplete and still under construction, but she had their furniture put in place and did not complain.

President Adams had high hopes he would be nominated to serve a second term, but Thomas Jefferson was nominated on the Democrat-Republican ticket, as was Aaron Burr, and they won over John Adams and Charles Pinckney, the Federalist candidates. Adams had negotiated a peace agreement with France by this time, but this achievement was not enough to enable him to win the race.

The election process was disrupted when Thomas Jefferson and Aaron Burr each received the same number of electoral votes. Jefferson was elected on the 36th ballot by the House of Representatives.

During his last hours in office, President Adams appointed many judges on the federal level in an attempt to influence the new administration; his appointees included John Marshall, named to be chief justice of the Supreme

Court. Many of the appointees did not receive their commissions before Thomas Jefferson was inaugurated.

On the morning of President Jefferson's inauguration, John Adams left by stagecoach for his home in Massachusetts. He did not attend the ceremony, but it is uncertain if he chose not to attend or if he was not invited. President Jefferson was outraged by Adams's attempt to "pack the courts" with Jefferson's enemies before leaving office.

Back home in Massachusetts, former president Adams tended his farm and started working on his autobiography. Despite his frequent statements throughout his life that he did not think he would live to reach old age, John Adams lived to the age of 90.

By a strange coincidence, John Adams and Thomas Jefferson both died on the same day — July 4, 1826, the 50th anniversary of the signing of the Declaration of Independence. They had resumed their former friendship in 1812 in the wake of personal troubles and losses of loved ones.

Bibliography

Burleigh, Anne Husted. *John Adams.* New Rochelle, N.Y.: Arlington House, 1969.
Hosmer, James K. *Samuel Adams.* American Statesmen Series. New York and London: Chelsea House, 1980.
Levin, Phyllis Lee. *Abigail Adams.* New York: St. Martin's Press, 1987.
Shaw, Peter. *The Character of John Adams.* Chapel Hill: University of North Carolina Press, 1976.
Shepherd, Jack. *The Adams Chronicles.* Boston: Little, Brown, 1975.
Smith, Page. *John Adams.* 2 vols. New York: Doubleday, 1962.

2. Thomas Jefferson

Thomas Jefferson served reluctantly as vice president for President John Adams. Their relationship was so stormy that the two men were not even speaking to each other by the time their four-year term ended.

Thomas Jefferson was born on April 23, 1743, on the Virginia family plantation called Shadwell. His father, Peter Jefferson, was a strong, vital Welshman who was a member of the Virginia House of Burgesses (the legislative body of the state before the Revolutionary War), a justice of the peace, sheriff of Albemarle County, and a lieutenant colonel in the Virginia militia. Thomas admired his father and probably got his passion for public service from him.

Thomas' mother, whose maiden name was Jane Randolph, was a member of one of Virginia's leading families. She was born in London and had come to Virginia as a young girl.

Some of Jane Randolph's relatives believed she had married beneath her station when she married Peter Jefferson. Possibly Thomas resented their attitude, for he and his mother were never close, even though he lived at home until he was twenty-seven years old.

Thomas Jefferson's education began at a small school operated by a tutor in the courtyard of the Jefferson family home, but at age nine, he entered a private school (at Dover Church). It was located several miles from his home, so young Thomas had to board with the operator of the school, the Reverend William Douglas, and his family. Thomas spent summers at home.

When Peter Jefferson died in 1757, Thomas returned home to serve as nominal head of the household and family. He enrolled at a school in Fredericksville, near enough so that he could spend weekends at home with his family.

The teacher at this school was the Reverend James Maury, an Anglican clergyman for whom Jefferson developed a strong dislike. When he was only fourteen or fifteen, Jefferson repudiated every principle espoused by Maury, and he did not forget his overwhelming objections to his teacher's ideas when he reached adulthood. One of his chief aims during the Revolution was to rid the country of the pervasive power of the Anglican church.

On January 14, 1760, Jefferson wrote his guardian, Colonel John Harvie, to ask permission to attend William and Mary College in Williamsburg, saying, "I

Thomas Jefferson. Reproduced from the collections of the Library of Congress.

suppose I can pursue my studies in the Greek and Latin as well there as here, and likewise learn something of the Mathematics."

The college was helpful to Thomas Jefferson in many ways, including broadening his social contacts. Williamsburg was the scene of balls and parties such as he had never seen, and he enjoyed the change. He graduated in April 1762.

From the time he left college until 1767, Jefferson studied law with attorney George Wythe in Williamsburg. He was not impressed by the language and usage of the laws, but after he was admitted to the bar in 1767, he was a success and attracted aristocratic clients from Virginia families such as the Pendletons, Pages, and Randolphs.

Jefferson married a wealthy widow, Martha Wayles Skelton, on January 1, 1772. They had a total of six children born of their marriage, but only two lived to reach adulthood. After Martha's death in 1782 at age thirty-three, Thomas never remarried.

In December 1768, Jefferson had been elected a member of the Virginia House of Burgesses, where he served continuously until 1775. His public duties required his absence from home frequently, and sometimes he was gone for several weeks at a time.

When sentiment developed against British rule, Jefferson was a willing participant in plans to alter relationships between Britain and her colonies. He was elected to serve as a delegate to the Continental Congress, which was formed to discuss and formulate requests to British officials to broaden and recognize the rights of American colonists.

Jefferson wrote a document entitled *A Summary View of the Rights of British America*, addressed to King George III, in which he told the king that "Kings are the servants, not the proprietors of the people."

The ultimate result of the efforts of Jefferson and his fellow dissidents was the Declaration of Independence, which was written by Jefferson and approved by the Continental Congress on July 4, 1776.

From 1776 until 1779, Jefferson served as a member of the Virginia House of Delegates, which was charged with formulating a code of laws for the new free state of Virginia. Thomas Jefferson also introduced a bill called "Establishing Religious Freedom," which was adopted in 1786. It stated specifically, "No man shall be compelled to frequent or support any religious worship, place or ministry whatsoever."

On June 1, 1779, Jefferson became the wartime governor of his state, but with an inadequate militia to repel the invaders, Virginia was occupied by British forces in May 1781. He resigned and told the legislators they needed a military governor. An inquiry concerning his actions ensued after Governor Thomas Nelson, Jr., took office, but Jefferson was declared innocent of any wrongdoing.

On September 6, 1782, Martha Jefferson died, and Thomas was devastated by grief for weeks afterward. He had been in constant attendance at her bedside for four months before her death.

When Jefferson resigned as governor, he never meant to go back into politics, but his loneliness after Martha's death was so profound that he decided to seek relief in public activity.

In May 1784, Jefferson was asked by the Congress to go to France to assist John Adams and Benjamin Franklin in peace negotiations with Great Britain. He went, taking along his oldest daughter, Martha, whom he enrolled in a convent school. He left his two younger daughters in Virginia with his sister-in-law, Elizabeth Eppes. Young Lucy Jefferson died of whooping cough in her aunt's home in October 1784.

In 1785, Jefferson's book entitled *Notes on the State of Virginia* was published. He was deeply saddened by the death of his young daughter and enraged by what he perceived to be neglect in her care. He determined to bring his other daughter, six-year-old Maria, to be with him in France, especially after he learned he would replace Benjamin Franklin as minister to France.

Finally, in May 1787, Maria Jefferson sailed for France, accompanied by her personal maid, Sally Hemings, as a companion. When she got to France, she did not remember either her father or her sister, whom she had not seen in the past three years.

It has been rumored for years that Thomas Jefferson took Sally Hemings, a slave at his Virginia home of Monticello, as his mistress while she and Maria lived with him in Paris. This theory has never been proved, however, and was disputed by relatives and friends who knew him well. Other men, including some of Jefferson's own relatives, could have been the fathers of Sally Hemings's children.

Thomas Jefferson was greatly impressed by the beautiful and gentle manners of French aristocrats, but he was appalled by the poverty and misery of the vast majority of ordinary French citizens. He supported the French Revolution as a necessary evil to improve living conditions in the nation.

If Jefferson was disappointed that he was not nominated to be the first president or first vice president of the United States, he never told anyone. General George Washington was a public hero who was elected to be the first president by an unanimous electoral vote, and he was the obvious choice. John Adams received the next highest number of electoral votes and became vice president. Jefferson was appointed by President Washington to be the nation's first secretary of state.

When President Washington announced near the end of his first term that he did not plan to seek reelection, both John Adams and Thomas Jefferson wanted to succeed him. They and their supporters were so vehement in their insistence on their rival claims to the office that President Washington became alarmed that the new government might collapse and agreed to accept the nomination for a second term.

Thomas Jefferson resigned as secretary of state at the beginning of President Washington's second term and returned to his home in Monticello.

When President Washington retired from politics in 1796, both Thomas Jefferson and John Adams were candidates for the highest office. John Adams received seventy-one electoral votes and became president; Jefferson got sixty-eight and became vice president. By this time their opposing viewpoints were well known, and there was little communication between them.

The lack of activity in his office as vice president bothered Jefferson. He was never consulted by President Adams about anything. To occupy his time when he was not presiding over the Senate, Jefferson wrote a manual of parliamentary practice that is still used by the Senate.

Thomas Jefferson, John Adams, and Aaron Burr all ran for president in the election of 1800. Jefferson and Burr received the same number of electoral votes, with Adams third. Jefferson was elected president by the United States House of

Representatives on the thirty-sixth ballot. Aaron Burr was named vice president, and they were inaugurated on March 4, 1801.

President Jefferson resented President Adams's last-minute appointments of judges chosen from a group of men who were known to be Jefferson's political enemies. He said, "It seemed but common justice to leave a successor free to act by instruments of his own choice" in a letter to former first lady Abigail Adams.

Jefferson considered the national debt a sacred obligation, and he protested Secretary of the Treasury Alexander Hamilton's negligence in paying the debt.

When he moved into the "great castle," which would be called the White House in later years, Thomas Jefferson found his new home had vast dimensions but no staff. Abigail Adams told him he needed thirty servants. His salary was $25,000 a year, and during the first year he spent $6500 for food, $2700 for servants' salaries, and at least $3,000 for wines.

President John Adams did try to leave seven horses and two carriages for the new president's use, but when Congress learned Adams had used money appropriated for furnishings to buy the riding equipment, the congressmen ordered the horses and carriages sold and the proceeds returned to the furnishings fund.

With $12,000 now in the furnishings fund, President Jefferson asked Dolley Madison, wife of his secretary of state, James Madison, to help him choose furnishings for the mansion, and he hired architect Benjamin H. Latrobe to make the "great castle" a suitable home for a president of the United States. Dolley Madison also served as the president's hostess at official state dinners and other functions.

President Jefferson reduced the size of the United States Navy by five frigates and the number of captains from nineteen to none. On March 16, 1802, an act was passed to reduce the army strength from about 4,500 men to 3,312. He planned to apply the money saved to make payments on the national debt.

President Jefferson fought the Federalist laws he did not like. He got a Judiciary Act passed in 1802 which nullified most of the judicial appointments President Adams made before he left office. The Alien and Sedition Acts were abolished, and the residency requirement for a person to become a naturalized citizen was reduced to five years. The federal tax on alcohol was repealed.

Thomas Jefferson was lonely in Washington without his family, and he begged his daughters to visit him. They exchanged letters frequently, but that was not the same as seeing them. When none of them came, he made a long visit home to Monticello and found they had had the measles and had been unable to travel.

In 1803, President Jefferson initiated the successful purchase of the Louisiana Territory for three cents per acre, for a total of $15 million. The acquisition doubled the land area of the United States.

In 1804 the Twelfth Amendment to the Constitution was ratified, which required electors to vote separately for a president and vice president. This amendment was the direct result of the tie vote for Jefferson and Burr in the last election and the controversy it caused.

Vice President Burr was unsatisfactory in his position, and for his second term, President Jefferson chose Governor George Clinton of New York to be his vice president. The two men held opposing views on many subjects, however. Clinton supported former vice president Burr and had been an active opponent to the ratification of the Constitution.

President Jefferson had been interested for years in the land west of the Mississippi River, and he commissioned Merriweather Lewis and William Clark to explore the West after he had concluded the Louisiana Purchase in 1804. Their exploration continued for thirty months, and they traveled eight thousand miles.

Jefferson was forced to partially lift the embargo imposed on both Britain and France between 1807 and 1809 because of serious financial repercussions to the American economy.

In March 1807, President Jefferson signed a bill into law which forbade the importation of slaves into the United States. While it did not stop the slave trade, the numbers were greatly reduced.

Thomas Jefferson was subpoenaed in 1807 as an official witness in the trial of Aaron Burr, his former vice president, for treason; he was requested to furnish documents to the court pertinent to the case. Jefferson invoked executive privilege and did not appear, nor did he release the papers.

At the end of his second term, Thomas Jefferson returned to his plantation at Monticello. "I resume with delight the character and pursuits for which nature designed me," he wrote a friend. "I talk of . . . seeding and harvesting with my neighbors, and of politics too, if they choose."

After his retirement, Jefferson stayed busy with daily tasks. He rode forty miles or more each week on horseback, supervising his farms, grist mill, and furniture shop. His real focus in retirement, however, was on founding a university in Virginia. He designed the buildings, helped select the library books, helped interview professors, and oversaw construction of the buildings in person.

Jefferson was a creative thinker who invented a clock which showed the day of the week as well as the time of day. He had a dumbwaiter lift installed in a fireplace cavity to bring up wine bottles from the cellars of his home, and he invented swivel chairs.

Thomas Jefferson had letters from inventors in various areas of the United States, including Robert Fulton, who was carrying out submarine navigational experiments, and Eli Whitney, who invented the cotton gin. Jefferson was especially interested in the cotton gin because of its importance to planters.

Thomas Jefferson never changed his opinion that big, active governments were oppressive to the people they governed. He insisted the states were "the wisest conservative power ever contrived by man." He feared the Supreme Court with its powers to enforce its own interpretations of the Constitution, and he said the Constitution did not erect any "such single tribunal" which was independent of "the will of the nation."

While he was still president, Jefferson had incurred debts, and in April 1815, he arranged to sell his library of six thousand volumes to the United States government for $23,950 to begin a new Library of Congress. (British forces had destroyed the first Library of Congress three years before when they burned the city of Washington during the War of 1812.) Ironically, about two-thirds of the books he sold to the government were also destroyed in a fire in 1851.

After he had sold his books, Jefferson began building a new library of his own immediately, saying, "I cannot live without books" in a letter to former president John Adams dated June 10, 1815.

In retirement he still remembered Paris fondly. He wrote a friend, William Short, in March 1815: "I should prefer that residence to any other. Paris is the only place where a man who is not obliged to do anything will always find something amusing to do."

In 1819 a series of bad crop years and general financial reverses in the country made Jefferson aware he was sinking deeper into debt. His entertainment of friends continued, however, to be as lavish as ever, because he could not bear to have anyone think him stingy or inhospitable.

When he was seventy-eight, Jefferson fell at Monticello on a step leading down from a terrace and broke his left arm and wrist. Since he had suffered a similar injury to his right arm years before, he could barely write now, which was particularly unfortunate because writing letters had been one of his favorite occupations.

Jefferson developed an enlarged prostate gland which in time rendered him unable to lie down completely flat, walk, or stand upright. He was forced to take laudanum for pain.

Both Jefferson and John Adams hoped to live until the fiftieth anniversary of the signing of the Declaration of Independence. Both men, though critically ill, did live to see the dawning of July 4, 1826, but both died during that day.

Jefferson was buried at Monticello in the family cemetery with graveside rites conducted by a local Episcopal rector.

Thomas Jefferson was nearly bankrupt at his death, and he left no money with which to keep Monticello in good condition. In 1926 a group of determined Virginia women decided to buy the property and have it restored to its former glory. Today Monticello, the "Mecca of Democracy," is visited by people from all over the world.

Bibliography

Brodie, Fawn. *Thomas Jefferson: An Intimate History*. New York: Bantam Books, 1974.
Malone, Dumas. *Jefferson and the Ordeal of Liberty*. Boston: Little, Brown, 1962.
———. *Jefferson, the President*. Boston: Little, Brown, 1970.

3. Aaron Burr

Aaron Burr, vice president during President Thomas Jefferson's administration, was the first vice president who did not become president. He had a brilliant intellect, but he had a conspiratorial nature which caused him to rebel against many of the beliefs and practices of the new United States government he served.

Burr was born on February 6, 1756, in Newark, New Jersey, the son of the Reverend Aaron Burr, minister and first president of the College of Princeton, and Esther Edwards, a daughter of Jonathan Edwards, a great religious teacher and evangelist in New England. The Reverend Edwards became the second president of Princeton when the Reverend Burr died in 1757.

Young Aaron was only seventeen months old at the time of his father's death, but he inherited a large estate, and his sister Sarah received nothing. Their mother died the next year, leaving her young children in the care of relatives.

When Aaron was four years old, he was sent to live with his aunt and uncle, Dr. and Mrs. William Shippen in Philadelphia. A few days after his arrival, Aaron ran away and was gone for three or four days before he was found.

A few months later, in 1761, Aaron and his sister went to live with their mother's brother, Timothy Edwards, in Massachusetts. In 1762, Timothy Edwards moved his whole family to Elizabethtown, New Jersey, where Aaron and Sarah began school work with a private tutor, Judge Tappen Reeve. Sarah Burr later married Judge Reeve.

In 1766 young Aaron ran away from his Uncle Timothy's home and worked as a cabin boy on a ship going to New York. His uncle soon located him and took him back home after a long discussion about what Aaron could expect when he got back home.

In 1769, at the age of thirteen, Aaron Burr enrolled in Princeton. He was a slightly built young boy, and officials placed him in the sophomore class, although he qualified academically as a junior. Burr liked studying and was an excellent student. He graduated from Princeton at age sixteen with highest honors.

In 1773, Burr went to visit a good friend of his grandfather's named Joseph Bellamy. Dr. Bellamy held a doctor of divinity degree, and he took Burr into his home to live for several months. During this time Burr studied religion until questions in his mind about religion had been resolved. Dr. Bellamy talked with him at length about his doubts and opened his extensive library to him.

Burr left Dr. Bellamy's to go live with his sister and brother-in-law, Judge and Mrs. Reeve, in Connecticut. There he devoted his attention to the study of military history, taxation, and the rights denied colonists living under British rule at the time. His friends and neighbors were also interested in these topics, especially the last two, and letters exchanged between Burr and more distant friends also reflected their absorption with the subjects.

After the battle at Lexington in April 1775, Burr was eager to join his fellow countrymen in repelling the British armed forces. By now he was five feet six inches tall, with a slender build but well developed. He had dark hair and black eyes and a courtly manner. He also had firm belief he was destined for greatness.

The rag-tag group of colonists Burr joined did not fit his dream of a glorious military career which would increase his knowledge of strategy on the battlefield and lead to his ultimate promotion and high honors for valor. Instead he found himself a member of a group of undisciplined men who were fond of squabbling among themselves over trifles; many of them became ill from bad sanitary conditions in their camp.

Burr decided to join a division of soldiers planning to launch an attack on British forces in Quebec. The attack was a disaster for the forces from Connecticut because their general, Richard Montgomery, one of his aides, and several other men were killed. The soldiers still standing were forced to flee back to the border of the United States.

In May 1776, Aaron Burr joined troops that were stationed in New York and commanded by General George Washington. Even with better conditions, Burr soon became restless. When he let it be known he was thinking of leaving the army, he was assigned to serve as an aide to Major General Israel Putnam, who was in charge of protecting New York City from enemy troops.

Finally Burr saved a brigade from certain capture and imprisonment by British forces at Bunker Hill when he insisted the troops under General Knox's command retreat from the enemy instead of defending their position. They had no provisions, no water, and little real protection from mortar fire.

In 1777, at age twenty-two, Burr was promoted to lieutenant colonel of his regiment by General Washington. He acquitted himself admirably in several battles and would often go more than twenty-four hours without rest or sleep. He was promoted to colonel after a time.

By October 1778, Aaron Burr was completely exhausted and requested a furlough to regain his health. The furlough was granted by General Washington. Burr's health was worse than he realized, however, and on March 10, 1779, he sent his resignation to General Washington.

After his army service ended, Burr decided he would study law. Because his inheritance had diminished during his days as a soldier as a result of his womanizing and partying, he now needed a job that paid well.

Aaron Burr. Reproduced from the collections of the Library of Congress.

Aaron Burr went to study law with Judge Paterson in New Jersey in the fall of 1780, but he left when he realized the judge intended for him to learn the law thoroughly. He moved on to Haverstraw, New York, where his mentor was Thomas Smith, a brother of the king's attorney general, William Smith. In autumn 1781, Burr went to Albany to gain admission to the bar, and he qualified without any great effort.

Burr set up a practice in Albany with Major W. Popham, who had served in the army with him, and on July 2, 1782, Burr married Mrs. Theodosia Prevost, a widow with several children still young enough to need education. Burr assumed their care willingly, and the next year his own daughter, also named Theodosia, was born.

In letters to his wife written when he was traveling on business errands, Burr complained frequently of being ill, and on more than one occasion he mentioned severe headaches.

In April 1788, Burr was nominated by the anti-Federalists of New York City to be a candidate for the New York Assembly. The next year he was named attorney general of New York State by Governor George Clinton. Burr had entered the political arena, from which he would never turn. On October 24, 1791, he was seated as a United States senator from New York, and in October 1792, he was named as a judge to the New York State Supreme Court.

Young Theodosia was much loved by her father, and they maintained a steady correspondence during his absences from home.

Mrs. Burr died in 1794, several years before their daughter's marriage to Joseph Alston in 1801. The newlyweds went to live in South Carolina, where Alston owned a plantation. Their homestead just south of Myrtle Beach is now a museum in a garden of statuary and sculptured pieces by Anna Huntington, a later owner of the property.

Burr was seen escorting Dolley Payne Todd around Philadelphia later in 1794, but after he introduced the young widow to statesman James Madison, she changed escorts permanently. She called Madison "the great little Madison," and they were married.

In 1800, Aaron Burr was chosen to be a candidate for vice president with Thomas Jefferson as the candidate for president, or at least that was the intended result. When the electoral votes were counted, Jefferson and Burr were tied with seventy-three each. The custom of the day demanded the man with the most votes would be inaugurated as president and the runner-up would be sworn in as vice president.

The tie caused controversy, however, when Burr refused to concede the presidential spot to Jefferson. The matter was referred to the United States House of Representatives, which after much wrangling decided Jefferson should be president. General Alexander Hamilton was a leading supporter of Jefferson, and he wrote letters criticizing Burr, which led to Jefferson's election on the thirty-seventh ballot.

Burr was bitterly disappointed, and he and Jefferson served the country as the two top officers in the government under an uneasy truce. President Jefferson refused to include Burr in official events, and Vice President Burr broke a tie vote in the Senate by voting against a bill promoted by Jefferson's administration. Their hostility continued through the entire four years of President Jefferson's first term in office.

President Jefferson negotiated the acquisition of the Louisiana Territory from France during his first term, and this purchase doubled the size of the area of the United States. He also brought about the repeal of the Excise Tax and passage of the Judiciary Act of 1801.

While President Jefferson's actions brought him increased public approval, Aaron Burr embarked on a route toward his own political destruction.

In the 1790s, New York City, where Burr lived, was the attraction for immigrants coming to the United States. Yellow fever was an ever-present danger for all residents, and as the population increased, the epidemics worsened. At last it was decided contaminated water sources spread the disease.

In 1798, Aaron Burr and a group of other businessmen formed the Manhattan Water Company and laid six miles of wooden pipes to homes from a spring-fed reservoir at Reade and Center streets. By the next year, water had been put in at least four hundred houses. The city continued to grow, and in 1800 the population was sixty thousand.

In 1803, Aaron Burr announced he would be a candidate for the governor of New York in the 1804 election. President Jefferson had chosen the current New York governor, George Clinton, as his running mate in his bid for a second term as president. Apparently Burr stood a good chance of being elected.

Burr was defeated in his campaign to be governor, however. His opposition was again led by Alexander Hamilton, who questioned Burr's integrity in public speeches. Earlier Hamilton had been asked to lead a group of New England senators who wanted to form a northern confederacy of New England states and New York and break away from the United States. When Hamilton refused, they asked Burr to lead them, and he accepted. Burr told Hamilton: "Our Constitution is a miserable paper machine. You have it in your power to demolish it."

Burr's words came back to haunt him, and when he lost the election as governor, he blamed Hamilton. Burr challenged Hamilton to a duel, and the two men met on July 11, 1804, in Weehawken, New Jersey.

Aaron Burr killed Alexander Hamilton in the duel, and he was indicted for murder. He was never tried, however, and the charges were dropped because of the circumstances of Hamilton's death. Ironically, Burr had prevented a duel between Hamilton and James Monroe seven years earlier.

Burr was bitter about his political failures, and he decided to go out West for a time. There he met and conspired with General James Wilkinson and other supporters to seize by armed force the land comprising the Louisiana Territory purchase. They planned to use the property to establish a separate, independent country, with Burr to be named emperor of the government. After they got their new country started, they planned to organize an army for their protection and use it to conquer Mexico.

News of the new army and Burr's dreams of glory filtered back to Washington, however, and Burr and his soldiers were stopped on their way down the Mississippi River in 1807. Burr was tried for treason. He had managed to convince Major General Andrew Jackson that he and his new army were defending the United States against an invasion by Spain, and he had requested Jackson's help. General Jackson, then serving with the Tennessee militia, had turned over two riverboats and several reliable officers to Burr to help thwart the "invasion."

President Jefferson wanted Burr convicted of treason, but sympathetic Chief Justice John Marshall disagreed and Burr was acquitted.

Burr left for Europe after his acquittal, as public opinion had turned against him in the United States and he hoped to secure British aid in his schemes.

Failing completely in his bid for British help, he went on to Sweden, then to Germany, by which time all officials in those countries were suspicious of his motives and his ideas.

On February 16, 1810, Burr arrived in Paris, where he again tried to interest officials of yet another government in his plot. He was not only refused any assistance, he was detained in France until July 1811 before being allowed to return to the United States.

The French ship on which Burr was a passenger on his return home was captured by the English navy, and he was forced to remain in England until 1812. He had been in Europe for four years.

Back in New York at last, Burr opened a law office and was moderately successful in gaining new clients. A month later, however, his son-in-law wrote him that Burr's grandson Aaron Burr Alston had died, and Burr's daughter, Theodosia, was in poor health. Alston explained he had to leave her to report for military duty in Columbia, South Carolina, and Burr asked Theodosia to come and stay with him in New York. She embarked on the *Patriot* about the first of January in 1813, but the ship was lost at sea during a violent winter storm.

In 1819, Aaron Burr was commissioned by the government officials of Venezuela to organize an army and navy for their country to protect them against a Spanish invasion. The invasion never materialized, but Burr continued with his grandiose plots and counterplots until 1834, when he suffered a stroke.

Aaron Burr returned to live on Staten Island, New York, where he remained until his death on September 14, 1836, at age eighty-one. He was buried at the Princeton burial ground with military honors.

Bibliography

Brodie, Fawn M. *Thomas Jefferson*. New York: W. W. Norton, 1974.
Davis, Matthew L. *Memoirs of Aaron Burr*. Volumes 1 and 2. 1836. Reprint. Freeport, N.Y.: Books for Libraries Press, 1970.
Lyman, Susan Elizabeth. *The Story of New York*. New York: Crown Publishers, 1964.

4. George Clinton

George Clinton devoted most of his adult life to the pursuit of government excellence, and he was a strong, effective leader in New York State politics. He also served as vice president for President Thomas Jefferson and President James Madison.

George Clinton was born on July 26, 1739, in Ulster County, New York, where his father, Charles Clinton, had established a homestead nine years earlier when he and his family had arrived from England. Mrs. Clinton, the former Elizabeth Denniston, had given birth to three children before Charles was born in New York, but two died on board ship on their voyage from England in a measles epidemic, and only son James landed with them in New York.

Charles Clinton did not confine his activities to farming, but also worked as a land surveyor, miller, and real estate investor. All his projects were profitable, and as his sons grew up, he employed a tutor for their schooling, a young Scottish clergyman named Daniel Thain.

About 1757, George Clinton left home to become a seaman on a privateer vessel named the *DEFIANCE*, which had a crew of one hundred forty men. The ship captured three French ships in the Caribbean which were being used in the French and Indian War against English forces. He served briefly later as a subaltern in the company commanded by his brother, Captain James Clinton.

Returning home to New York in 1760, George was named to be a clerk of the Court of Common Pleas in his home county. He needed training in law for his new job, so he went to New York City to study with attorney William Smith. In 1764, George Clinton was admitted to the New York bar, and he returned to Ulster County to practice law; he also worked as a surveyor and farmer.

In 1768, Clinton was elected a member of the New York Assembly, and his political career began. The move toward independence from British rule of the American colonies began about this same time, but Clinton was no rebel and often voted for laws supporting the Crown. When the Quartering Act was proposed, however, which gave British soldiers the right to demand citizens to allow them to live in their homes, Clinton voted against it. He was also opposed to the Townshend Acts, which further increased taxes imposed on imported British goods such as tea, paper, and woolens.

In December 1769, George Clinton was converted to the rebel cause when the Assembly had opposition leader Alexander McDougall arrested because he believed a £2000 stipend proposed for the support of British troops stationed in the New York area was wrong. Clinton believed McDougall had a right to oppose the law, if he so chose, and Clinton was respected by the patriot group Sons of Liberty for his stand.

In February 1770, George Clinton had returned to Ulster County, and he married Cornelia Tappen there on February 7 of that year. Cornelia was the daughter of a wealthy Dutchman named Peter Tappen. She was described by witnesses as a "pretty Dutch girl," but her health was not robust and she would be troubled by illnesses throughout her life.

The newlyweds went to live on a farm in New Winsor, New York. Their first two children, daughters Catherine and Cornelia, were born on the farm.

George Clinton was chosen a delegate to the Second Continental Congress and took his seat on May 15, 1775. He met General George Washington for the first time at the Congress, where they became good friends.

Clinton supported General Washington's appointment as commander in chief of the American army. Clinton was made a brigadier general of the New York State militia later that same year, and he and his forces were charged with defending the highlands of the Hudson River area against attacks by the British.

The Clintons named their son born during this period George Washington Clinton, and they named their third daughter Martha Washington Clinton.

At first, Clinton's command included the Ulster and Orange county militias, but the forces of both Westchester and Duchess counties were soon added. He was serving in the Hudson River area with his troops when the Declaration of Independence was signed, and his signature is not on the document.

In 1777, Clinton was elected the first provincial governor of New York, and he took office at the temporary capital at Kingston. He served as New York's governor for the next eighteen years.

After the Revolutionary War ended, New York City again became New York's capital, and in January 1784, the first session of the New York State legislature convened, with all the recently elected senators and assemblymen present. (Albany did not become New York's capital until 1796.)

General George Washington came to visit Governor Clinton after the war and bought land in the state of New York. He asked the governor's advice about the establishment of a standing army in the state, as Washington believed the militia in the state was not adequate for defense purposes.

Governor Clinton was opposed to the ratification of the United States Constitution because he thought it bestowed too much power on national officers of government. He was for states' rights above all else. He wrote seven letters to the *New York Journal* in which he outlined his reasons for opposing ratification. He signed the letters "Cato."

When General George Washington was inaugurated the first president of

George Clinton. Reproduced from the collections of the Library of Congress.

the United States on April 30, 1789, at Federal Hall in New York City, which served as the temporary capital of the United States, Governor Clinton staged an elaborate celebration for his old friend. There were fireworks in the sky, candles in the windows of homes all over the city, a huge parade, an elaborate dinner party for dignitaries, and other honors. New Yorkers were thrilled to have the new national government located in their city, even if it was only temporary.

Governor Clinton believed the educational system in New York needed improvement, as did other citizens. The years of war had taken a toll on colleges. King's College in New York City (now Columbia University) had closed for a while during the war.

Clinton and his supporters placed special emphasis on establishing free public education for all citizens because the new democratic form of government needed an informed citizenry.

In 1782, Governor Clinton said: "It is the peculiar duty of the government of a free state, where the highest employments are open to citizens of every rank, to endeavor by the establishment of schools and seminaries to diffuse that degree of literacy which is necessary to the establishment of public trusts."

Governor Clinton also devoted much of his time and energy while in office to the advancement of higher education in the state, and his efforts led to the opening of New York State University.

In President Washington's administration, Secretary of the Treasury Alexander Hamilton wielded a great financial influence. He put the fledgling United States government on a sound financial basis by levying taxes to pay off debts incurred by the war, and he campaigned for the creation of a national bank.

Patriot James Madison agreed with Governor Clinton that Hamilton was too Federalist in his thinking, and Madison worked to bring Philip Freneau to Philadelphia in 1791 to establish an anti-Federalist newspaper. It was the seed of the development of the Republican party.

The Republicans supported the appointment of Edmund Charles Genet, French minister to the United States, who arrived on August 8, 1793. Governor Clinton extended a warm welcome to the young man, even though Genet had spent weeks traveling from Charleston, South Carolina, where he landed, to the latest temporary capital of Philadelphia to present his credentials to President Washington.

On his long journey north, Minister Genet endeavored to recruit men to help him invade the Louisiana Territory and free the area from Spanish control.

Secretary of State Thomas Jefferson, who remembered his days in France with fondness, indicated to officials in Kentucky, where Genet made a speech about his project, that he approved of Genet's plans for Louisiana. Soon Jefferson realized his approval was inappropriate, however, and he warned President Washington that Genet could wreck the new government if he was allowed to proceed with his recruitment.

President Washington asked French officials to recall Genet, and they sent Jean Antoine Joseph Baron Fauchet to replace him. Fauchet told the president that Genet should be arrested immediately and returned to France, where he would probably be sentenced to death by guillotine.

Washington did not condone such punishment, and he allowed Genet to remain in the United States. Governor Clinton's twenty-year-old daughter, Cornelia, married the young Frenchman on November 6, 1794, in her parents' home; she viewed Genet as a great defender of the oppressed people of Louisiana. Genet spent the rest of his life working on impractical inventions and living the good life, protected by Clinton's money and prestige.

Governor Clinton and President Washington were alarmed by Genet's attempts to cause a war with Spain because of the lack of United States military capability. Governor Clinton went to work improving conditions in his own state by recruiting volunteers to build a fort on Governor's Island off the coast.

George Clinton retired from politics in 1793 and devoted the next several years to his business affairs. He bought land in Poughkeepsie and had a home built on it for his and Cornelia's retirement years.

After Cornelia Clinton died on March 25, 1800, George was distraught with grief. They had been married for thirty years.

Clinton's family and friends believed a return to politics would fill his life with other interests and help him cope with his deeply felt loss. He was approached about his willingness to serve as vice president with Thomas Jefferson, the presidential nominee in the election of 1800. He was willing, but Aaron Burr was nominated instead. After Vice President Burr's deceitful actions, George Clinton was elected to serve as vice president during President Jefferson's second term.

Clinton presided over the Senate for the first time on December 16, 1805. Unfortunately, his age was advancing, and he found it difficult to concentrate on Senate business. Also, he had never been a presiding officer before, and he made a poor showing compared to the younger, more skillful Aaron Burr.

While serving in Washington, Vice President Clinton and his daughter Maria, who accompanied him, lived with a good friend of President Jefferson's named John Beckley. They did little entertaining. After Beckley's death in 1807, the Clintons lived in a boardinghouse.

President Jefferson and his vice president were friends during most of Jefferson's second term, but near the end of the term, the president ignored the vice president and did not consult him on political appointments made in New York or on foreign policy. Jefferson even proposed that New York State should be divided into two states, which Clinton opposed.

When the election of 1808 approached, Vice President Clinton hoped he would be the presidential nominee, but Virginian James Madison was chosen. Clinton was renominated to be vice president, and he and Madison were elected.

Vice President Clinton did not attend President Madison's inauguration, and he was late arriving to the first session of the Senate in 1809. He was beginning to lose interest in politics because of his failing health.

Clinton was opposed to many of the policies of President Madison, and his relationship with Madison was cordial but distant. On February 20, 1811, Clinton broke a tie vote in the Senate on rechartering the Bank of the United States by casting his vote against it. He believed the Constitution did not grant the federal government powers to create a corporation.

President Madison and Secretary of the Treasury Albert Gallatin had supported the measure and were disappointed, but not surprised, by the vice president's vote. He was known to be opposed to central authority in finance and banking.

The health of the vice president continued to worsen. He complained that presiding over the Senate and sitting for three hours continuously was tiring. As the 1812 election neared, everyone knew Clinton was not able to run for reelection, and candidates began jockeying for position. First Lady Dolley Madison deplored "the electioneering for his office that goes on beyond description."

George Clinton died in Washington on April 20, 1812, of pneumonia. His daughter Maria, his son George, now a congressman, and his nephew DeWitt Clinton were with him.

President Madison attended the military-style funeral of his vice president, who was buried in Washington in the congressional cemetery. There were eleven months remaining in his term, but the Constitution did not require replacement and he was not replaced.

Clinton's body was later moved to Kingston, New York, where a monument was erected in his honor.

Bibliography

Kaminski, John P. *George Clinton: Yeoman Politician of the New Republic.* Madison, Wis.: Madison House, 1993.

Ketcham, Ralph. *James Madison: A Biography.* New York: Macmillan, 1971.

Lyman, Susan E. *The Story of New York.* New York: Crown, 1964.

Spaulding, E. Wilder. *His Excellency, George Clinton.* Port Washington, N.Y.: Ira J. Friedman, 1964.

5. Elbridge Gerry

Elbridge Gerry was a close friend of radical Samuel Adams and a strong advocate of independence for the American colonies. Gerry was named a delegate to the Massachusetts Provincial Congress in 1774 and to the Continental Congress in Philadelphia in 1776. He felt privileged to be one of the signers of both the Declaration of Independence and the Articles of Confederation.

Elbridge was born July 17, 1744, in Marblehead, Massachusetts, to Thomas Gerry and his wife, the former Elizabeth Greenleaf. He was the middle child of five in the family to reach maturity. Six Gerry children died in infancy.

Thomas Gerry was a trader and shipper in codfish, which he sold to Spain, Portugal, and the West Indies. After unloading his codfish, he refilled his ship with products of each region, which he then transported back to Massachusetts for resale. He soon became a wealthy man. He was active in local politics also and served as a captain in the local militia.

Young Elbridge probably had a tutor for his beginning education, and he qualified to enter Harvard College at age fourteen, the typical age for freshmen at the college. He was the only son in the Gerry family to attend college, and he graduated in 1762. Subsequently, he joined his father in working in the family shipping business.

The passage of the Townshend Acts caused the citizens of Marblehead to decide to boycott British products. After the Boston Massacre in 1770, they were convinced their lives were no longer safe under British rule, and their rights were being increasingly violated. Massachusetts men were often forcibly removed from local ships sailing in the sealanes they normally used and forced to serve as seamen on British ships. The people were convinced that strong action of some sort was in order.

Elbridge Gerry was appointed town inspector of Marblehead to prohibit local citizens from using tea imported from England. Anyone caught using such tea was ostracized.

In 1772, Gerry was elected to serve as a representative to the General Court, and he began his lifelong struggle to safeguard the rights of American citizens.

In 1773 a smallpox epidemic occurred in Marblehead, and Elbridge's brother John and some other men requested permission to build a hospital on a small island offshore where people of the town could be vaccinated and kept in isolation while their bodies built immunity to the disease. Town officials approved the plan, and the hospital was built.

From the beginning, the local citizens were split into two groups — those who trusted vaccination to protect them and their families from getting smallpox and those with an unreasoning fear of the disease who believed the hospital would contribute to its spread.

Acting on their fears, Marblehead residents would not allow their neighbors who were returning home after treatment in the hospital to land on shore. They drove the boats away from the beach with barrel staves. Finally on January 26, 1774, a group of townspeople with blackened faces rowed over to the island and burned the hospital, completely destroying it.

Elbridge Gerry was so shocked by the event that it later affected his opinions about direct elections of government officials by voters. He had learned public reaction could be both uncertain and dangerous.

When Gerry was nominated to be a delegate to the First Continental Congress, he refused the honor. In addition to the disillusion he had suffered from the actions of his neighbors during the smallpox epidemic, both his parents had recently died, his father only two months before.

Gerry did assume an active role in the Massachusetts Provincial Congress, however, and he spent long hours procuring needed supplies for the militia to use in the event of an attack by British forces. He had a personal interest in the preparations also, as the British Parliament had recently passed a law forbidding any colony business to trade with another country, effective July 1, 1775. The law would cause the Gerry codfish business to cease operation because all its commerce involved selling to and buying from other countries.

Three of the Massachusetts delegates to the Continental Congress were unsure how they felt about full independence for the colonies, while delegates John Adams and Samuel Adams supported the idea without reservation. The two Adamses welcomed the election of Gerry to the Congress on December 15, 1775, because they knew from correspondence with him that he was also heartily in favor of independence. Gerry replaced delegate Thomas Cushing, who had not decided what he thought about the issue.

Elbridge Gerry did not hesitate to express his views in the congressional sessions, and when he believed the new government in process was being formed according to aristocratic views rather than republican ones, he went back to his home in Massachusetts in 1780 and did not return until the autumn of 1783.

Shortly after his return, Gerry mounted fierce opposition to the establishment of a standing army and a permanent military training school, which would be operated by the government. The men supporting the military proposals included General George Washington, General Henry Knox, Alexander Hamilton, and James Madison, all patriots who had been members of their local militias and believed the militias were inadequate for any permanent defense. Gerry

Elbridge Gerry. Reproduced from the collections of the Library of Congress.

feared, however, that the military forces they were forming could be used to overthrow the new government.

Elbridge Gerry was over forty years old, and he had never married, but in late 1785 he fell in love with Ann Thompson, a twenty-year-old New York socialite who was considered by some observers to be "the most beautiful woman in the United States." Her father, James Thompson, was a wealthy merchant in New York, and he had sent his daughter to Europe to complete her education.

When Elbridge married Ann on January 12, 1786, in New York City, he left his old home in Marblehead forever. Ann had no wish to live in a town which smelled strongly of its fish trade, and they went to live in Cambridge, Massachusetts, in an elegant mansion called Elmwood.

Elbridge and Ann entertained extensively and lavishly. He was blissfully happy in his new marriage. He proudly took his new bride to visit friends and relatives and gave serious consideration to retiring from public life.

In late 1786, however, Daniel Shays led a rebellion of his destitute fellow farmers against the courts in Massachusetts to stop mortgage foreclosures on their farms. There was no federal force in place to put down the protest, and one had to be assembled hastily.

Elbridge Gerry understood that mob action could destroy a government as effectively as a standing army, and he relented in his opposition to having a standing army. He continued to fear a military takeover of the government until the 1790s, however.

When the Constitutional Congress convened on May 29, 1787, Gerry was a delegate. He found himself at odds with other delegates about allowing the executive branch of the government to appoint federal judges. After he presented his reasons for opposing the law, the Congress voted to let the senators appoint judges at the federal level.

With Shay's Rebellion still in his memory, Gerry supported the view of delegates from South Carolina, who believed the average voter would not be a "fit judge" of candidates nominated to serve in the House of Representatives and that the representatives should be elected by indirect votes by states legislators. James Madison, a delegate from Virginia, insisted, however, that direct election was preferable.

Madison and Gerry agreed that Congress should establish post offices and that Congress should reserve the right to declare war, with the executive branch only having a right to "repel sudden attacks."

Gerry opposed ratification of the final draft of the Constitution because of the weakening of states' rights and the vast amount of power being granted to the federal government officials. Other delegates opposed the document as drafted for various other reasons, and opposition began to increase. When the Bill of Rights was added and an authorization for future addition of amendments was included, however, the Constitution was ratified.

Gerry had become a father for the first time shortly before the Congress began. Elbridge and Ann would have a total of ten children during their years of marriage; one son died in infancy. Gerry brought his wife and their baby daughter Catharine with him to Philadelphia, but they left to go to New York within a few days to visit Ann's parents because of their fear of summer fevers in Philadelphia.

Gerry was elected to serve in the United States House of Representatives in 1789 in the first session ever held. Again he expressed his political views freely, and this time found himself agreeing with many of Secretary of Treasury Alexander Hamilton's ideas.

When Gerry began his second term in 1791, he was less interested and made few speeches. He wanted to be at home with his family, which was steadily increasing. When his second term neared its end, he did not campaign for a third.

From 1793 to 1797, Gerry did not hold any public office, but in 1796 he served as a member of the Electoral College and cast his vote for John Adams to be the second president of the United States.

Late in 1797, President Adams asked Gerry to join Charles C. Pinckney and John Marshall on an official diplomatic mission to France to try to end the threat of war between the United States and France.

Upon the trio's arrival in France, Talleyrand, the minister of French foreign affairs, sent a delegation to talk with the United States representatives instead of meeting with them himself.

The French agents made it clear that peace with France could be bought if enough money was offered. Talleyrand wanted a large loan made to the French government and a cash payment to himself for his efforts in negotiations.

President Adams was angry when he learned of Talleyrand's demands, and he reported the attempted extortion to the United States Congress. Instead of naming the three French agents for Talleyrand, Adams referred to them as X, Y, and Z.

Members of Congress resented Talleyrand's attitude toward the United States government, and they publicized the demands, causing much anti-French sentiment in the United States.

Talleyrand was embarrassed by the furor he had caused with his greedy demands, and he offered to negotiate with Elbridge Gerry individually. Gerry wrote President Adams requesting permission to conduct such negotiations alone with Talleyrand and asked for full authority to make a treaty with him. United States Ambassador William Vans Murray confirmed in a letter also to President Adams that the French officials were prepared to negotiate only with Gerry.

President Adams could not understand what had happened to cause his other two delegates to be shut out. On June 13, 1798, First Lady Abigail Adams wrote her sister Mary Cranch that the president was distressed about the problem and that John Marshall and Charles Pinckney would be ordered to leave by French officials.

Abigail wondered if Gerry was assuming too much responsibility on his own. Referring to Gerry, she wrote her sister: "If he stays behind he is a ruined man. . . . This is all between ourselves. You will be particularly reserved upon the subject. I do not wish to have Mrs. Gerry's feelings hurt by believing I am judging hardly an old and steady friend."

Instead of granting Gerry full negotiating powers, President Adams ordered him to return home at once, as Marshall and Pinckney had done earlier. The president then sent Oliver Ellsworth, chief justice of the Supreme Court, and Governor William R. Davie of North Carolina to France to join Ambassador William Vans Murray. They were all ordered to act only together.

France and the United States signed the Treaty of Morfontaine on September 30, 1800, and the threat of war ended.

Elbridge Gerry was elected governor of Massachusetts in 1810. He approved a redistricting plan that ensured Republican victories in future elections by creating peculiar configurations for some of the districts. The editor of the *Boston Sentinel* said one district resembled a salamander, and he said the district had been "gerrymandered."

Ann Gerry did not move to Boston to live while her husband served as governor, but he wrote her every day. They had so many children that she believed moving their household would be too difficult.

In 1812, Gerry was chosen to run for vice president with presidential nominee James Madison, who was seeking a second term. They were elected, and the two men had a harmonious relationship, both politically and personally.

Vice President Gerry supported the president when he urged a declaration of war against England in 1812; his recommendation was granted by Congress. Vice President–elect Gerry wrote him: "War is declared. God be praised, Our country is safe."

When President Madison became seriously ill with a liver ailment in 1813, newspapers began a vehement denunciation of his support for the war. Their editorials also speculated about the vice president's qualifications and his ability to be head of the government in the event of President Madison's death. Fortunately, President Madison recovered.

Ann Gerry did not bring their family to live in Washington either. The vice president carried on extensive correspondence with her and his children. He was not lonely because Washington hostesses were delighted to have a vice president as an extra man at their dinner parties. He attended levees and parties, as well as dinners hosted by the president and first lady.

Vice President Gerry presided over a Senate that was unhappy with President Madison's administration, the war with Great Britain, and almost every other subject that came to their attention. The senators' discontent was so profound that when Congress adjourned on August 2, 1813, Gerry refused to vacate his position as presiding officer. He feared President Madison might die, and since Gerry himself was sixty-nine years old and his own future was uncertain, he wanted to make sure Speaker of the House Henry Clay would become president if the worst happened instead of Senator William Branch Giles or some other malcontent in the Senate who might be named president pro tem.

Gerry had suffered what he termed a "sun stroke" the year before while President Madison was ill. It was plain to all that Gerry's health was failing, and no one was surprised when he was stricken with what was probably a heart attack while riding in his carriage to the Senate chambers on November 23, 1814. He died later that day. For the next twenty-seven months, the United States did not have a vice president.

Ann Gerry died in Massachusetts on March 17, 1849, at the age of eighty-six.

Bibliography

Billias, George Athan. *Elbridge Gerry: Founding Father and Republican Statesman.* New York: McGraw-Hill, 1976.
Ketcham, Ralph. *James Madison: A Biography.* New York: Macmillan, 1971.

6. Daniel D. Tompkins

Vice President Daniel D. Tompkins probably prevented the British armed forces from regaining control of the United States during the War of 1812. He was not a soldier himself, but he furnished the money to pay soldiers of the United States government by using his own property as collateral for defense loans made to the government, which had little money to spend for defense.

Daniel Tompkins was born on June 21, 1774, in Westchester County, New York, at Fox Meadow (now Scarsdale). His parents, Jonathan and Sarah Ann Hyatt Tompkins, were the owners and operators of a large farm situated in an area largely populated by aristocratic Loyalists who supported the British Crown.

As the drive for independence in the American colonies had escalated, Jonathan Tompkins, a Whig militant, was obliged to move his family to live in Duchess County during the battle of White Plains. Their safety was threatened by even their Tory neighbors, as well as by British soldiers.

The family returned to their Westchester farm after the Revolutionary War ended. In addition to farming, Jonathan Tompkins served as supervisor of Scarsdale from 1783 until 1792. He also served in the New York State legislature and was a member of the board of regents for New York State University.

With all the political involvement and interests of his father, it was natural that young Daniel would develop similar interests as he became an adult.

Young Daniel attended a boarding school located in New York City that was operated by Malcolm Campbell, who had been extensively educated in Scotland. Daniel commenced his education in September 1787, but the next year his father moved him to the Academy of North Salem in Westchester County.

Daniel D. Tompkins entered Columbia College in 1792, where entrance requirements for applicants for admission included being "able to render into English Caesar's Commentaries of the Gallic War, translations of the four orations of Cicero against Cataline, the ability to read the first four Books of Virgil's Aeneid and the Holy Gospels from the Greek, to explain the government . . . to turn English into grammatical Latin and . . . understand the first four rules of Arithmetic, with the Rule of Three, and Vulgar and Decimal Fractions."

It was evident that to meet these requirements, Tompkins had spent many hours studying. He qualified to enter as a sophomore.

Daniel D. Tompkins. Reproduced from the collections of the Library of Congress.

Columbia College (now Columbia University) was located in the midtown area of New York City, which had thirty thousand inhabitants in 1792. Columbia College had eighty students enrolled during 1792–93.

While he was at Columbia, Tompkins wrote in an essay that he thought an exorbitant amount of study time was devoted to Latin and Greek; he suggested that a study of modern literature was also desirable for a student receiving a broad liberal education. Surprisingly, he also urged the offering of higher educational opportunities to women.

In other essays, of which there were many, Daniel Tompkins denounced slavery and deplored the current attitude toward native American Indian tribes, which involved "an unnatural war against them." He was opposed to capital punishment and considered it to be barbaric.

In May 1795, Tompkins graduated from Columbia; he delivered the valedictory address as the top student in his class. His oration ended with the advice, "Go on then, students of Columbia, with eminence and glory in your view."

Tompkins enjoyed politics, and he decided his best chance to advance in that field was to become a lawyer. He began study immediately, was admitted to the New York Bar in 1797, and opened a law practice in New York City.

On February 20, 1798, Tompkins married Hannah Minthorne, a pretty, charming girl of Dutch background and a member of a wealthy New York family. Her father, Mangle Minthorne, had been accused of selling English tea during the boycott prior to the Revolution, but he had many business interests and had prospered throughout his life without such activity.

On January 31, 1800, Tompkins became a father when his and Hannah's daughter Arietta was born. She was followed by a son Griffin, born on November 22, 1801, Hannah Ellsworth born September 21, 1803, Sarah Ann born December 19, 1805, Minthorne born December 26, 1807, Daniel Hyatt born March 17, 1810, Susan McLaren born September 10, 1812, and Ray born January 20, 1814.

Daniel Tompkins entered politics the same year their first daughter was born. He was elected to serve as alderman of the Seventh Ward in New York City, where he and his family lived.

Mangle Minthorne was an active Republican, and Tompkins knew he could expect help from him when he sought political appointments. In 1801, Tompkins was named a commissioner of bankruptcy in federal court and a counselor in the New York Supreme Court.

As his career continued, Tompkins was elected a representative in the New York State Assembly in 1802, serving from January of that year to April 1803. In 1804 he became an associate justice in the New York State Supreme Court when a justice retired.

Later that year, Tompkins was elected to represent New York State in the United States House of Representatives, but he resigned before the opening session, preferring to remain as a justice with the New York State Supreme Court. There he was noted for his honesty, fidelity to duty, and strict impartiality.

When Daniel Tompkins was elected governor of New York in 1807, Hannah Tompkins served as a gracious hostess at both formal and informal parties in the governor's mansion, as she had been reared in a home where entertaining was a way of life.

Tompkins had speculated in profitable real estate deals prior to his election as governor. He and his wife owned their three-story brick home in the Bowery area, and he was able to provide his family with a pleasant life. He was a young man on the way up in the world.

Tompkins had an interest in fine arts, and he promoted their enjoyment in New York City, where he signed an agreement to create a society for the purpose. He and other art patrons bought shares in the society at fifty dollars each, and the money was used to import plaster casts of well-known sculptures that formed the basis of the New York Fine Arts Academy. In 1808 the Academy was incorporated.

President Thomas Jefferson was opposed to the involvement of the United States government in the British and French hostilities that were then increasing, and he ordered British ships to leave ports in the United States on July 2, 1807. The United States Congress then agreed with President Jefferson that American ships should remain in port to prevent their capture and use by enemy European armed forces. The Long Embargo remained in effect until 1809.

Governor Tompkins gave his full support to the embargo ordered by the president, even though it drew increasing opposition from New York voters as time passed. Tompkins believed the embargo was necessary to preserve the United States government. When insurrectionists defied the embargo, Tompkins ordered the New York State militia to repress the defiance of federal authority.

Soon after Governor Tompkins was first elected, an English warship, the *Leopard*, attacked the United States frigate named the *Chesapeake*, forcibly boarded it, and captured four of the crewmen to work on the *Leopard*.

President Jefferson notified Governor Tompkins that 12,704 militiamen should be equipped and ready to move at a moment's notice to defend the property of U.S. citizens. The total defense force from all the states would number one hundred thousand. In 1808, Tompkins was ordered to equip 14,389 more soldiers, and in April 1812, another 13,500.

Governor Tompkins began urging the New York State legislature to appropriate funds to build forts on the frontier to protect the state, especially along the borders with Canada.

On January 26, 1808, when the second contingent of militia was ordered by President Jefferson, he also told Governor Tompkins the federal government could not pay for any defense measures, that "reliance must be on the means to be provided by their respective states." The federal government ignored requests for guns and ammunition for New York soldiers.

By the time the 1809 election was held, New York citizens were agreeing that the governor had been right when he supported the embargo, and he was reelected; the Republicans also regained control of both legislative houses.

On June 18, 1812, the United States formally declared war on England and aid was vital. Many New England citizens were still in awe of Great Britain, and officials of other states opposed the war. They refused to assign active duties to the militias in their states which would protect national interests. Smuggling, piracy, and aid to British forces among these dissenters were commonplace.

In England, newspapers reported gleefully that "the proud seat of that nest of traitors," Washington, D.C., had been destroyed by fire. They hoped Loyalists in New England would urge renewal of political control of the United States by England.

When British forces invaded Maryland at Bladensburg in September 1814,

Governor Tompkins knew his state would probably be the site of another invasion, and the recruitment and equipping of more soldiers was crucial.

Governor Tompkins appealed to New York political leaders Rufus King and DeWitt Clinton to help him. They managed to secure promises of support from business leaders, but banks would not lend money to the government of the state to finance an army unless Governor Tompkins endorsed the notes as an agent of New York State.

Federalist leader Rufus King told Tompkins bluntly that he must do all he could to save the United States from England. "Ruin yourself if it becomes necessary to save your country, and I pledge you my honor that I will support you in all you do," King assured Tompkins.

With this promise from the leader of the Federalists in his state, Tompkins endorsed the notes amounting to $4 million to finance immediate mobilization of troops. Some New York citizens who belonged to the Federalist party wanted to secede from the Union rather than fight with the British again, however.

During this period, newly elected James Madison asked Daniel Tompkins to serve in his administration as secretary of state, but Tompkins declined. He preferred to remain the commander in chief of the New York militia, believing he would be regarded as the man who saved New York. He hoped he might even be elected president of the United States at a future date.

As soon as Governor Tompkins was nominated vice president in 1817, the question of his default on the war debts arose. The war had ended in 1814, and some of the money had been repaid to the banks, but Tompkins's opponents claimed his accounts of expenditures did not total the amount borrowed. The failure on his part to keep receipts of expenditures and payments made led to his being accused of dishonesty. Martin Van Buren, United States senator from New York, and presidential candidate James Monroe, also from that state, defended the governor. They tried to explain the discrepancies, but many would not accept the explanations.

Both James Monroe and Daniel Tompkins were elected despite the controversy. In his last message to the New York legislature in 1817, Tompkins recommended the passage of a law setting all the slaves living in New York free by July 4, 1827, and the law was passed.

Vice President Tompkins took the oath of office on March 4, 1817, with a huge debt he had guaranteed still unpaid. The Federalist party, which had been in control of the legislature, was destroyed by the members' refusal to pay for soldiers and supplies with which to fight the War of 1812. Even Rufus King's promise of support was hollow. He made no effort to pay any of the debts incurred, nor did he try to help Tompkins collect.

Meantime, the Tompkins family now had eight children, and the United States Congress voted to withhold the vice president's annual salary of $5000, leaving him with no money to support his family. He was bankrupt.

Vice President Tompkins spent most of his time while in office trying to appease his creditors. He began to drink excessively in his frustration while he pressed his claims of $660,000 due him from the United States government.

The *Evening Post* had often been critical of Tompkins while he was governor, but now its editors insisted Tompkins should be paid $136,799.97, by their calculations, owed to him by the federal government.

Tompkins and President Monroe were reelected for a second term, but living with such stress and having his integrity questioned publicly wrecked Tompkins's health before all the charges were disproved. He reached the point where he could no longer preside over the Senate, and in March 1822, he returned to his family in New York and never came back to Washington.

Tompkins finally collected $97,229 from congressional action in May 1824; the amount was to be paid in two successive payments. His other claims were denied because he had no proofs of his claims to present.

Daniel Tompkins lived in failing health until his death on June 11, 1825, in New York. Hannah Tompkins lived until February 18, 1829, and probably resided with some of their children.

Both Daniel and his wife were buried in the cemetery of St. Mark's Church in New York City, the Minthorne family church.

Bibliography

Irwin, Ray W. *Daniel D. Tompkins*. New York: New York Historical Society, 1968.
Niven, John. *Martin Van Buren*. New York: Oxford University Press, 1983.

7. John Caldwell Calhoun

John Caldwell Calhoun was involved with politics from his earliest years. He was born on March 18, 1782, in Abbeville District, South Carolina. His father, Patrick Calhoun, was from Donegal in Ireland and had been a member of the South Carolina legislature since 1769. John's mother, Martha Caldwell Calhoun, was his father's third wife. It was she who taught young John his courtesy, gave him religious instruction, and bequeathed him her emotional intensity.

Young John listened when his father denounced the United States Constitution to neighbors when the child was only five years old. Patrick Calhoun insisted the document gave federal government officials the right to tax citizens of South Carolina, and he believed that was taxation without representation.

The little boy adored his father, and he was an attentive audience when his father related tales of oppression in Ireland and Scotland, massacres in this country by Indian raiders, and battles fought during the Revolutionary War.

John started school when he was seven years old in a log cabin school located two or three miles from his home. He learned to read, could write his name, and knew how to add and subtract simple numbers, which was all the school had to offer.

John's sister Catherine was married to Moses Waddel, a lawyer and a teacher who had started his own academy in Columbia County, Georgia. They welcomed thirteen-year-old John into their home in 1795 so he could get more education.

John had barely got started with the new lessons when his sister died following a brief illness. Moses Waddel was so distraught he could not teach for some months, but John read the books in his library.

When John began a project, he devoted his full attention to it, often going without sleep for extended periods and eating only when someone reminded him that he should. His health suffered, and Waddel took John back home to his mother.

Upon reaching his South Carolina home, John learned his father had died on February 15, 1796, of tuberculosis. Only Mrs. Calhoun and John's brother Patrick were living now in the main house. His two older brothers had left home to find jobs.

John C. Calhoun. Reproduced from the collections of the Library of Congress.

John Calhoun's childhood ended with the deaths of two relatives dear to him, but he had his mother and younger brother to care for, and he went to work on the family farms. Fortunately, he loved farming, from plowing and planting to hoeing, weeding, and harvesting the crops. Of course, he had help from the slaves who also lived on the Calhoun property, but supervision of the work was his primary responsibility.

Since John's education had been so tragically interrupted, his older brothers, William and James, came to talk to him about returning to school. John said he would go if he could get a complete education, including a law degree. His brothers agreed to assist him, and he entered Yale.

In 1804 John Calhoun graduated from Yale at age twenty-two with high honors. It was most remarkable since the graduate had only a total of twenty-four months of formal education before entering Yale. It is evident that he had a brilliant intellect and much ability.

Calhoun went to Litchfield, Connecticut, to study law with Judge Tappen Reeve in 1805 and returned to South Carolina in 1807, when he began his own law practice in Abbeville. Later that year he was elected to serve in the South Carolina General Assembly. In 1810 he was elected to serve the first of three terms in the United States House of Representatives.

In his first speech in the House, John Calhoun defined congressional duties as being those of "a diplomatic corps . . . sent here to protect the states' rights."

While he was still a student at Yale, Calhoun had been invited to visit a cousin's family at their summer home in Newport, Rhode Island. His cousin, John Ewing Colhoun (*sic*) had been a United States senator before his death in 1802.

Mrs. Colhoun was of Huguenot background, and she enjoyed living well. John liked her and her children, but he was never envious of their wealth or social position in either Newport or their winter home in Charleston, South Carolina.

On January 8, 1811, John Calhoun married Floride Colhoun, the daughter of his cousin. The wedding was held in the home of the bride at Bonneau's Ferry in South Carolina and was a gala occasion with many guests present. John was madly in love with his young bride and had been waiting impatiently for their wedding for almost a year. Floride's mother approved of the match as she felt they were well suited in temperament. Their marriage was happy, and as years passed they had nine children, seven of which lived to reach adulthood.

His marriage to beautiful Floride gave Calhoun an entry to Charleston society with its influence in politics and the aristocracy of wealthy plantation owners. He received no direct monetary benefit, however, and always supported his family with his own income.

Representative Calhoun supported President Madison in his decision to go to war with England in 1812. He thought soldiers and sailors should be drafted, but a conscription was not used.

Calhoun was a dedicated supporter of the Union all of his life. As Southern domination of the federal government lessened, he feared some of the more radical Southerners would urge secession, and he insisted the Union was both desirable and necessary.

In 1817, President James Monroe named Congressman John Calhoun to be secretary of war in his cabinet. In this post Calhoun was a supervisor of policies at West Point Academy and a negotiator for more land purchases from members of Indian tribes; he also directed activities for explorations in the Northwest Territory.

John Calhoun assumed his new duties with his usual enthusiasm and established such a solid War Department that neither the Mexican or Civil Wars caused any difficulties.

Calhoun sent two expeditions to the Northwest Territory to establish army outposts there for defense against unfriendly Indians and marauding British traders. President Monroe, both houses of Congress, and newspaper reporters gave Calhoun's efforts their hearty approval, and he won general public approval also.

When problems surfaced with the design of the steamboat being used for exploration, Calhoun's political enemies took the opportunity to diminish his popularity with the public. During the winter of 1819–20, with the connivance of Speaker of the House Henry Clay and Secretary of the Treasury William H. Crawford, Congress requested reports on the expeditions and other activities being conducted by the War Department. Why had expenditures in the department doubled since 1811, while army strength remained about the same?

Secretary of War Calhoun furnished a report containing more than five thousand words, in which he enumerated the reasons for the increase in expenditures and the benefits to the public good produced by his efforts. Newspaper accounts praised his actions, and future contenders for office of the president took notice that a new political star was rising which might pose a threat to their own future political ambitions. Calhoun would bear watching.

John Calhoun did enter the presidential race in 1824, but he withdrew when he decided he could not win. Presidential candidate John Quincy Adams asked him to be his running mate, and he accepted. Together they won the election.

As vice president, John Calhoun was more secure financially, and in 1825 he bought a plantation for his family in Pendleton, South Carolina. They named their home Fort Hill. Their chief crop was cotton, and as a planter, Calhoun became aware that tariff protection imposed by Northern officials was detrimental to the Southern economy.

By 1827 Calhoun could not sell his own cotton crop for a profit, and Southern extremists were insisting secession from the Union was the solution to their problems. Tariff laws supported by Northern politicians were bankrupting the South.

When the Woolens bill, yet another tariff proposal, came to the Senate floor early in 1828, Vice President Calhoun cast the deciding vote against it. As a result, President John Quincy Adams did not ask his vice president to run with him for a second term, but presidential candidate Andrew Jackson did.

Andrew Jackson was elected to the new president, and John Calhoun became vice president in a new administration headed by a different leader.

Floride and the children came to Washington to live for a time to reunite their family so often separated by circumstances. There were now six Calhoun children, and Floride was pregnant again.

Not many months of President Jackson's administration had passed before someone told Jackson that his vice president, while secretary of war, had recommended that Jackson be reprimanded for his military activities in Florida a few years earlier. President Jackson was proud of his exploits as General Jackson, and he became furious with Vice President Calhoun.

When Floride Calhoun snubbed Peggy Eaton socially a few weeks later, the Calhouns were persona non grata to the president, who considered her a good friend.

Mrs. Eaton had reportedly had a romantic affair several years earlier with John Eaton, now secretary of war in President Jackson's cabinet. Mrs. Eaton was married to her first husband at the time of her involvement with Eaton, and even though she finally married Eaton, most of the women in Washington society ostracized her, including Floride Calhoun.

President Jackson's deceased wife, Rachel, had been the object of similar gossip and shunning by society years earlier, and the president reacted to Mrs. Eaton's predicament as if it were his own.

In 1832, a year before his term as vice president would end, John Calhoun resigned his office and returned to South Carolina. There he found the state government in an uproar; state officials who insisted they constituted South Carolina's only government had nullified the national tariff law. They would no longer pay tariffs imposed by the federal government. Others argued the state government did not have authority to nullify a federal law.

President Jackson threatened to send armed soldiers to South Carolina to collect the tariff, but resistance continued unabated. At last the South Carolina officials were forced to reinstate the law because President Jackson declared that if they did not, he would have former vice president Calhoun hanged "higher than Haman." Calhoun was venerated in his state and officials yielded.

Later that year, John C. Calhoun was elected to serve in the United States Senate for South Carolina, and in 1834 he opposed President Jackson's national bank proposals.

For the next several years, Senator Calhoun was torn between his senatorial duties and his family. His oldest daughter, Anna Maria, had married mining engineer Thomas Clemson several years before, and she had difficulty bearing children and usually became dangerously ill.

Anna was more like her father than were the other Calhoun children because she had a quick mind and wide range of interests; Calhoun loved her dearly and worried about her often.

Calhoun's oldest son, Andrew, had borrowed money from Anna's husband in 1838 to buy a plantation in Alabama, and in 1843 Clemson told Andrew he needed the loan repaid. Andrew thought he should have more time, and there were hurt feelings.

An even greater source of concern was that Floride Calhoun had suffered a stroke the year before and was having a painfully slow recovery.

John Calhoun decided he should go home in 1843. He needed to help Floride, he needed to be with his younger children, and he hoped to settle the quarrel between his son and son-in-law.

Calhoun could not be idle, so he turned to putting his ideas and beliefs on paper. He wrote two books during this time. One was entitled *A Disquisition on Government* and the second was *A Discourse on the Constitution of the United States.*

The reason Calhoun gave for his writing was "to lay a solid foundation for political science." He did his work well and his books are still considered invaluable in the study of political science.

On March 6, 1844, John Calhoun returned to Washington when he was named secretary of state in President John Tyler's administration. Tyler had become president when President William Henry Harrison died after serving only one month in office.

Secretary of State Calhoun helped President Tyler negotiate a treaty to annex Texas, an ardent dream of Tyler's. Texas was annexed, and later war with Mexico followed.

In 1845, James K. Polk was elected president, and Calhoun was reelected to the United States Senate. Now Calhoun defended the practice of slavery with his usual vehemence. He insisted abolitionists from Northern states were wrong in their views, and he believed they were trying to make the Southerners their political subjects and ruin the Southern economy.

Before his death, Senator Calhoun predicted the Civil War and the terrible consequences his beloved state of South Carolina would suffer. As he aged, he became obsessed with the belief that a probable break-up of the Union would occur and said, "The dissolution of the Union is the heaviest blow that can be struck at civilization and representative government." His doctor told him he was "thinking himself into the grave."

John C. Calhoun died on March 31, 1850, in Washington. Floride came to be with him as soon as she could from Fort Hill, but she arrived too late to tell him goodbye.

Calhoun's funeral was held in the Senate Chamber, and he was buried in the churchyard of St. Philip's Church in Charleston, South Carolina.

Bibliography

Bemis, Samuel Flagg. *John Quincy Adams and the Union.* New York: Alfred A. Knopf, 1956.
Coit, Margaret L. *John C. Calhoun: American Portrait.* Boston: Houston Mifflin, 1950.
Niven, John. *John C. Calhoun and the Price of Union.* Baton Rouge: Louisiana State University Press, 1988.

8. Martin Van Buren

Martin Van Buren did not allow his humble beginnings or his lack of formal education to stand in the way of his success as he progressed from being a surrogate lawyer in his home county of Columbia in New York State to being a president of the United States.

Van Buren was of Dutch ancestry, and he was born on December 5, 1782, in Kinderhook, New York, just five days before the provisional Treaty of Paris was signed, which ended the Revolutionary War between the United States and England.

His father, Abraham Van Buren, was the owner of a farm and a tavern located on the post road to Albany. The post road was a busy thoroughfare, and the tavern would have been an extremely profitable business in the right hands, but Abraham Van Buren was a free spender and could not manage his money.

Martin was one of six Van Buren children born to Abraham and Maria Van Buren, and their home was always crowded. His older brothers, James and John Van Alen, born of his mother's first marriage, were admitted to the bar to practice law when Martin was still a child.

Abraham Van Buren rented the large tavern room in their home to both Federalists and Jeffersonians for political meetings. Politics was a favorite topic of conversation among the adults in Martin's family and the patrons of his father's tavern. When he was only seventeen, Martin actively campaigned for the nomination of his friend John P. Van Ness to be the Republican candidate for the United States Congress.

Young Martin received only a village school education, and he felt the lack of education keenly all through his life. He did not use it as an excuse for failure, however, but instead he endeavored to broaden his education by reading and listening to the ideas and beliefs of men more educated than he was. He also learned to curb a nature that tended to be passionate and impetuous.

Martin Van Buren was apprenticed in a fashion to Francis Sylvester, one of Kinderhook's most respected attorneys. For the law training he received from Sylvester, Van Buren was obligated to sweep out the store building in which his bedroom was located and keep the law office clean. He also worked as a clerk in the store.

Martin Van Buren. Reproduced from the collections of the Library of Congress.

After four years of devoted study, Van Buren was admitted to the New York bar as his brothers had been before him. United States Representative John Van Ness remembered Van Buren's assistance years earlier in his bid for a congressional seat, and he offered to pay Van Buren's fare to New York, where his brother William Van Ness had a thriving law practice. Van Buren had a job with William Van Ness if he wanted it.

Van Buren accepted the job gratefully and he was working in New York City during the political maneuverings and plots and counterplots of Aaron Burr and

DeWitt Clinton, Republican party leaders. It could be truly said that he received political instruction from masters of intrigue.

Romance took Van Buren back to Kinderhook, and he married a local girl there named Hannah Hoes on February 21, 1807. They moved to Hudson, fifteen miles away, to begin their life together. The next year Van Buren was appointed surrogate attorney for Columbia County, in charge of overseeing sales and other property transfers between parties.

Another attraction Hudson held for Martin and Hannah Van Buren was its excellent school, Hudson Academy, which would furnish a quality education for future little Van Burens. In time they had four sons who reached maturity: Abraham, John, Smith Thompson, and Martin Jr.

In 1812, Van Buren was elected a New York State senator, and he and Hannah moved their family to Albany, where educational facilities were even better. In 1816 he was elected attorney-general of the state, and he felt confident about his political abilities. His law practice was thriving too.

Hannah Van Buren's health began to fail in January 1817, following the birth of their last son, however, Martin was reminded of Hannah's great importance in his life, and he tried to spend more time at home with her and his children. He enjoyed the excitement of the political arena, and he was soon involved again with public events.

As attorney general, Van Buren prosecuted General William Hull for dereliction of duty during the War of 1812 when Hull surrendered the city of Detroit to British forces. Van Buren was removed from the attorney general's office in 1819, the same year his wife died from tuberculosis. He spent several weeks in deep mourning and finally returned to politics to stay busy and take his mind from his grief.

In 1821, Van Buren was elected to serve in the United States Senate, to which he was reelected in 1827. Maria Van Buren, Martin's sister, had assumed the care of Martin's four sons. Hannah's sister, Mrs. Moses Cantine, lived not far away in Albany, so when Van Buren first began serving in the Senate, he left his sons with relatives and took a room in a Washington boardinghouse.

Two years later Abraham Van Buren entered West Point Military Academy, and John entered school in New York City, where he lived in the home of Rufus King, one of his father's longtime friends and political supporters.

Van Buren took his Senate duties seriously. His position as chairman of the Judiciary Committee and the finance Committee required long days and hard work.

When he was reelected to the Senate in 1827, Van Buren decided to move his household from Albany to Washington, D.C. because he missed the comforts of a real home.

Van Buren sold his house in Albany and planned to rent a large house in Washington and then rent rooms to other government officials. His sons Martin and Smith were in boarding schools and spent holidays in Kinderhook with some of their many relatives. John was a student at Yale, and Abraham was a lieutenant in the United States Army.

Senator Van Buren decided to throw his political influence into the campaign of General Andrew Jackson for president in the 1828 election. Van Buren did not like President John Quincy Adams, but he discovered Adams was popular with New York voters when he visited relatives in Kinderhook.

It was during this period that anti-Masonic sentiment arose. A man in New York named William Morgan had published the secrets of the Masonic Order the year before and had subsequently disappeared under mysterious circumstances. Rumors were rampant that Masons had murdered Morgan. Unfortunately, candidate Andrew Johnson belonged to the Masonic order, and Van Buren wondered if he was supporting the wrong candidate.

In the 1828 election, Andrew Jackson was elected president, Jackson's Democratic party elected eighty-one members to the House of Representatives, and Senator Martin Van Buren was elected governor of New York State. He would be returning to Albany, it seemed.

Van Buren only served as governor for a little more than two months, however, and then he resigned to become President Andrew Jackson's secretary of state.

Van Buren enjoyed his greatest success in this post. He was charming and tactful by nature, and he was highly respected by diplomats in France, England, and Turkey. They had considered President Jackson to be boorish and uncouth, and it was a relief to have urbane Van Buren taking part in negotiations between nations.

In France, Van Buren negotiated a settlement of American damage claims for losses during the Napoleonic wars. In England he worked out a trade agreement for United States trade with the West Indies, and in Turkey he got officials to allow Americans to have access to the Black Sea.

Vice President John C. Calhoun viewed Van Buren as his greatest potential rival to be the presidential candidate in 1832, and he blocked Van Buren's confirmation as minister to Great Britain when there was a tie vote in the Senate.

Calhoun was also motivated by his knowledge that President Jackson liked Van Buren. The vice president and President Jackson had become hostile in their own relationship because Calhoun had opposed Jackson's military activities in Florida years before. Mrs. Calhoun had also pointedly snubbed President Jackson's good friend Peggy Eaton on a recent occasion, and Calhoun had endorsed South Carolina's nullification of the Federal tariff laws when South Carolina voters decided the laws were not "binding upon this state."

Vice President Calhoun enjoyed knowing he had kept Van Buren from becoming the official minister to Great Britain, and he hoped Van Buren would go back to New York and stay.

"It will kill him dead, Sir, kill him dead," Calhoun said. "He will never kick, Sir, never kick."

Senator Thomas Hart Benton disagreed with Calhoun's assessment of the result of his actions. He told Calhoun he had broken a minister, but elected a vice president.

Senator Benton was a prophet. President Jackson was so angry with Vice President Calhoun that he asked Martin Van Buren to be his vice presidential candidate in the 1832 race, and dumped Calhoun from the ticket.

President Jackson was reelected, and Martin Van Buren was the new vice president. He supported the president on all his programs, although he had private doubts about the wisdom of withdrawing federal funds from the United States Bank. In public they were in total agreement.

With President Jackson's endorsement, Vice President Van Buren was elected president in 1836, and Richard M. Johnson, United States representative from Kentucky, was his vice president.

It was not a good time to be elected to the highest offices. As a result of President Jackson's banking activities during his last term in office, a financial panic occurred in 1837, only two months after Van Buren took office. This panic led to a depression which lasted for the next six years.

In 1839 hostilities broke out along the United States-Canadian border in the area of Maine. The border had never been clearly defined, and both countries claimed twelve thousand square miles of territory along the Aroostook River. The dispute was not settled until 1842 after President John Tyler was in office.

Texas had gained independence from Mexico in 1836 and presented a petition to join the United States. President Van Buren was opposed, however, because Texas would be a slaveholding state. Trouble seemed to pile on trouble.

A fortuitous event occurred during Van Buren's presidency when his son Abraham married former first lady Dolley Madison's niece, Angelica Singleton, in 1838. President Van Buren had found it difficult to keep track of household needs and entertaining without a wife to help him, but Angelica now assumed the duties of the official White House hostess.

President Van Buren ran for a second term in 1840 after being renominated by a unanimous vote of the Democratic National convention delegates. The delegates refused to renominate Vice President Johnson because of his life-style, and no candidate was nominated for vice president.

Van Buren was defeated by the Whig candidate, General William Henry Harrison. The former president returned to his home in Kinderhook, but not before he had spent some time in New York City attending the theater, opera, dinners, and other social gatherings.

When Van Buren reached Kinderhook, he was given a hero's welcome and escorted to his new home in the former Van Ness mansion. He had bought the property earlier and had it refurbished to his tastes. He named it Lindenwald (German for "linden forest").

Van Buren enjoyed the next few years he spent traveling to visit old friends in the United States and Europe. His sons had all married and were presenting him with a new grandson or granddaughter regularly. He loved his beautifully decorated and elegantly furnished mansion, but he could not quite let go of politics.

In the 1844 election, Van Buren wanted to be the Democratic nominee for president again, but James K. Polk from Tennessee was nominated and elected. In 1848, Van Buren ran for president on the Free Soil ticket, but he was defeated by Whig candidate General Zachary Taylor. Lewis Cass was the Democratic nominee for president that year.

When the Civil War started unofficially in 1860 with the secession of South Carolina and then other Southern states from the Union, Van Buren believed President Lincoln was doing the right thing to ask Northern states to provide soldiers and supplies to suppress the rebellion.

Van Buren spent the winter of 1860–61 in New York City, where he contracted pneumonia and began having circulatory problems. His health continued to decline steadily, and he died on July 24, 1862, at Lindenwald. He was buried beside his beloved wife, Hannah, in the Van Buren family plot in the village cemetery at Kinderhook.

Martin Van Buren left a legacy of honesty, loyalty, and honor in politics. Few politicians today will do the same.

Bibliography

Curtis, James C. *The Fox at Bay*. Lexington: University Press of Kentucky, 1970.
Niven, John. *Martin Van Buren*. New York: Oxford University Press, 1983.
Remini, Robert V. *Martin Van Buren and the Making of the Democratic Party*. New York: W. W. Norton, 1970.

9. Richard Mentor Johnson

Although he was a hero of the War of 1812, and possessed a brilliant intellect, Richard Mentor Johnson's unusual life-style prevented his being nominated for president or even renominated for vice president after the completion of his first term in that office. He was a kindly man who was concerned about the welfare of those less fortunate than he, and he established a school to educate young Indian boys.

When campaigning, Richard Johnson often said he was "born in a cane break and cradled in a sap trough," but to be more accurate, he was born in Beargrass (now Louisville), Kentucky, on October 17, 1780. His father, Robert Johnson, and his mother, the former Jemima Suggett, were in the process of resettling in Kentucky at the time Richard was born. They had been living in Virginia with their other four children, but they believed Kentucky offered greater opportunities than relatively crowded Virginia.

Robert Johnson found the water supply to be "sluggish" at Beargrass, and he soon moved his family on to Bryant's Station, near the present city of Lexington, Kentucky. He worked as a surveyor with Daniel Boone, another pioneer settler of the region. Johnson helped Boone and some of the other men in the area build the wagon roads that connected the various settlements.

Young Richard grew up enjoying outdoor activities, all the while keeping a sharp eye out for any sign of an Indian attack. He received his first basic education from his parents, but he began studying Latin at age fifteen when he enrolled in Elijah Craig's Latin School in nearby Scott County. It was a good opportunity for Richard to learn subjects his parents had not been taught.

After completing the courses at the Craig School, Johnson entered the Transylvania University in Lexington, where he studied law. He was admitted to the Kentucky bar in 1802. He did not formally graduate from the University, however, and incorrect reports later circulated that he had no formal education. He began the practice of law at Great Crossings, Kentucky.

Johnson was elected to serve in the Kentucky State legislature in 1804 and 1805. In 1806 he was nominated by the Democrat-Republican party in Kentucky to be its candidate for Kentucky's representative in the United States House of Representatives. He won the election.

Richard Mentor Johnson. Reproduced from the collections of the Library of Congress.

Representative Johnson supported President Thomas Jefferson when Jefferson decided to impose an embargo on all ships in American ports. The president hoped to avoid another war with England or France by economic means. England imported thirty-one million pounds of cotton each year from the United States to use in manufacturing cloth and other items, and many Englishmen would lose their jobs if the shipments of cotton stopped. Also foreign ships could not unload their cargoes in American ports.

France sold many of its exported products to the United States, and it was hoped France would be forced to respect the neutrality of United States ships if its trade was also cut off.

Instead of the plan working as Jefferson had hoped, United States merchants went bankrupt, everyone connected with shipping had no work, and farm products piled up in dock warehouses. President Jefferson admitted his error indirectly when he approved the Non-Intercourse Act in 1809, which partially restored shipping between the countries.

When President James Madison urged a declaration of war against Great Britain in 1812, Representative Johnson agreed the United States government had to establish sovereignty over its ships at sea. In fact, Johnson left Washington and returned to Kentucky, where he was named a colonel of a regiment of mounted riflemen preparing to help in any conflict.

Colonel Johnson had a talent for military strategy, and he enjoyed a remarkable success in his militia activities. His regiment under the command of Governor Isaac Shelby joined General William Henry Harrison at the border of the United States and Canada, where it was engaged in the Battle of Thames with the British and their Indian allies on October 5, 1813.

Colonel Johnson was seriously injured in the battle, during which he reportedly killed the great Indian chief Tecumseh. His regiment repelled the enemy, and soon other United States troops joined the battle.

Richard Johnson returned to the Kentucky home of his parents to recuperate from his wounds. His mother died on January 23, 1814, shortly after his return, and his father married a seventeen-year-old girl a few months later.

His father died on October 15, 1815, and under the terms of his father's will, Richard inherited a mulatto slave girl named Julia Chinn. His mother had liked Julia and had educated her in household affairs. She was the person Johnson turned to during his bereavement and recuperation.

Johnson had to wait for his wounds to heal before he could return to his seat in the House of Representatives, which he had not resigned when he left Washington earlier.

Representative Johnson finally returned to Washington in March 1815, but he still had a long way to go to be fully recovered. This was evident from a comment made by Attorney General Richard Rush in a letter written on September 8, 1840, which appeared in the *Louisville Public Advertiser*. Rush said he often attended gatherings in First Lady Dolley Madison's drawing rooms, where he and many others enjoyed her hospitality. One conspicuous guest, he wrote, was a man upon crutches; his frame all mutilated; moving with difficulty, yet an object of patriotic interest with everybody. The guest he mentioned was Representative Richard M. Johnson.

During his years in Congress from 1807 to 1819 and his years as a senator in the Congress from 1819 to 1829, Johnson lived in the home of the Reverend O.B. Brown, a Baptist preacher/politician. He did not set up a household of his own until he was elected vice president later.

When Johnson went home to Kentucky, Julia Chinn, his mulatto slave, became his mistress or his common-law wife. A widely published report in both the

Lexington Observer and *Kentucky Reporter* said Johnson had married Julia, and the report was never contradicted by anyone. According to Johnson's contemporaries, Julia was a beautiful woman.

The couple had two daughters, whom they named Adeline and Imogene, and Richard Johnson acknowledged they were his children. Julia was mistress of his household, and they lived together as a family.

On December 5, 1825, a resolution was adopted by the local Baptist board of the General Convention and the War Department of the federal government to allow Senator Richard Johnson to establish a school on his estate for the purpose of providing education to young Choctaw Indian youths. Johnson hired the Reverend Thomas Henderson to teach the students. Twenty-one Indians were enrolled with the understood purpose of providing them with sufficient education to enable them to enroll later in Transylvania University for higher education. By the next year, twenty-six Choctaws and ten local white boys were attending Choctaw Academy, including Johnson's own nephew, Robert Ward Johnson.

Senator Johnson wanted his two daughters to receive an education too, so he asked the Reverend Henderson if he would include them as students. Henderson agreed, saying, "I engaged on evenings, after the ordinary duties of the Academy were over, to give lessons to about six or eight servants, and the two females spoken of before. I soon discovered such uncommon aptness in those two girls to take in learning, that my mind became much enlisted in their favor. A stranger would not suspect them to be what they really are — the children of a colored woman."

In Washington, President John Quincy Adams stated his belief that federally sponsored internal improvements were a needed function of the new government. Secretary of State Martin Van Buren disagreed, saying many projects should be denied or stopped before demands on the national Treasury became overwhelming. Senator Andrew Jackson agreed with Van Buren.

When Richard Johnson, again a member of the House of Representatives, presented in April 1830 a request for a good turnpike to be built between Lexington, Kentucky, and Maysville, Kentucky, newly elected President Andrew Jackson vetoed it, with Van Buren's encouragement.

Their veto plans reached the ears of Representative Johnson, and he rushed to talk to the president about the importance of the road. He told President Jackson that his friends back in Kentucky would "be crushed like a fly with a sledge hammer" if the president vetoed the turnpike bill.

President Jackson asked him, "Have you looked at the condition of the Treasury — at the amount of money it contains . . . at the amount of other claims upon it?" Richard Johnson admitted he had not.

"Well, I have," President Jackson said. "I stand committed before the country to pay off the National debt. . . . There is no money to be expended as my friends desire."

President Jackson liked Johnson even if he did veto the turnpike bill. He knew Johnson was a courageous leader of the troops he led during the War of 1812, the same war in which Jackson served as a general of the army. While most Southerners despised Johnson for his choice of a mulatto woman as a mate, the president did not condemn him.

In July 1833, during a cholera epidemic, Richard Johnson's beloved Julia died. Their daughters both married white men. Adeline Johnson had already married Thomas W. Scott the year before her mother's death, and Imogene married Daniel B. Pence a few years later. Richard Johnson gave each of them a deed to a large tract of land for a wedding present.

As the election of 1836 neared, Martin Van Buren, a Democratic senator, was the heir-apparent to the presidency, fully supported by outgoing President Andrew Jackson. Politician Amos Kendall urged Van Buren to choose Richard Johnson to run for the vice president.

When the election results were tallied, presidential candidate Van Buren received 170 electoral votes, but vice presidential candidate Johnson only got 147 because Virginia electors refused to vote for him. The Senate then chose Richard Johnson to be vice president at Van Buren's urging, as the Constitution specified in the event no candidate for the office of vice president received a majority vote.

Just after the president and vice president had taken their oaths of office, a financial panic swept the country. There had been several bad crop years, the nation had an unfavorable trade balance with England, and banks failed due to unsound loans they had made previously.

In an attempt to improve his own financial status, Vice President Johnson opened a tavern, hotel, and resort on his Kentucky farm and spent much of his time there.

In Washington, Johnson rented a large house and entertained occasionally with the aid of a mulatto woman said to be a niece of Julia Chinn's. She always addressed her employer as "My dear Colonel." Washington society matrons were appalled by Johnson's living arrangements and boycotted most of his efforts to entertain socially.

Johnson was always an unusually casual dresser, preferring the rumpled look. He never wore a cravat, even when he presided over the Senate.

When the Democratic Convention of 1840 was held, President Van Buren was renominated, but the delegates refused to renominate Vice President Johnson. They left the post vacant. There was no ensuing problem since Whig candidate General William Henry Harrison was elected president, with John Tyler elected the new vice president.

In 1841, Richard Johnson retired to his Kentucky farm and gave his full attention to his resort called White Sulphur Spring. A friend of politician Amos Kendall reported after a visit to the resort: "I stopped yesterday evening at Colonel Johnson's watering establishment and stayed until today. The old gentleman seems to enjoy the business of *tavern-keeping* as well as any host I ever stopped with, and is a bustling a landlord as the most fastidious traveler could wish. . . . The Vice President . . . seems to be so happy in the inglorious pursuit of tavern-keeping—even giving his personal superintendence to the chicken and egg purchasing and watermelon selling department."

Before the election of 1844, Richard Johnson traveled to various states and talked with political leaders in an attempt to get the Democratic nomination for president, but he received little encouragement.

Johnson's Choctaw Academy closed in 1845 when the Choctaw tribe established a school on its reservation, but Johnson deserves credit for starting the education of young Indians and proving they were capable students.

Johnson remained in White Sulphur Spring until he was elected to serve in the Kentucky legislature in 1850. He was an affable, friendly man who continued to be popular with Kentucky voters. The *Kentucky Statesman* reported on July 24, 1850, "Few public men of this present day and generation can boast of such continued manifestations of public confidence within the limits of their home districts."

When Richard Johnson was seated in the legislature, he had been ill and he had gone to Frankfort against the advice of his doctors. The *Louisville Daily Journal* reported on November 9, 1850: "Colonel R. M. Johnson is laboring under an attack of dementia, which renders him totally unfit for business. It is painful to see him standing on the floor attempting to discharge the duties of a member."

On November 18, 1850, his death was announced in the Kentucky House of Representatives. He had died earlier that morning in his lodgings after suffering a stroke.

Richard Johnson was buried in the cemetery at Frankfort on November 23, 1850, "in the ground appropriated to the burial of Kentucky's illustrious dead," to quote the *Louisville Weekly Courier.*

Johnson was survived by two brothers, John T. and Henry Johnson, and his beloved grandson, Robert Johnson Scott, to whom he had deeded property in 1848.

Bibliography

Meyer, Leland Winfield. *The Life and Times of Colonel Richard M. Johnson of Kentucky.* New York: Columbia University Press, 1932.
Niven, John. *Martin Van Buren: The Romantic Age of American Politics.* New York: Oxford University Press, 1983.

10. John Tyler

When President William H. Harrison died after serving only one month in office, Vice President John Tyler did not hesitate to seize the reins of power and become president. He even returned mail addressed to him as "Acting President."

It was fortunate that he acted promptly, for the United States government could have been tied up for years in legal controversy about what the Constitution really meant when it said, "in case of the removal of the President from office, or of his death, resignation or inability to discharge the powers and duties of the said office, the same shall devolve on the Vice President."

Did "the same" mean the office or the duties? Some diehards never believed President Tyler had a right to be president and referred to him as "His Accidency."

John Tyler was born on March 29, 1790, into the aristocratic family of Judge John Tyler, Sr., and his wife, the former Mary Armistead. The family lived on a twelve-hundred-acre plantation called Greenway, which was located between Richmond and Williamsburg, Virginia.

It is not certain where young John began his education, but it was probably with a tutor in his home. His mother died when the little boy was only seven years old, so she did not have long to be his teacher, as mothers often were then.

When he was twelve years old, John enrolled in the preparatory division of William and Mary College in Williamsburg. He progressed to classical college courses in languages, English literature, history, and economics. In 1807 he graduated at age seventeen.

John's father taught him to play a violin, and he also taught his son law and indoctrinated him with his political and economic beliefs. Judge Tyler was an unabashed friend and admirer of Thomas Jefferson.

Young John Tyler was elected to serve in the Virginia House of Delegates in 1811, and in his first term, he managed to get a resolution passed asking that the Virginia legislature retain the right to instruct the United States senators it sent to Washington about voting and other issues.

With his growing law practice and his demonstrated ability to exert political influence in high places, the young man decided he was ready to marry. He

John Tyler. Reproduced from the collections of the Library of Congress.

and Letitia Christian of Cedar Grove Plantation in New Kent County were married on March 29, 1813. She was a member of a wealthy Virginia family that was also prominent in politics.

It was a happy, serene marriage that produced seven children as time went by. They lived at Mons-Sacer, a five-hundred-acre tract inherited by John Tyler from the Greenway estate when his father died earlier that year.

No sooner had the newlyweds settled into their new marriage and home than John was called to military duty in action against the British. Judge Tyler had hated the redcoats, and his son shared his views on that subject too.

John Tyler reported for duty with the local militia, the Charles City Rifles, where he was given a commission as a captain. They were ordered to go to Williamsburg.

When they reached their destination, the new recruits were quartered upstairs in a building on the William and Mary College campus. Night after night went by with no sign of enemy redcoats, until rumor had it one night that redcoats had been seen entering Williamsburg.

The recruits were drowsy, having been awakened from a sound sleep, and all of them rushed toward the stairs at the same time, tumbled down them, and landed in a tangled heap at the bottom. The rumor turned out to be false.

The company was reassigned to the Second Elite Corps of Virginia, but members returned to their home a month later without ever seeing a redcoat. John Tyler laughed often when he recalled his military career.

After the War of 1812 ended, Tyler turned his attention back to politics and was elected to represent the Richmond district in the United States House of Representatives in 1816.

Washington, D.C., was a muddy mess at that time in our nation's history, and Letitia Tyler chose to remain on their plantation in Virginia with their children. When Congress was in session, John stayed in the capital city in a boardinghouse operated by Mrs. McDaniels. He kept in close touch with his wife and children through correspondence. His living conditions bordered on the primitive and the food was barely edible, but he believed it was his duty to represent the people of Virginia.

John Tyler was elected to the House for three consecutive terms but resigned in January 1821 because he was in the minority opposing high tariffs, funding internal improvements with federal money, and chartering the Bank of the United States. Believing his efforts were ineffectual, he went home.

In 1823, Tyler returned to the Virginia House of Delegates, and he was elected governor of Virginia by the state legislature in 1825. As governor, Tyler advocated improvements in public transportation, with a program of canal and road constructions all over the state. He also wanted public schools established for education statewide, but he failed to gain either of his projects. He resigned as governor to take a seat in the United States Senate.

Between 1820 and 1830, Letitia Tyler had five more babies, bringing the total to seven. One of the children died when only a few weeks old. John had acquired a small crowd of children to feed, clothe, and educate, but he was not a good financial manager. His political jobs, prestigious as they were, did not pay well, and he was in constant need of more money.

The Virginia legislature elected Tyler to serve as one of its United States senators in 1826, and he served in the U.S. Senate until 1836.

At first, John Tyler was a loyal supporter of President Andrew Jackson, but as time passed, he came to consider Jackson a virtual dictator who tried to impose his will on the American people through the use of force. Tyler had adopted the political beliefs of the new Whig party, and he joined their ranks.

Tyler was elected to the Virginia House of Delegates by the Whigs: he served from 1838 until 1840 and was named Speaker of the House in 1839.

The next year, Tyler was named vice presidential nominee by the Whigs on a ticket with presidential candidate William Henry Harrison. They won the election and were inaugurated on March 4, 1841. President Harrison died one month later, on April 4.

Vice President Tyler had returned to his home in Virginia after the inauguration, and he had to ride horseback all night to hurry back to Washington to be sworn in as president. He took the oath of office on April 6 and went to President Harrison's funeral the next day.

From the beginning, Tyler insisted he was President Tyler, not acting president, not temporary president, not an illegal usurper of the office. He firmly believed that he was the legal president as provided by the Constitution and he acted accordingly.

On April 14 that year, the Tylers moved into the White House. Letitia came to Washington with John this time, but her health was so poor from a recent stroke she had suffered that her death was considered to be imminent. She remained in her upstairs bedroom most of the time she was first lady, while her daughters and daughter-in-law served as hostesses at state dinners and other gatherings.

President John Tyler set off a fire-storm of protest when he vetoed the measure to recharter the Bank of the United States. He was threatened in letters that he would be assassinated. Mutterings of "He ought to be impeached" were heard. His entire cabinet resigned in protest except for his secretary of state, Daniel Webster.

President Tyler stood firmly by his principles and ignored his critics, but the price he paid was high. The Whig party expelled him from its ranks.

He was still president, however, and he settled some thorny issues during his administration. The border between the United States and Canada was established from the Atlantic coast to the Rocky Mountains, the United States finally gained entry to Chinese ports for trading, and Texas statehood was assured.

First Lady Letitia Tyler died on September 10, 1842, and was taken back to Cedar Grove, her family home, for her burial. She and John Tyler had been married for twenty-nine years.

President Tyler was introduced to Julia Gardiner of Long Island, New York, at a White House reception in 1842 shortly before his wife's death. He began seeing Julia socially in January 1843, and they were married in New York City on June 26, 1844. John was fifty-four years old, and his bride was twenty-four.

The Tyler children were stunned by their father's remarriage. Julia was five years younger than Mary, John's oldest daughter. His daughter Letitia never accepted Julia as her stepmother.

The newlyweds went back to live in the White House after a wedding trip to Philadelphia. Julia loved her new importance as first lady. In the last month of her husband's term as president, she arranged a White House ball for three thousand guests.

John Tyler retired with his new wife to Sherwood Forest, a twelve-hundred-acre plantation in Virginia he had bought earlier. It was located only a few miles from where he was born. There Julia gave birth to seven more little Tylers, and John's financial problems continued.

When the nation became divided on the slavery question, Tyler pleaded with the delegates at a convention of representatives from twelve states held in an effort to compromise and preserve the Union. His attempts as peacemaker failed, however, and the Civil War began.

In November 1861, Tyler was elected to a seat in the Confederate House of Representatives, but he died on January 18, 1862, in Richmond before he was seated. Julia was with him.

Tyler's body was taken to the Hollywood Cemetery in Richmond for burial, where his grave is beside that of President James Monroe.

Union government officials took no notice of Tyler's death, even though he was a former president. Finally in 1915 the United States Congress had a memorial stone marker placed at his grave.

Julia Tyler survived John by twenty-seven years and loyally supported the Southern cause even after she returned to Staten Island in New York to stay with her mother.

Julia came back to live in Virginia after the war had ended. She died in Richmond on July 10, 1889, after suffering a stroke and was buried beside her husband.

Bibliography

Chidsey, Donald Barr. *And Tyler Too*. Nashville, Tenn.: Thomas Nelson, 1978.

Morgan, Robert J. *A Whig Embattled: The Presidency Under John Tyler*. Lincoln: University of Nebraska Press, 1954.

Seager, Robert. *And Tyler Too: A Biography of John and Julia Gardiner Tyler*. New York: McGraw-Hill, 1963.

11. George Mifflin Dallas

George Mifflin Dallas received more praise and honor as a diplomat than he did as vice president in President James K. Polk's administration. It was not that Dallas was not an effective vice president, but rather that times were troubled as the Civil War approached.

George Dallas was born July 10, 1792, in Philadelphia to Alexander and Arabella Smith Dallas. Alexander Dallas was a lawyer, had been involved in politics for many years, and had served as secretary of the treasury in President James Madison's administration.

Young George began his education in a school in Germantown, moving on to a Friends' school in that city. He went to Princeton University in 1807 to complete his education and graduated at age seventeen as the top student in his class.

George studied law in his father's office for the next three years to prepare for the bar examination required to practice law. He found himself bored by the endless study, and in 1813 he volunteered to serve in the Pennsylvania militia. Alexander Dallas had another son serving in the United States Navy, however, and he did not think the family should provide a second son for the defense structure in the nation. He ordered George to come home.

Reluctantly, George returned home as his father wished, but then his luck changed. Albert Gallatin was going to Russia on a diplomatic mission for President Madison to seek a mediated settlement by the czar in the War of 1812 between the United States and England.

Diplomat Gallatin was a friend of George's father, and he promised Mr. Dallas he would take the young man with him to Russia as his private secretary if Alexander Dallas would pay his son's expenses. All arrangements were made, and George was ecstatic to be visiting Europe. He was twenty-one years old and ready for adventure.

Gallatin was also taking along his own sixteen-year-old son, James, and John Payne Todd, President Madison's stepson. Todd seemed to be uncertain about what he wanted to do in life, and President and Mrs. Madison thought the trip to Russia and his association with men involved in government affairs might be beneficial to the young man, who was also twenty-one years old.

George M. Dallas. Reproduced from the collections of the Library of Congress.

The delegation left for Russia on May 9, 1813, and arrived on July 21 that year. There they learned that English officials had turned down prior settlement proposals offered by Russian officials. The Russians were involved themselves in a war with France, now governed by Napoleon Bonaparte.

George Dallas was excited to be in a foreign country, and he traveled throughout Russia for the next few weeks. He was greatly impressed by the Russian czar, Alexander I, and later described him as "the best bred gentleman in Europe."

Albert Gallatin decided to send George Dallas to England to be the "eyes and ears" for the American government, although he had no power to enter into negotiations with officials there. Dallas spent several weeks in England in limbo before he learned Gallatin had left Russia to go to Amsterdam, and Dallas went to join him and the others there.

In late August 1814, Gallatin sent Dallas back to Washington with a preliminary peace treaty for President Madison's approval. When Dallas reached Washington in late October, he found President and Mrs. Madison were getting settled in the Octagon House, having been forced to leave the White House when it was burned by British forces.

His part in diplomacy finished, Dallas turned his attention to a young lady in Philadelphia named Sophia Chew Nicklin, the daughter of a prominent businessman in the city.

George Dallas knew he needed to have a job if he planned to marry, so he took and passed the bar examination and started a law practice with Charles J. Ingersall, a good friend, in 1815. They handled a wide variety of legal matters, but the income was only adequate.

George and Sophia were married on May 23, 1816, however, and they lived with his mother for the next several years. The elder Mrs. Dallas was a widow, and she was glad to have their company, her husband having died several months before their marriage.

George and Sophia Dallas had a total of eight children during their years together — two sons, Alexander James and Philip, and six daughters, Julia, Elizabeth, Sophia, Catherine, Susan, and Charlotte. Their oldest son was born hydrocephalic and died when he was only nine years old.

Despite his law duties, Dallas was a loving, devoted father who took time to play with his children. He often played a variation of "follow the leader" and other active games with them.

Political parties were in a state of flux during the early 1800s, with the Federalists calling themselves Independent Republicans and the Democratic-Republican party divided into new school and old school factions.

George Dallas, Thomas Sargeant, Richard Bache, Samuel Ingham, William Wilkins, and other Pennsylvania politicians decided to found a new political party. Since most of the charter members were either relatives or in-laws of the others, it was called the "Family party."

George Dallas was serving as the deputy attorney general of Pennsylvania when a movement arose in 1819 to impeach the Pennsylvania governor for corruption and malfeasance in office. Dallas defended Governor Findlay, and the governor was cleared of all charges after a long trial. The verdict was not popular with voters, however, and Dallas resigned as deputy attorney general before a newly elected governor could fire him.

During this time of turmoil, George Dallas was also legal counsel for the Bank of the United States in his state, which brought in extra income with which to support his increasing family. He also worked as an attorney for other clients after he left the deputy attorney general position, but he did not neglect his political activities.

Dallas and other Family party members believed Secretary of War John C. Calhoun could be elected president in 1821, and they promoted his campaign vigorously, while belittling the qualifications of Secretary of State John Quincy Adams, Calhoun's likely rival in the 1824 election.

Despite their early start, the best Dallas and his fellow Family party members could do for Calhoun was to get him elected as vice president on a ticket with John Quincy Adams.

In the 1828 election, Vice President Calhoun was reelected, but the new president was General Andrew Jackson, hero of the War of 1812, who defeated incumbent President Adams.

In 1831, George Dallas was named as one of Pennsylvania's members in the United States Senate when Senator Isaac D. Bernard resigned because of bad health.

By 1833, the Family party's influence was reduced dramatically by its prior support for Vice President John C. Calhoun. This endorsement returned to haunt the party when Calhoun threatened nullification of the tariff bills of 1828 and 1833 in his home state of South Carolina. Both bills were helpful to Pennsylvania citizens, and they would not support a candidate who opposed the bills.

Sophia Dallas did not move to Washington when her husband was elected senator in 1831, and it was the first time they had been apart for a significant length of time since their marriage. Even though she visited him in Washington occasionally, both were unhappy apart, and as a result, George Dallas did not seek reelection in 1833.

Dallas really believed he was through with politics, and he returned to his law practice with relief. When Martin Van Buren of New York was elected president in 1836, however, Pennsylvania Democrats, who had campaigned and won their states' votes for Van Buren, thought the new president should appoint a Pennsylvania citizen to his cabinet. Instead, he offered the post of minister to Russia to George Dallas of Pennsylvania, and that was all.

Dallas was pleased with the offer because Pennsylvania financiers had blamed him for the failure to have the Bank of the United States chartered as a state agency. He had openly opposed the idea, and as punishment, he and his family were being shunned in Quaker Philadelphia by bankers and businessmen. None of the Dallas family was invited to any gatherings of a social nature, and their society friends refused to attend parties hosted by the Dallases.

George and Sophia Dallas, accompanied by seven of their children, arrived in Russia on July 29, 1837. They were soon settled in a "snug house" belonging to a Russian count in St. Petersburg. There George and Sophia were presented at Court to the Emperor Nicholas I and Empress Alexandra. George and Sophia Dallas were pleasantly surprised by the relaxed and pleasant atmosphere prevailing at the Peterhoff Palace where the emperor and his family lived.

Dallas's efforts to arrive at a diplomatic solution in the Russian-American disagreement about territorial claims north of the 54°40' parallel were unsuccessful, largely because of the intransigent attitude of Count Nesselrode, vice-chancellor to the czar.

Despite the count's rejection of Dallas's proposals, Mrs. Dallas and their daughters enjoyed the Russian social season of parties and balls, but they sensed their social activities were closely monitored. Because of the intense scrutiny, Dallas was unable to learn anything significant about Russia's internal affairs or government activities.

Another problem encountered by the Dallas family was the stinginess of the United States government in providing for their living expenses. Dallas complained to a Philadelphia colleague, Henry Gilpin, about his insufficient salary, writing, "The expense of living here exceeds all belief. . . . Food prices and rent are enormously high." Also, the only schools available for young Phillip Dallas to attend were expensive military academies.

Former first lady Louisa Adams had complained of much the same conditions when she and her husband, John Quincy Adams, had lived in Russia during his diplomatic mission. Mrs. Adams had been forced to make her own ball gowns.

Since George Dallas was not able to come to any agreement with Russian officials anyway, he requested that he be recalled home, and his request was granted.

Home had never looked better to the Dallas family members than when they got back to Philadelphia in autumn 1839. Dallas returned to his law practice, where he stayed for the next four years.

The issue of the annexation of Texas by the United States arose during the period after the return of George Dallas, with President John Tyler fully supporting the annexation. Texas had been an independent territory since 1836, and the citizens there wanted to join the United States. George Dallas voiced his own approval, but he had no idea what would result from his opinion.

Tennessean James K. Polk was named the presidential nominee of the Democrats for the 1844 election, and Polk also favored annexation of Texas.

Polk wanted a like-minded candidate on the ticket with him for vice president, and with the urging of the Pennsylvania delegates at the convention,

George Dallas was nominated as vice president. He would have been pleased if he had known about it, but he was not there.

A delegation of sixty men from the convention arrived at the Dallas home at three o'clock in the morning on May 31. When George Dallas opened his front door, he was stunned by the sight of the crowd of men standing there, and even more amazed by their startling news.

Members of the Whig party were quietly confident their candidates, Henry Clay for president and Theodore Frelinghausen for vice president, would win the election, so they did not get too excited about the opposition. They too received a surprise a few months later when President Polk and Vice President Dallas were elected.

As vice president, George Dallas worked hard, and he and President Polk had a harmonious relationship. The president kept Dallas fully informed about government activities.

Although Dallas had previously favored a high protective tariff to aid the Pennsylvania economy, when President Polk wanted to lower the tariff in 1846, Vice President Dallas supported the move and cast the tie-breaking vote in the Senate for the Walker Tariff Bill, which reduced import taxes.

Pennsylvania citizens were outraged by Dallas's vote and considered his action treasonous to the state. They hanged him in effigy from telegraph wires only recently installed in Philadelphia, and newspapers were vehemently opposed to any possibility Dallas might run for president in the next election.

The daily barrages of insults were so violent that Vice President Dallas feared for the safety of his family, still in Philadelphia. He urged Sophia to bring the children to live in Washington for a while until tempers cooled. They came and stayed with him for several weeks, and when they returned to Philadelphia, they encountered no problems.

As his term as vice president drew to a close, George Dallas was eager to return to his home and family, and they were glad to have him back. In January 1849, he wrote Sophia that it was only one more month until they could begin spending the rest of their lives together.

President Polk had become more distant in his attitude toward Dallas in recent weeks, possibly viewing him as a potential rival in upcoming elections. He ignored his vice president's recommendations for appointments to offices and did not even invite him to a presidential dinner for government officials he and Mrs. Polk hosted in December 1848.

George Dallas retired thankfully and went back to his law practice, now much more active since he had been a vice president. He was one of Pierce Butler's lawyers when Butler divorced British actress Fanny Kemble. (Butler was a wealthy South Carolina plantation owner.) Dallas continued to handle railroad mergers, business contracts, and other business matters.

The slavery issue continued to grow in American society, and Dallas expressed the view that since the Constitution did not refer to a nation, the United

States was a confederation of sovereign states that had the right to decide on an individual basis about slavery and its abolishment.

When incumbent President Franklin Pierce realized Dallas might be a rival candidate for president in 1856, he offered him a diplomatic mission to London in January of that year. Dallas accepted because he had little confidence in his supporters' abilities to get a nomination for him as the next president.

At the Democratic Convention in 1845, it was painfully evident that former vice president Dallas would not receive a groundswell of support for his nomination. James Buchanan was the obvious favorite and won the nomination and later the election.

The Dallas family arrived in England on March 13, 1856. In the group accompanying George were Sophia, her sister, three unmarried Dallas daughters, and Philip Dallas, their son, who would serve as his father's secretary.

George Dallas had been sent to England to clear up the differences in interpretation of the Clayton-Bulwer Treaty which had been signed in 1850 and to make it clear to the government officials in England that American men could not be recruited to fight for British causes.

In the matter of the recruitment, it turned out that some British officials and a number of private citizens had expressed their disapproval of the practice, so it was not too difficult to get the recruitment stopped legally.

George Dallas failed in his attempt to get the amended Clayton-Bulwer Treaty accepted by British officials. The treaty concerned the construction of a canal in Central America to provide a passageway between the Atlantic and Pacific oceans. Each country would maintain neutrality, with neither having absolute control over the canal. Neither England nor the United States could fortify the area around the canal, colonize Central America, or exercise dominion in the region.

Even though George Dallas and his family remained in England for four more years, President Buchanan ignored his presence and used Secretary of State Lewis Cass to negotiate with the British government. No final action occurred until 1901, when England conceded to the United States the right to build, exclusively police, and operate a canal across the country of Panama, if the United States would agree to keep the canal open to ships of all nations, with fees to be uniformly charged.

When the British began seizures and recruitment of American men again in 1858, Dallas protested forcefully to the British officials, and they agreed to end the practice at once, claiming they had boarded the ships to ascertain their nationality. Both they and Dallas, for the United States, agreed that flying flags on ships would be wise, and their identification by that method proved sufficient.

George Dallas felt vindicated by this success, and he was glad to return home to Philadelphia in June 1861, although he had enjoyed his stay in England more than his previous assignment in Russia.

With a Civil War now raging in the United States, railroads were vital to the war effort. British owners of the Atlantic and Great Western Railroad asked Dallas to serve as the president of their railroad not long after he got back to Philadelphia.

Dallas was relieved to be offered a job not connected with politics that paid well, and he accepted. On December 30, 1864, he went out to shop and take care of business matters. He appeared to be in good health, but he died the next night of an apparent heart attack.

George Dallas had died without a fortune to leave to his family, for his social and political connections had always outranked his income. Young Philip took care of his mother until his own death in 1866, at which time Sophia went to live with a married daughter. Sophia died in 1869.

All three, George, Sophia, and Philip Dallas, were buried in St. Peter's Church cemetery in Philadelphia.

Bibliography

Belohlavek, John M. *George Mifflin Dallas: Jacksonian Patrician.* University Park: Pennsylvania State University Press, 1977.

Klein, Philip Shriver. *President James Buchanan: A Biography.* University Park: Pennsylvania State University Press, 1970.

Nichols, Ray Franklin. *Franklin Pierce: Young Hickory of the Granite Hills.* Philadelphia: University of Pennsylvania Press, 1931.

Sellers, Charles Grier, Jr. *James K. Polk, Jacksonian.* Princeton: Princeton University Press, 1957.

12. Millard Fillmore

Millard Fillmore was born January 7, 1800, to Nathaniel and Phoebe Millard Fillmore. He was their first son. Nathaniel Fillmore was a farmer in the Finger Lakes area of central New York State. Young Millard spent his early years helping his father hoe corn, plow fields, and clear more land for farming.

When he was fourteen, Millard was apprenticed to a processor of cloth whose workplace was located near the Fillmore home. That apprenticeship lasted only four months, but Millard's next apprenticeship lasted until the boy reached the age of nineteen. The work was also in a cloth mill, but the owners were better suited to teach him his trade.

By this time in his life, the cloth trade was the most Millard Fillmore had learned. He could read little but the Bible. It was the establishment of a new academy at New Hope, a small town nearby, that led him to broaden his education.

Despite his age, Fillmore enrolled in the academy as soon as it opened, and it was here he met his future wife, who was a teacher in the school. The young woman's name was Abigail Powers. She inspired Millard to work diligently at his studies, which he enjoyed anyway.

Fillmore was surprised and pleased when his father made arrangements in 1819 for him to work as a clerk in the law office of the county judge, Walter Wood. Judge Wood accepted Millard on a probationary basis.

When Fillmore's two months of employment in the law office had passed, Judge Wood told him that if he could pay off his apprenticeship at the cloth mill, he would teach him fundamental law so he could go into practice.

Millard Fillmore was thrilled to be given such a wonderful opportunity, and he accepted a job teaching in one of the local schools to earn money to buy out his apprenticeship. He believed he was on the road out of poverty when he was finally free of the cloth mill. He paid $30 for his apprenticeship release.

Judge Wood's heart may have been kind, but he proved to be impossible to please. He became highly indignant with Fillmore when the young man accepted a case to try in a justice of the peace court in 1821.

Fillmore tried to explain he needed money to pay living expenses, and the case was settled out of court anyway, but the judge would not accept his explana-

Millard Fillmore. Reproduced from the collections of the Library of Congress.

tion. Fillmore decided the judge simply planned to keep him on to work as a drudge instead of allowing him to be a real lawyer, and he left his job in Judge Wood's office.

His dreams of a better life shattered, Fillmore went back to helping his father work on the family farm. His father had bought another farm and moved the family nearer to Buffalo, New York, and he urged Millard to visit lawyers in Buffalo to see if one of them would hire him as a clerk.

Early in 1822, Fillmore got a job with the law firm of Rice and Clary. The attorneys agreed that he could continue teaching school for the three months each year it was in session and then work for them studying law for the other nine months. About a year later, he was admitted to the bar.

Millard Fillmore set up his own law practice in East Aurora, New York, while he continued to study law to fill in the areas with which he was unfamiliar. He was moderately successful in his practice because he was the only lawyer in town, and after two years he decided he could afford to marry Abigail, who was still waiting patiently.

On February 5, 1826, Abigail and Millard were married in her hometown of Moravia, and they went to live in East Aurora. The next year their son, Millard Powers Fillmore, was born.

Soon Fillmore became involved in local politics, as lawyers often do. When a local man was rumored to have been murdered by members of the town's Masonic Order, an anti-Masonic political party was formed, and Fillmore joined it. The anti-Masons elected him to serve in the New York General Assembly, but since he knew little about legislative matters, he maintained a low profile during his first year in the Assembly.

Millard Fillmore was a quick study, and by 1830, he was making speeches and introducing bills in the legislature. He projected an image of bluff sincerity when he spoke slowly and simply, using ordinary words in his speeches. He discovered he enjoyed political maneuvering and intrigue.

That same year Millard and Abigail took their son and moved to Buffalo to live in a six-room frame house at 180 Franklin Street. Here he rejoined his former law colleague Joseph Clary, and they formed a law partnership.

In Buffalo the Fillmores were accepted into local society with no questions asked, which pleased them greatly. They joined the Unitarian church, where they made more acquaintances and friends. Their daughter Mary Abigail was born in Buffalo a few months later.

In November 1832, Fillmore was elected to the United States House of Representatives by the anti-Masons. His present law partner, Joseph Clary, was also a justice of the peace, which occupied much of his time, and with Fillmore gone for long periods of time, they were forced to dissolve their partnership. Fillmore asked his law clerk, Nathan K. Hall, to join him in his practice.

New York political leader, Thurlow Weed was an editor whom Fillmore admired, and when Weed decided he preferred the new Whig political party over the anti-Masons, Fillmore followed his lead and joined the Whigs also.

In 1840 the Whigs elected their first president, General William Henry Harrison, a war hero. Representative Fillmore was named chairman of the House Ways and Means Committee, an important and pivotal post for advancement in politics.

Millard Fillmore did not seek reelection to his House seat in 1842 because he was hoping to be elected to the United States Senate instead in 1844 or possibly to be named a candidate for vice president. Instead, Thurlow Weed insisted Fillmore would be an excellent candidate for election as governor of New York, but he was mistaken. Fillmore was defeated in the 1844 campaign for governor, his first political defeat.

In 1848 the Whig party was split into two factions — the Southern plantation owners, who were in favor of continuing slavery, and the Northern industrialists, who were mostly abolitionists.

General Zachary Taylor was nominated to be the presidential candidate, as he was both pro-Union and a slaveowner. When Fillmore was offered a place on the ticket as vice president, he accepted with pleasure. Taylor and Fillmore were elected, and they were not even introduced until after the election.

President Taylor and his staff ignored Vice President Fillmore after the inauguration on March 5, 1849. Fillmore was not consulted about cabinet appointments or policy formulation. He was not even allowed to make patronage suggestions about appointments in his own state of New York.

When the Compromise of 1850 was introduced in the Senate, President Taylor was opposed to the measure, but Fillmore told him he believed it was in the national interest to pass the Compromise and he would vote for it if the Senate deadlocked.

The Compromise of 1850 was seen by many as the last hope to avert a civil war in the country. States formed from territory recently acquired from Mexico could decide for themselves about slavery. The measure also established the borders of the state of Texas, New Mexico, and Utah and provided that the federal government would return runaway slaves to their masters.

Before a final vote was taken in the Compromise of 1850, however, President Taylor died on July 9, 1850, after a short illness, and Millard Fillmore was sworn in as president the next day in a joint session of Congress.

The Compromise of 1850 was adopted, but the Whig party was permanently split because of it.

Millard Fillmore, Jr., became his father's presidential secretary. He was now a lawyer, following in his father's choice of career. Mary Abigail filled in as White House hostess when First Lady Abigail was not able to attend state dinners and other social affairs.

President Polk had attempted to buy Cuba from Spain for $100 million during his term as president. Spain refused to sell, and a Venezuelan soldier-of-fortune, Narciso Lopez, decided to lead an invasion of the island. Unfortunately, he outfitted his fellow invaders in the United States.

Great Britain became alarmed and proposed a treaty between its government, France, and the United States which would guarantee none of the three would ever take possession of Cuba. When Lopez and his companions were either killed during their landing on Cuban shores or were shot by Spanish troops as hostile invaders, it became evident that the United States was not engaging in a ruse to acquire Cuba. President Fillmore believed the acquisition of Cuba would cause more problems than it was worth, and the controversy ended.

President Fillmore decided not to seek reelection in 1852. Tensions between Northern and Southern factions remained high, and he was not sure he could continue to hold the nation together.

Because he was well-liked, Fillmore received messages of support for his candidacy for a second term from all over the country. Seventy-year-old Secretary of State Daniel Webster decided to enter the presidential race if Fillmore did not run.

At the convention, Webster could not get the votes necessary from the delegates. He received only twenty-eight out of two hundred and ninety-six. After fifty-three ballots were taken, Winfield Scott of New Jersey was nominated to be the Whig candidate for president.

Poor Daniel Webster was humiliated by his lack of support after devoting most of his adult years to government service, and he died a few months later in October.

President Fillmore and his wife began preparing to return to Buffalo when his term ended. After all their household possessions had been shipped ahead, only one duty remained — that of attending the inauguration of incoming President Franklin Pierce.

The cold March wind blew in strong gusts across the portico where the Fillmores watched the inauguration of the new president, and it had been snowing from time to time. Mrs. Fillmore was severely chilled, and the next morning doctors discovered she had developed pneumonia. The Fillmores were told they would have to remain in Washington until she recovered.

After three weeks of battling the illness, Abigail Fillmore died on March 30, 1853. Instead of beginning the retirement she and Millard had planned, she returned to Buffalo to be buried in Forest Lawn Cemetery there.

About a year later, at the end of July 1854, young Mary Abigail Fillmore died from cholera. The loss of both his wife and daughter in such a short time brought on a severe depression in Fillmore, who decided to travel. For the next sixteen months, he traveled extensively through the United States and Europe. He returned to run for president again in 1856, but he was defeated by James Buchanan.

On February 10, 1858, Fillmore married Caroline Carmichael McIntosh in Albany. Caroline was the widow of a wealthy Albany businessman, Ezekiel McIntosh.

Fillmore and his new wife became active in civic affairs in Buffalo, and they bought a house. He worked diligently to help establish the Buffalo Fine Arts Academy and to preserve and improve the Buffalo Historical Society. From the founding of the University of Buffalo in 1846 until his death, Fillmore served as chancellor of the university.

In their later years, Caroline Fillmore's health declined, and they went to Europe in 1866 to see if there was any sort of treatment that would benefit her. Millard Fillmore continued to feel well, and on January 7, 1874, he wrote his friend Corcoran, "My health is perfect, I eat, drink and sleep as well as ever."

On February 13, 1874, however, Millard Fillmore suffered a stroke, which was followed by two others and he died on March 8, 1874. He was also buried in Forest Lawn Cemetery.

Caroline Fillmore lived seven years after her husband's death. She was an invalid in their Buffalo mansion and required constant care before her death on August 11, 1881.

Bibliography

Hamilton, Holman. *Zachary Taylor: Soldier in the White House.* Indianapolis: Bobbs-Merrill, 1951.

Rayback, Robert J. *Millard Fillmore.* Buffalo, N.Y.: Henry Stewart, Incorporated, for the Buffalo Historical Society, 1959.

13. William Rufus Devane King

Vice President William Rufus Devane King was a descendant on his father's side of colonists who settled along the James River in Virginia in the 1600s. On his mother's side, he was a descendant of a prominent French Huguenot who left France to go to Scotland and then came to America in the early 1700s. These earlier settlers felt an obligation to serve their fellow citizens and government, and William King continued the tradition.

Young William was born in Sampson County, North Carolina, on April 7, 1786, to William and Margaret Devane King. William King was a wealthy land owner who was able to provide well for his seven children, Thomas, William, John, Tabitha, Helen, Margaret, and Ann.

When William Jr. was born, the country was still being governed under the Articles of Confederation and the United States Constitution had yet to be written.

The boy began his education in Grove Academy in nearby Duplin County, and he moved on later to Fayetteville schools in Cumberland County, both near his home. The schools were operated by Presbyterian ministers, and subjects taught included Greek and Latin, all sciences, English literature, and mathematics.

William transferred to the preparatory school at the University of North Carolina in Chapel Hill in 1800, where an instructor noted, "In this class James Battle and William King are the best; and bid fair to be good scholars; as they are diligent in their Studies and punctual in the performance of all their duties."

When the board of trustees of the university examined William's class on June 22, 1801, he was found to be "outstanding" in spelling, reading, and Caesar's *Commentaries*, and "distinguished" in English, Latin, and mathematics.

When he was fifteen years old, William was judged to be ready to enroll in the freshman class at the university. He may have learned enough from books to qualify him for college courses, but he was immature in his behavior, as were some of his classmates. The boys brought a calf into chapel, stole beehives and spread the honey on the floors of classrooms, cut down corn in nearby farmers' fields, and generally made nuisances of themselves. Records show William was fined on several occasions for rule infractions.

William R. King. Reproduced from the collections of the Library of Congress.

William King left the university in the summer of 1804 before graduation, and there is no record why he did so. He had decided to study law, and he may have thought a degree would not be necessary. King began studying with William Duffy of Fayetteville a few weeks later. He was admitted to the North Carolina bar in 1806 and opened a practice in Clinton.

From 1808 to 1818, King laid a foundation on which to build a future in politics. He was elected to the North Carolina House of Commons in 1808 and to the United States House of Representatives in 1810. He was always a loyal Republican, supporting President Thomas Jefferson's policies and later those of President Andrew Jackson. When President James Madison advocated a declaration of war against England in 1812, Representative King voted for war.

On April 23, 1816, William King was commissioned to go to Italy, Sicily, and Russia as secretary of the legation headed by Ambassador William Pinkney. King resigned from the House of Representatives.

In Europe, the American legation was formally presented to the king of Italy, and William King was sent on to Russia in advance of the other members of the legation to make sure Ambassador Pinkney would be received by the Russian czar.

In July 1817, King left Russia alone to return to the United States. It is not clear why he left, but it may have been the Russian winter cold was more than he could stand. He had already been sick several times while he was there.

After his return King bought a plantation in the Cahaba area of the Alabama Territory. He helped organize a state government, and Alabama was admitted to the Union a few months later. He named his plantation in Alabama "King's Bend."

King was elected by Alabama voters to serve in the United States Senate in 1819. He supported the Missouri Compromise and Land Act of 1820, which relaxed mortgage payments on land bought earlier by farmers from the government. The intent was to extend settlements on the frontier when the land was sold and to give the farmers a deserved break.

Senator King was reelected to the Senate in 1822, 1828, 1834, and 1840. In 1844 he was named by President John Tyler to be United States minister plenipotentiary to France. His mission there was to persuade French officials, especially the king of France, Louis Philippe, not to oppose the annexation of Texas by the United States government.

King successfully convinced the French ruler that a protest against the annexation would not prevent it and would only cause American citizens to feel hostile toward France. Texas became a state in 1845, and neither England or France protested.

King stayed on in France for several months after he had completed his mission and entertained American and French officials liberally. With his preferences for wearing silk scarves, glittering jewelry, and a powdered wig, William King felt at home in Paris. He soon missed his friends back in the United States, however, and in 1846 he asked to be recalled and his request was granted.

Shortly after his return, William King was elected to fill a vacant seat in the United States Senate caused by the resignation of Senator Arthur P. Bagby. King held the seat until December 20, 1852, leaving the Senate only after his election to serve as vice president of the United States.

Senator King and Senator James Buchanan, both bachelors, were roommates in Washington for several years, and they discussed the possibility of running for president and vice president as a team in 1844. James Buchanan decided he was not well-enough known to the voters yet to be elected president, but he urged his friend King to try for the vice presidency at the Republican Convention that year. King was bypassed, however, and George M. Dallas was chosen instead.

King and Buchanan's dream did not end while the former was in France, and they decided to try again in 1852. James Buchanan was not nominated for president that year, but William King was nominated for vice president. Franklin Pierce was the presidential nominee.

Pierce and King won the election, but Vice President King had become seriously ill several weeks earlier and had gone to Havana, Cuba, in an attempt to regain his health.

A special act of Congress allowed Vice President King to take the oath of office in Cuba on March 4, 1853; he was the only vice president to that date to take the oath on foreign soil.

Vice President King returned to his Alabama plantation six weeks later on April 17 and died the next day from tuberculosis. He had never actually presided over the Senate for a day as vice president.

William King was buried in a vault on his plantation, but was later reinterred in City Cemetery in Selma, Alabama.

Bibliography

Henderson, Dr. Archibald. "North Carolinian Elected Vice President; Died Soon After." *Uplift Magazine* 29, no. 28 (July 5, 1941).
Klein, Philip S. *James Buchanan.* University Park: Pennsylvania State University Press, 1962.
Martin, John M. "William R. King and the Compromise of 1850." *North Carolina Historical Review* 39 (October 1962).
———. "William R. King and the Vice Presidency." *Alabama Review* 16 (January 1963).
———. "William R. King: Jacksonian Senator." *Alabama Review* 18 (1965).

14. John Cabell Breckinridge

John Cabell Breckinridge was proud of his successful election to serve as vice president with President James Buchanan in 1856. The slavery issue waxed hotly in his state of Kentucky, but few believed it could not be settled if reasonable men presented their views. When the problem exploded, requiring a choice between secession or remaining in the Union, the state of Kentucky chose the Union and John Breckinridge chose secession and traveled south to join Confederate forces.

John Cabell Breckinridge was born on January 16, 1821, in Lexington, Kentucky, on the family plantation called Thorn Hill. His mother was the former Mary Clay Smith, and his father, for whom he was named, was secretary of state in Kentucky's state government. The senior Breckinridge died in 1823 during a fever epidemic, leaving his widow with four young children to rear alone.

Mary Breckinridge took her children to live with their father's mother, Polly Breckinridge, at Cabell's Dale, one of the finest homes and estates in Bluegrass country.

Grandmother Polly had extremely bad eyesight, and young John would hold her hand as they walked over the estate grounds and visited the grave of the elderly woman's husband.

Polly Breckinridge still grieved for her husband, and always wore a mourning bonnet on her head. Little John gave her the name of "Grandma Black Cap." Her husband had served as a state representative in Kentucky's legislature many years before, and she told the little boy about his struggle to ensure the rights of voters.

Another fascinating feature at Cabell's Dale was the site of an Adena Indian village, abandoned by the tribe many years earlier. There were plenty of arrowheads and tomahawks still concealed in mounds of dirt where the Indians had hidden them many years before. They furnished John and his playmates with inspiration for mock battles and hunting expeditions.

John's education began when his mother taught him to read and write and continued when he went to Kentucky Pisgah Academy at age ten. In November 1834, he went to Dannville, Kentucky, to enroll in Centre College, where one uncle, John Young, served as college president and another uncle, William

John C. Breckenridge. Reproduced from the collections of the Library of Congress.

Breckinridge, was a professor. John lived with Dr. Young while he attended college and graduated in 1838.

Yet another uncle, Robert Breckinridge, invited John to stay in his home in Princeton, New Jersey, and take graduate courses in the college there.

After spending six months in Princeton, John Breckinridge went back to Kentucky to study law with Judge William Owsley, who required him to read Blackstone twice. After studying with the judge, Breckinridge entered Transylvania University's law school in Lexington, and he received almost perfect grades in his studies.

John C. Breckinridge was a handsome man during his college years, and he had several female admirers. He was six feet, two inches tall, weighed 175 pounds, and had black hair and eyes of such a dark shade of blue that they sometimes appeared to be black.

Breckinridge started a law practice with his cousin, Thomas Bullock, in Burlington, Iowa. They were not overnight successes, but their practice did grow.

One of the highlights of these years for Breckinridge was a buffalo hunt he went on in 1842 with some Sauk and Fox Indian warriors. He had been intrigued by Indian lore since childhood, and he admired the red men. He welcomed their invitation to the hunt, during which he met Keokuh, a mighty chief. He wrote his Uncle Robert, "In person, voice and manner the Chief was the most impressive man I have ever seen."

When he went back to Kentucky to visit relatives in 1843, John Breckinridge became engaged to Mary Cyrene Burch, who was seventeen years old and a cousin of Breckinridge's law partner, Thomas Bullock. They decided to live in Kentucky after they married, so John had to go back to Iowa to settle accounts and say goodbye to his friends.

Mary Cyrene Burch and John Cabell Breckinridge were married on December 12, 1843, and bought a house in Georgetown, Kentucky. John went into law practice with Samuel Bullock, Thomas's cousin.

In 1844, James K. Polk from Tennessee was nominated to be the Democrats' candidate for president, and Breckinridge became an ardent supporter of Polk. He made speeches for Polk and told citizens they should vote for him. Breckinridge considered entering a local race of Scott County court clerk, but Mary was expecting their first child and her health was delicate.

On December 29, 1844, Mary Breckinridge gave birth to a son they named Joseph Cabell, but it was a difficult birth and John had to spend time helping her with housework and the care of the baby for weeks after.

On November 22, 1846, Clifton Rhodes Breckinridge was born. John had moved his law practice back to Lexington earlier that year, and they had bought a house there formerly owned by Congressman Richard Menefee.

The Mexican War also started in 1846. When soldiers killed in the battle of Buena Vista were brought back to Kentucky for burial, Breckinridge was invited to speak at the military funeral for the men. His speech was eloquent and moving, according to the thousands of people attending the services, and it moved John Breckinridge to decide to join the army himself.

On September 6, 1847, Breckinridge was commissioned a major to serve with the Third Kentucky Volunteers. The regiment went to Mexico within a few weeks, but Major Breckinridge spent most of his time there as a lawyer defending erring soldiers. After eight and half months, the war had ended and the regiment went back home to Louisville.

Major Breckinridge went on to Lexington and home as rapidly as possible because he had learned he was the father of a new daughter named Frances. He found his family were all doing well, and returned to Louisville to help muster out the soldiers.

On June 11, 1849, Breckinridge was nominated as a candidate to serve in the Kentucky House of Representatives. He thought there was only one overwhelming problem in the country, and that was the drive for emancipation. He continued to be against slavery, as he had been all his life, but he believed the best solution lay in sending slaves to live in the colony of Liberia in Africa rather than setting them free to roam around without shelter, food, clothes, or money.

Breckinridge was elected to serve in the Kentucky legislature, and two years later he was elected to represent Kentucky in the United States House of Representatives. He served there from 1851 to 1855.

In 1856, John Breckinridge was elected vice president of the United States; at age 35 he was the youngest man yet to be elected to that office. The newly elected president was James Buchanan. Even though Breckinridge was a fervent believer in states' rights, he presided over the Senate without showing any partiality.

In March 1857, John Breckinridge brought his wife, Mary, back to Washington with him for the inauguration on March 4. They lived in rented rooms in the Willard Hotel.

Breckinridge was dismayed by President Buchanan's refusal to meet with him a few days later. He wanted to be friendly, at least, with Buchanan, but the president ignored him coldly.

A downturn in the economy later that year forced the Breckinridges to sell their house in Lexington. They had a new house built in Washington, but it was not completed for many months, and they had to continue living in rented rooms.

In Washington, John and Mary were active on the social scene, attending dinner parties with Washington elites, except for gatherings hosted by President Buchanan or his niece, Harriet Lane. The vice president was seldom invited even to official state dinners.

Vice President Breckinridge was insulted and hurt by the president's attitude. To make his feelings perfectly clear, President Buchanan offered Breckinridge an appointment as minister to Spain while he was still vice president.

Of course, an acceptance of the offer would have effectively removed Breckinridge from the 1860 presidential election, in which he would be a possible rival candidate for president. Breckinridge declined to accept the offer.

Despite President Buchanan's dislike of his vice president, the senators over whom he presided liked him. Massachusetts Senator Henry L. Dawes said in

1858 that Vice President Breckinridge was "an honorable man, an honest man and was conscientious in the discharge of every official duty, never betraying a trust and never doing a mean thing to advance a cause." In 1859 the Washington correspondent for the *New York Times* wrote, "Vice President Breckinridge stands deservedly high in public estimation."

President Buchanan was successful in foreign policy, but he was never able to realize how deep the divisions were between citizens in the North and those in the South. He kept insisting, as late as 1858, "the prospects are daily brightening."

In President Buchanan's opinion, the federal government could not prevent secession legally and could only defend itself if attacked. He was unable to get any domestic programs he had hoped for because of the total split of the Democrats into two sectional factions.

Before Buchanan's term as president ended in March 1861, seven states had already seceded from the Union — South Carolina, Mississippi, Florida, Alabama, Georgia, Louisiana, and Texas. When a provisional government was organized at the beginning of 1861 for the Confederacy, Buchanan had not acted.

Breckinridge entered the presidential race in 1860, and he carried eleven Southern states, but he and the other candidates were defeated by Republican Abraham Lincoln. Breckinridge had run on the National Democrat ticket. He received 18% of the popular vote to Lincoln's 40%.

John Breckinridge won election to the United States Senate, however, and took office in 1861. His last remaining duty as vice president was swearing in his successor, Hannibal Hamlin, after which Breckinridge took his own Senate seat.

Throughout the next few weeks, Senator Breckinridge urged Kentucky officials to send delegates to a border state convention to settle the slavery question for the area, but when Fort Sumter, under federal control in the harbor at Charleston, South Carolina, was attacked on April 12, 1861, the Civil War became the reality.

Senator Breckinridge's son, Cabell, then only sixteen, went promptly to Tennessee and joined Confederate forces, to his father's dismay. Another son, Clifton, joined the Confederate navy at age fifteen.

Even though Breckinridge continued to plead with officials in Kentucky to work toward a compromise settlement between the North and the South, on September 18, 1861, Kentucky legislators voted to keep Kentucky in the Union.

Senator Breckinridge was accused of spying for the Confederacy, and orders were given to take him into custody. He was left no choice but to "go South." He did not want to stay in Kentucky, where he believed tyranny reigned and the Constitution was being flouted by the Union government. He was formally expelled from the United States Senate.

When he joined Confederate forces at Richmond, Virginia, Breckinridge was commissioned a brigadier general. He had made a long circuitous journey to avoid capture, and he was relieved to be among friends. After the battle at Shiloh, he was promoted to major general in 1862.

Mary Breckinridge joined her husband at Murfreesboro, where she remained for several months and where he returned to her when he could.

Major General Breckinridge was a good soldier, brave and resourceful. His regiment defeated Union forces under the command of General Franz Sigel at Newmarket, Virginia and he served with General Robert E. Lee in the Wilderness Campaign and with General Jubal Early in Shenandoah, where he was second in command.

By February 1865, it became apparent the Confederate cause was lost. There was no money to pay soldiers, buy food or uniforms, or even guns and ammunition. General Sherman's army was systematically burning every building in the South in its march to the Atlantic Ocean. The Confederate government surrendered on April 26, 1865, and the war was over.

John Breckinridge had been serving as secretary of war in the cabinet of the Confederate president, Jefferson Davis, and he and Mary had been living in Richmond.

Fearing capture and possible charges of treason, John Breckinridge and other former members of the Confederacy went to Cuba after the war ended. When he learned his movements in Cuba were being noted and reported back to government officials in Washington, he left Cuba and went to Toronto, Canada.

In Toronto, Breckinridge had a reunion with his wife and four of their children. Clifton entered Washington College back in the United States, where he studied military tactics.

For the next two years, the Breckinridges traveled with friends to England, France, Greece, Egypt, and Palestine, returning to live in Niagara on the Canadian side. Friends and relatives begged them to return to Kentucky, but John Breckinridge would not consider returning until a general amnesty was granted to all Confederates.

In July 1868, the family were all together in Niagara. Mary's health had suffered from all the stress she had endured, but she believed better days were ahead now. She wrote her friend, Sallie Johnson, "I cannot tell you how happy we were as it was the first time we had been together since the war."

At last amnesty was granted, and the Breckinridges returned to the United States in February, 1869. They all agreed it was good to be back home when they reached Lexington. Later that year Cabell married young Sallie Johnson, the daughter of Mary's friend.

Mary and Frances were both students again in Kentucky schools, and Clifton was doing well at Washington and Lee College. Young Owen dropped out of school for a time and took a job as a clerk in a hardware store. Later he moved to California, where he practiced law and served as a state senator.

John Breckinridge's new law practice prospered, but he worked without success to get a railroad line connecting the area to the main Chesapeake and Ohio Railroad line.

On May 17, 1875, John Breckinridge died in Kentucky of complications of cirrhosis of the liver. Mary lived until 1907, dying at the age of eighty-one. Both are buried in the Lexington Cemetery.

Bibliography

Davis, William C. *Breckinridge: Statesman, Soldier, Symbol.* Baton Rouge: Louisiana State University Press, 1974.

Heck, Frank H. *Proud Kentuckian: John C. Breckinridge, 1821–1875.* Lexington: University Press of Kentucky, 1976.

Stillwell, Lucille. *John Cabell Breckinridge.* Caldwell, Idaho: Caxton, 1936.

15. *Hannibal Hamlin*

Hannibal Hamlin served as vice president during President Abraham Lincoln's first term, the most traumatic and divisive period in our nation's history, when the soldiers of the Union army from Northern states invaded the Southern states, meeting stiff resistance from the Confederate army.

Hannibal was born on August 27, 1809, in Paris Hill, Maine, to Cyrus and Anna Livermore Hamlin. His father was a doctor. Hannibal was the seventh child of nine in his family.

Hannibal was large for his age as a child and had pronounced athletic abilities. He had a dark tan complexion, giving rise later to the rumor that some of his relatives had been black or mulatto, which he denied.

In his early years, Hannibal attended the local village school, and in 1826 he enrolled in Hebron Academy. He had to leave school the next year when his elder brother became ill. Hannibal had to assume the operation of the family farm until his brother recovered his health to a degree that he could again do the agricultural work.

Unfortunately, Hannibal Hamlin never had an opportunity to attend another educational institution. He worked some as a surveyor and taught in the local school until he reached the age of twenty. At that time, he moved to Columbia, Maine, so he could study law with his brother Elijah.

Dr. Hamlin's death the next year forced Hannibal to again return home and take care of the farm and his mother. All his brothers and sisters had married and had homes of their own.

Hannibal Hamlin attempted to continue his law studies while he farmed and even carried books to the fields with him, but it was too difficult. His mother encouraged him to find a lawyer in Portland nearby to help him, and the law firm of Fessenden and Dubois agreed to tutor him in exchange for janitorial duties.

The year 1833 was an important year in Hamlin's life. He passed the bar exam, and later that year he married Sarah Jane Emery on December 10. Sarah Jane was the daughter of a local judge, and she was a qualified school teacher.

The newlyweds lived briefly in Lincoln, Maine, before moving on to Hampden, where Hamlin opened his own law practice.

Hannibal Hamlin. Reproduced from the collections of the Library of Congress.

In 1835, their first child, a son named George, was born. A son Charles was born in 1837, a son Cyrus in 1839, and a daughter, Sarah Jane (called Sally), in 1842.

Hamlin's first entry into politics was as a state representative in the Maine legislature. He also belonged to a militia company called the Hampden Rifles, in which he held the rank of captain.

In 1840, Hamlin was chosen as a delegate to the Democratic National Convention being held in Baltimore. There he voted for the nomination of Martin

Van Buren for president. In July of that year, Hamlin was nominated as a candidate for the United States House of Representatives.

It was not a Democratic year, however, and the Whigs won locally and nationally. William Henry Harrison was elected president, but after only a month in office, he died and Vice President John Tyler became president.

Hamlin focused his attention on his law practice for the next three years; he was then elected to serve in the United States House of Representatives, and he went to Washington.

The national capital was a dirty town that was dusty and muddy by turns; pigs and cows roamed freely in the streets. Hamlin despised Washington and rarely had any of his family accompany him there.

The annexation of Texas occupied the thoughts of many congressmen in 1840s. President John Tyler and Secretary of State John C. Calhoun were one hundred percent in favor of annexation because Texas would enter the Union as a slave state, and they were both from Southern states. Northern Democrats, including Hamlin, were heartily opposed to annexation for the same reason.

In 1844, Representative Hamlin was reelected, and Democrat James K. Polk became the new president. Texas was admitted as a state in 1846, and President Polk then turned his attention to annexing California.

President Polk sent envoy John Slidell to Mexico to offer the bankrupt Mexican government $5 million for the area, but the offer was ignored and Mexican soldiers came to prevent the hostile takeover of California by Americans.

President Polk ordered United States soldiers under the command of General Zachary Taylor into the region, and war did begin on May 11, 1846.

Northern congressmen hastily composed the Wilmot Proviso, which would forbid slavery in the proposed new state of California. When Representative David Wilmot of Pennsylvania, for whom the bill was named, was late reaching the voting session on the measure, Representative Hamlin who had helped draft the proposal introduced the Proviso in Wilmot's absence. When the bill went to the Senate, it was rejected.

In 1848 Hannibal Hamlin became a United States senator when he was elected to fill a vacancy caused by the death of Senator John Fairfield of Maine, and President Zachary Taylor was elected. By now, Hamlin was an active, recognized abolitionist who lost no opportunity to promote his views.

The slavery question pervaded entire sessions of both houses of Congress, and nothing got done. There was no subject on which Northern and Southern legislators could agree. The Southerners insisted the Constitution allowed them to continue slavery under states' rights, while Northerners insisted slavery should be abolished everywhere in the nation.

Senator Hamlin did not take seriously the threats made by Southern members to secede. He could not believe they would be so shortsighted as to do anything that drastic. Hamlin wrote his friend, Leonard Andrew: "We have disunion men here certainly, but they are few and harmless. I set them down with our abolitionist. And the disunionists of the south will destroy our Government just about as soon as the abolitionists of the North. It is and has been all stuff, gasconade and bluster." Unfortunately, time would prove the problems were deeper than Senator Hamlin believed.

In 1850, Hamlin was elected to a full six-year term as senator from Maine, and President Millard Fillmore was now living in the White House. Fillmore had become president when President Zachary Taylor died on July 9, 1850.

Senator Hamlin introduced a reform bill in February 1851 that limited liability for shipowners, and later he promoted a bill to abolish the custom of flogging sailors aboard naval vessels. He was pleased when both bills became laws.

Most of the time Sarah Jane Hamlin stayed home in Hampden, and she always mentioned in her letters to Hannibal how much she missed him when he was away. She did, however, occasionally spend time enjoying the social life there in Washington while her husband was a senator and she wrote their son Charles that they had attended a crowded dance at the Jefferson Davis home in February, 1854, as well as a dinner party at the residence of the French minister. She said Senator Hamlin received about ten invitations to gatherings of various kinds each week.

In July 1854, Sarah developed a fever and a cough that stayed with her. Hannibal left Washington to be with her. She lived in steadily declining health until her death on April 17, 1855, of tuberculosis.

In November of that year, leaders of the Republican party asked Hamlin if he would be interested in being Maine's governor. He said he did not seek the honor, but the next year some of the delegates presented his name in nomination anyway. He warned his backers he would also campaign for reelection to the Senate and that he would choose to be senator rather than governor.

Hamlin was elected to both offices. He served one month as governor and then resigned to return to Washington and his seat in the Senate.

On September 25, 1856, Hamlin had remarried. His new wife was Ellen Vista Emery, his first wife's half-sister, who was at least twenty-five years younger than him. She had come to live in their Maine home and keep house for the family while Sarah was so ill. Hannibal's pet name for her was Ellie.

On March 4, 1857, Senator Hamlin got back officially to his job in the Senate, and President James Buchanan was inaugurated the same day. Two days later the Supreme Court ruled the Missouri Compromise of 1850 was unconstitutional, which, in effect, made slavery legal in every state.

Senator Hamlin was outraged by the ruling, but President Buchanan was hopeful it had resolved the slavery issue.

Later that spring, Hamlin went back to his Maine home, and he and his young wife planted a garden. He tried to put the developing sectionalism in the Senate out of his mind and enjoy being with his family. His son Charles had decided to study law, which pleased his father.

When Hamlin returned to Washington in December that year, Congress was in a chaotic state. Pro-slavery Democrats insisted slavery should be protected. Republicans insisted, however, that slavery must be abolished everywhere because the welfare of three and a half million slaves was at stake. No one mentioned where the huge numbers of black people would go once they had gained their freedom. Indiana even passed a law that no more black people could move into the state.

In the midst of the turmoil, Senator Hamlin received the good news in January that Ellie had given birth to their first child, a son they named Hannibal Emery Hamlin. "How I would like to see the blessed little boy and hold him in my arms, and his mother too," Hannibal wrote Ellie.

The political upheaval grew worse by the day, and in 1859 some Republican leaders asked Hamlin if he would be willing to run for president.

Hamlin did not think he could win, and he suggested they ask Judge John M. Read of Pennsylvania to be the nominee. Judge Read did not attract enough support, however, and Senator Abraham Lincoln of Illinois was nominated for president instead of Read.

Hamlin respected Lincoln, and he believed the Republicans had made a wise choice at their Chicago convention. Hamlin did not attend the convention, so he did not know he had received the nomination for vice president until some of his friends in Congress rushed into his hotel suite in Washington to give him the news.

Proudly, he wrote Ellie: "I presume you were as much astonished as myself on the nomination for Vice President. I was unprepared for it. I neither expected nor desired it. . . . As a faithful man to the country, it leaves me no alternative but to accept it."

Lincoln and Hamlin won the election, and the new president-elect asked Hamlin to come to Washington in November, where they talked about which New England men would be the best choices for cabinet posts. Hamlin stayed on until he and President Lincoln had been sworn into office, and then he returned to Maine.

Vice President Hamlin was in a gloomy mood about the future of the nation, which was rapidly approaching a civil war. When his friend Colonel James Dunning of Maine asked him if he thought there would really be war, Hamlin said: "Yes, there's going to be a war, and a terrible one. . . . We ought to lose no time in getting ready."

On April 13, 1861, Fort Sumter off the coast of South Carolina came under fire from Confederate guns, and President Lincoln ordered his vice president to go to New York City "to aid the leading men . . . in formulating and executing plans to defend the Union." Hamlin's base of operations was the Astor House in New York, and he talked with various men in authority from all over the United States.

While Hamlin was in New York, Washington, D.C., was threatened by a secessionist riot in Maryland and all communications between the capital and the outside world were cut off. For a few days, Vice President Hamlin was in actual charge of running the emergency government.

The country was engaged in a bitter struggle between the Northern states and Southern states almost before either group quite realized what had happened. As months passed, Vice President Hamlin urged President Lincoln to issue an emancipation proclamation, but Lincoln kept postponing the date to do so.

Ellen had been in Washington with Hannibal most of the time he served as vice president, but they went back to Maine in April 1862 and bought a house in Bangor. Ellen was pregnant again, and she probably wanted to live in a different house from the one Hannibal had shared with his first wife. Their second son, Frank, was born late that year.

While he was in Maine, Hamlin learned his son Cyrus had recently joined the Union army, as had Charles earlier. Charles was a full-fledged lawyer, having been admitted to the bar in 1858, and he had been in private practice before the war started.

With his own two sons in the army, when Vice President Hamlin returned to Washington, he made a habit of visiting army hospitals to chat with the patients there. He worried about his sons constantly.

As time passed, Hamlin went back to Maine more often than previously. His friendship with President Lincoln had cooled under the strain of war, and he complained in a letter to Ellie: "I am not consulted at all, nor do I think there is any disposition to regard any counsel I may give." Later Vice President Hamlin characterized himself as the most unimportant man in Washington, ignored by the president, cabinet, and congress.

Even with all his difficulties, Hamlin was surprised to learn he had not been renominated for vice president in the 1864 election. Republican delegates at the Baltimore convention and President Lincoln had decided Andrew Johnson from Tennessee was a better choice, being both pro-Union and from a border state.

Hamlin did not suspect President Lincoln of taking any part in having Johnson replace him as vice president until he talked with Judge J. Newton Pettis in March 1889, at the inauguration of President Benjamin Harrison. Hamlin was deeply saddened when Judge Pettis told him President Lincoln had engineered his replacement.

Later in 1864, Hamlin, now fifty-five years old, enlisted as a private in the Maine Coast Guard, Company A, in which he served two months as cook.

President Lincoln was reelected, but Hamlin lost his bid to return to the Senate. He was depressed by his loss, and his mood was not improved by his daughter Sally's marriage to Captain George Batchelder, whom Hamlin did not like.

Sally and her new husband were at Ford Theater the night President Lincoln was assassinated and witnessed the sad event. Vice President Andrew Johnson was now the new president, and Hamlin went back to farming in Maine.

After the Civil War ended, Hamlin got the post as port collector in Boston; it was a position that paid well. As President Johnson proceeded with reconstruction in the South, Hamlin found he disagreed vehemently with Johnson's leniency toward Confederates. President Johnson realized the war had ended, however, and had cost the South much more than it had the North. He wanted everybody to get along, but Hamlin resented Johnson so much that he resigned his port job in Boston.

Cyrus Hamlin died of yellow fever in New Orleans on August 8, 1867, while he was still serving in the army on the staff of General Fremont. Hamlin was deeply grieved by his death and returned to politics to keep busy.

In 1868, Hamlin was reelected to the United States Senate, where he served until 1881, at which time he retired to accept a post as minister to Spain. President James Garfield had appointed Hamlin in one of his last official acts before he was assassinated.

Ambassador Hamlin and Ellie left Philadelphia on November 5, 1881, and made a brief stopover in London before going on to Spain.

Hamlin found the Duke of Westminster's estate the most impressive sight in England with its flower beds and fruits. To him the estate was "perfect" and like a "fairyland." The palaces and cathedrals interested him less.

The French language seemed to Hannibal incomprehensible. He compared French conversations to the sound blackbirds made when feeding in a field where they all chattered at once. "For all the world it seemed to me they talked just as fast as the birds," he said. He liked Paris despite the conversational difficulties, however.

When they finally arrived in Spain on December 8, Hamlin noted the beauty of the Pyrenees, which he compared to the Allegheny Mountains in America. He was surprised by the barren, rocky soil around Madrid, and he found the crop yields were low indeed.

Hamlin had an audience with King Alfonso XII of Spain just before Christmas and was introduced to the Spanish queen. About ten days later, he and Ellen visited the royal couple, who invited them to accompany them ice-skating. The Hamlins declined with regret because they could not skate.

In February 1882, the Hamlins went to Italy on a tour, then on to Switzerland and back to France. Hannibal was an observant traveler who noted differences in governments and the living conditions of the ordinary citizens in each country; he also remarked that in Spain "mañana" was the best time to conduct business.

The Hamlins got back to Maine in January 1883 and were glad to be home. They became involved in the social activities in Bangor, where Hannibal still enjoyed dancing at parties.

Hamlin continued working on his farm until he was almost eighty years old, even though in 1877 he had suffered a heart attack in the cloakroom of the Senate chambers. His heart had been gradually weakening since that attack, and on July 4, 1891, he was playing cards with friends at the Tarantine Club when he collapsed. A few hours later he died.

Hannibal Hamlin willed the bulk of his estate to Ellen and stipulated that each of his sons should receive two thousand dollars and personal items. His daughter had died in 1878, apparently from cancer.

Bibliography

Hunt, H. Draper. *Hannibal Hamlin of Maine.* Syracuse, N.Y.: Syracuse University Press, 1969.
Oates, Stephen B. *With Malice Toward None.* New York, London, and San Francisco, Harper and Row, 1977.
Scroggins, Mark. *Hannibal: The Life of Abraham Lincoln's First Vice President.* Lanham, Md.: University Press of America, 1994.

16. Andrew Jackson Johnson

Andrew Johnson was born on December 29, 1808, in Casso's Inn in Raleigh, North Carolina, to Jacob Johnson and Mary McConough (Polly) Johnson. The Johnsons were employed by the owner of the inn, Peter Casso. Jacob was a porter, and Polly worked as a cook. They lived in a cottage near the inn.

Andrew's father drowned when the little boy was only three years old. Jacob was trying to save two of his acquaintances from a watery grave, and while the two friends managed to reach the banks of Walnut Creek, Jacob did not.

Polly Johnson tried to support Andrew and his older brother, Bill, by weaving, but she could not earn enough. The boys were apprenticed to a tailor named J. J. Selby when Andrew was fourteen years old.

James Litchford was foreman of the tailor shop, and he and a regular customer named Dr. William Hill helped Andrew learn to read as he worked.

Andy and Bill were rowdy and got in trouble frequently. After they threw rocks at an old woman's house in Raleigh in June 1824, they had to leave town to avoid being put in jail. They stopped in Carthage, a town about seventy-five miles from Raleigh.

There the two young men opened their own tailor shop and were soon doing a fair amount of business. They learned, however, that Selby had offered a reward through a newspaper advertisement for their return, and they moved on to Laurens, South Carolina, where they stayed for about a year.

Andy was nagged by guilt about his desertion of Selby and his apprenticeship, and early in 1826 he persuaded Bill to go back with him to Raleigh to make amends. They found Selby was no longer working as a tailor, and Litchford would not rehire the runaways. It was at this low point in their lives that Andy, Bill, their mother, and her new husband, Turner Dougherty, decided to move to Tennessee and make their home there.

They left in August 1826 and followed the Daniel Boone Trail. On their journey they passed General Andrew Jackson riding the trail on horseback, an exciting event to the two boys.

About a month later, they arrived in Greeneville, Tennessee, and Andy got a job in a tailor shop the day after his arrival. By March 1827, he was ready to open his own shop after the only tailor in Greeneville decided to quit.

Andrew Johnson. Reproduced from the collections of the Library of Congress.

Andy Johnson's shop became a meeting place for local politicians, and there were many spirited discussions on issues of interest at the time. Johnson was drawn into the arguments, and he developed a passionate interest in politics.

Bill Johnson got a job as a carpenter shortly after their arrival in Tennessee, but he left a few months later for Texas to seek his fortune in greener pastures.

During this time in the nation's history, debating was an exciting form of entertainment in rural America, and debating clubs were a part of every community. Andy Johnson requested and received permission to join a debating club at Greeneville College, and he remained an active debater for several years. When Greeneville College closed, Andy joined a debating club at Tusculum College, about four miles from his home.

Johnson met his wife-to-be in Greeneville shortly after his arrival. Her name was Eliza C. McCardle. They were married on May 17, 1827, in Greeneville.

The newlyweds lived in a back room of his tailor shop until 1831, when Andy bought a house with a separate building on the property he could use for his tailor shop. Their first two children, Martha and Charles, had been born while they lived in the one-room apartment. The couple eventually had three more children: Mary, born in 1832, Robert, born in 1834, and Andrew (Frank) born in 1852.

In 1829, Andrew Johnson was elected alderman of the town of Greeneville, and he served three terms before being chosen to be mayor. From this humble political start, Johnson continued to progress to ever higher offices. He represented both Greene and Washington counties combined in the Tennessee legislature from 1835 to 1837. That year he was defeated in his campaign to be elected a state senator, but in 1839 he was elected to serve in the state senate.

In 1841, Johnson proposed the formation of a new state in the area that would be composed of counties in east Tennessee, western North Carolina, southwestern Virginia, and northern Georgia. He believed the geography of the region isolated the people from other citizens in their states. Few people in the area owned slaves, and their attitudes and needs were different. The new state would bear the name of Frankland. He managed to get approval of the plan from the Tennessee Senate, but it died there.

In 1843, to the surprise of the elite members of the Democratic party in Tennessee, Andrew Johnson, a humble tailor, was elected to the United States House of Representatives from Tennessee, winning out over Colonel John Aiken, a lawyer from Jonesboro. Johnson served five terms in succession.

Johnson hated bigotry and intolerance and was adamantly opposed to slavery, and these attitudes led to sharp disagreements between him and fellow Southern Democrats. President James K. Polk considered him to be a traitor to the region, and during his campaign for governor of Tennessee against Johnson, lawyer M.P. Gentry said, "I have come forth from my retirement to remove that curse . . . and that curse is Andrew Johnson."

Despite the vituperation heaped upon him, Johnson was to be governor of Tennessee in August, 1853. As governor, he obtained money from the legislature to establish colleges and improve schools in Tennessee. He started agricultural and mechanical fairs in the state and was credited with the beginning of a statewide library system. He was perceived to be an honest, effective governor, and he was reelected in 1855.

In 1857, Governor Johnson went to Washington to offer former president Andrew Jackson's Tennessee home, called the Hermitage, to the United States government for use as a military academy. The Tennessee legislature had approved the offer, but federal officials declined to accept.

On his way back to Tennessee by train, Governor Johnson's railway car was one of several which plunged down a sixty-foot embankment when the train derailed. Johnson's right arm was seriously injured in the wreck, and it would cause him pain and difficulty for the rest of his life. He was unable to return to Nashville and his duties as governor until February 3, 1858.

Governor Johnson made it clear to his supporters he did not plan to seek another term as governor, but he hoped to move on to the United States Senate as Tennessee's representative there. He was elected and took office in 1857.

As the Civil War approached, Senator Johnson begged his fellow Tennesseans not to secede from the Union. In December 1860, he said: "I love the Constitution and swear that it and the Union shall be saved as 'Old Hickory' Jackson did swear in 1832. Senators, my blood, my existence, I would give to save this Union."

All his efforts failed, however, when Tennessee voted to secede, Senator Johnson was the only Southern senator to stay with the Union and retain his Senate seat.

In April 1861, Senator Johnson learned his wife Eliza was ill in Greeneville. Their five children were with her, but he believed he should be with her too.

Johnson left Washington shortly after Tennessee had seceded, and he was attacked by angry mobs on his way home. Another passenger, Senator Jefferson Davis, interceded and saved him from injury. Davis would later be named president of the Confederacy.

By June 12, 1861, Johnson realized it was dangerous for him to stay in Tennessee, and he returned to Washington by way of Cumberland Gap. He did not return to his Greeneville home for the next eight years. He was hung in effigy by angry Tennessee citizens.

Eliza and their children did not go with him in June, but increasing harassment forced them to leave also. Finally they were given permission to pass through enemy battle lines and join Andrew in Washington.

In 1862, President Abraham Lincoln appointed Johnson to be a brigadier general in the Union army and named him military governor of Tennessee. His duties were to establish a government in the state under federal authority. He and his family lived in Nashville from 1862 to 1864, even though Confederate forces threatened to take over the city several times. By the time war drew to a close, Governor Johnson had a civil government in place and operating.

When the campaign of 1864 began, President Lincoln felt a Southern Democrat candidate with Union beliefs might be a better choice for vice president than Hannibal Hamlin, the current vice president. Hamlin was a radical Maine Republican, and President Lincoln preferred moderate approaches.

Since Lincoln was elected by the Republicans originally and Johnson by the Democrats, they were chosen candidates by the National Union party.

President Lincoln was correct in his belief that Andrew Johnson would help him get reelected. President Lincoln received 55% of the popular vote over his Democratic opponent George B. McClellan's 45%.

Vice President Johnson worked hard to get Tennessee's government stabilized before he left for Washington, but as the Civil War was still in progress, he could not complete all the details. He also became ill, probably from stress.

Leaving Eliza and their children in Tennessee, the new vice president-elect went to Washington for the inauguration on March 4, 1865. He had a tiring trip because of his recent illness. He ate dinner, including drinks, with his good friend John W. Forney the night before the inauguration. The next day he was not feeling much better, but he felt he had to attend the ceremony and take his own oath of office as vice president. To fortify himself, he drank three more shots of whiskey.

Since he rarely drank alcohol at all, Vice President Johnson was obviously drunk by the time he reached the site of the inauguration. When he made the customary speech to the senate, his words were slurred and his audience of government officials and their guests listened in stunned silence to his rambling, incoherent speech.

A few days later President Lincoln defended his vice president when he told the new secretary of the treasury, Hugh McCulloch: "I have known Andy Johnson for many years; he made a bad slip the other day, but you need not be scared. Andy ain't a drunkard."

Vice President Johnson had lived in Washington for several years while serving in Congress, and no one saw him inebriated before or any time after his taking the oath of office.

On April 14, 1865, Vice President Johnson retired early in Kirkwood House where he boarded. About 10:15 P.M., he was awakened by a fellow boarder, former governor of Wisconsin, Leonard J. Farwell, who told him President Lincoln had been shot and seriously wounded at Ford's Theater in an assassination attempt.

Vice President Johnson and Farwell went immediately to the Peterson house across the street from the theater, where the wounded man had been taken. It was fairly obvious to all those present that the president was on his deathbed.

Vice President Johnson left within a few minutes to return to his boardinghouse, where he spent the rest of the night pacing the floor and worrying. After Lincoln's death the next morning, Johnson took the oath of office at Kirwood House about 10:30 A.M. and became President Johnson.

Former first lady Mary Lincoln was so distraught with grief that she was unable to move out of the White House until late May. The new first lady, Eliza

Johnson, and their daughter, Martha, arrived in Washington in June, and the family then moved into their new home.

As the new president of a divided nation, Andrew Johnson argued that Southern states had not really seceded from the Union, as such an action was both illegal and impossible. Therefore, he had no plans to deprive Southern citizens of their voting rights as long as they swore an oath of allegiance to the Union government.

Slaves had really been freed, or course, and Johnson expected all the states to allow black men to vote if they were literate and responsible people. He believed each state should set its own policy on the question, however.

Radical Republicans in Congress did not trust Southern goodwill, and they incorporated Civil Rights protection for black citizens in the Fourteenth Amendment. To be officially readmitted to the Union, Southern states had to ratify the amendment.

In 1866 the Ku Klux Klan was organized in Pulaski, Tennessee, to affirm white supremacy in the United States and to thwart Reconstruction efforts by intimidating former slaves.

In 1867, Secretary of State William H. Seward negotiated the purchase of Alaska from Russia for $7.2 million. Citizens of Alaska had the option of staying on as American citizens or moving to Russia to keep their citizenship there. That same year the Midway Islands in the Pacific were annexed.

Congress passed the Tenure of Office Act in 1867 over President Johnson's veto. The act called for Senate approval for removal from office of any government official President Johnson wanted to remove from office.

Republican Edwin M. Stanton, secretary of war, had been undermining the president's policies for some time, and when President Johnson dismissed him in February 1868, the House of Representatives voted overwhelmingly to impeach the president.

President Johnson had not violated any specific rule in dismissing Stanton, but the House leveled a vague charge that President Johnson was guilty of "high crimes and misdemeanors."

At the impeachment hearing, it was evident the charges were not proved, and President Johnson was acquitted. Seven Republican senators joined Democrats in clearing the president.

President Johnson hoped his reelection in 1868 would be, as he said, "a vindication such as no man had ever received," but his Democratic party did not even nominate him as its candidate for president. They chose Horatio Seymour instead.

The Republican candidate, General Ulysses S. Grant, defeated Seymour by a vote of 53% to 47% of the popular vote and 214 electoral votes for Grant to 80 for Seymour.

President Johnson was eager to return to Tennessee when his term ended, and he did not attend President Grant's inauguration. All the Johnson family were glad to be going back to their Greeneville home. First Lady Eliza Johnson's health had been so poor during the time she lived in Washington that she had rarely served as hostess at official dinners and parties. Daughters Martha Patterson and Mary Stover had served instead.

Once back in Tennessee, however, Andrew Johnson could not forget politics. He had been given a hearty welcome home by his friends and neighbors with a banner strung across the main street that read, "Andrew Johnson, Patriot"—a vast improvement over one eight years earlier that had said, "Andrew Johnson, Traitor."

Johnson ran for the United States Senate in 1871 and the United States House of Representatives in 1872, but was defeated both times. Finally in 1875 he was elected to the Senate by the Tennessee legislature, becoming the only former president of the United States to serve as a senator.

The Senate called a special session in March that year, and Senator Johnson made a speech criticizing President U.S. Grant's Reconstruction policy.

On July 28, 1875, Andrew Johnson was visiting his daughter Mary in Carter County, Tennessee, when he suffered a stroke. The next day he suffered another, more severe stroke and he died two days later on July 31, 1875. Following a funeral conducted with Masonic rites, he was buried on his own land near Greeneville.

Eliza survived until the next year, dying on January 15, 1876. She was buried beside her husband.

Although Johnson was denied a second term as president, it is probable that he helped remake the country with his reasonable, magnanimous treatment of Southern rebels. A guerrilla-type war might have been waged for years if Southern nerves had not been soothed, and such a war would have divided the United States indefinitely.

Bibliography

Lomask, Milton. *Andrew Johnson: President on Trial.* New York: Farrar, Straus, and Giroux, 1960.
Winston, Robert W. *Andrew Johnson: Plebian and Patriot.* New York: AMS Press, 1970.

17. Schuyler Colfax

Schuyler Colfax was vice president during President Ulysses S. Grant's first term; both men worked to reunite the nation during the tumultuous period of Reconstruction in the South. Both had been abolitionists before the Civil War started, both believed the war had been necessary, and both had little sympathy for the secessionists who tried, in their opinion, to destroy the country.

Schuyler Colfax was named for his father, who died six months before his son's birth on March 23, 1823. Schuyler, Sr. had been employed in a bank on Wall Street before his death from tuberculosis. His wife, the former Hannah Stryker, continued to live in New York with her mother until her child was born and for several years afterward.

Little Schuyler attended the local public school until he was ten years old, at which time financial hardship forced him to leave school to go to work to support himself and his mother.

When the boy was eleven, his mother moved to Brooklyn, and on November 6, 1834, she remarried. Her second husband was George W. Matthews from Baltimore, and he became the guiding influence in his stepson's life. Since Schuyler had never known his own father, it was not difficult for him to develop a real affection for the kind-hearted Matthews.

The family lived in Brooklyn for two years before moving to New Carlisle, Indiana, in 1836. After he had lived in a large city, this new area seemed like the wild frontier to thirteen-year-old Schuyler.

Matthews started a general merchandise store, and the village post office occupied a part of the building. Young Schuyler worked as a clerk and also found work on nearby farms during planting and harvest seasons.

In 1841, Schuyler Colfax's stepfather was elected to be the auditor of Saint Joseph County, Indiana. The family moved to South Bend to live, and Colfax was employed by his stepfather as a deputy auditor.

From his service in this minor political office, Colfax developed an interest in politics. He studied law at the urging of his parents, but he could not get his interest level high enough to succeed. He explained, "My mind was . . . so full of other subjects."

One of the more interesting subjects was a young lady named Evelyn Clark

Schuyler Colfax. Reproduced from the collections of the Library of Congress.

from Argyle, New York. They were married on October 10, 1844, in her home, and they started housekeeping in South Bend, Indiana.

About this same time, Colfax began writing articles on political subjects for newspapers and expressing his views to local politicians. In 1845 he entered into partnership with Albert W. West to buy the South Bend *Free Press*, which they renamed the *St. Joseph Valley Register*. The newspaper was issued weekly, and Schuyler was actively involved in its operation as the editor. The publication became one of the most influential newspapers in Indiana during the eighteen-year period in which Colfax was at the helm as editor. He was a loyal member of the Whig party, but he made an honest effort to be fair in his political editorials.

Talkative and pleasant in nature, Colfax was an ideal personality to enter politics. In fact, he was dubbed "Smiler" Colfax because of his good-humored approach to life.

On one subject Colfax was fiercely dedicated to his belief, and that subject was the abolishment of slavery. He was opposed to any addition of territory to the United States that would allow slavery. He said the motto of the North ought to be, "Not another inch of slave territory!"

By 1854, the Whig party had split along sectional lines, and the New Republican party was formed, although it was called the anti-Nebraska party for several months in the beginning.

Schuyler Colfax was nominated to be the Whig candidate in Indiana's 9th District for the United States House of Representatives that year, and he was successfully elected. He and Evelyn left for Washington, D.C., with high hopes he could make a difference and help reunite the badly divided nation. The furor raised about the election of a Speaker of the House demonstrated how bitter the divisions were at the time.

Representative Colfax was named a member of the Elections Committee, and his first term was relatively uneventful. He was renominated in 1856 and was again elected. President James Buchanan replaced President Franklin Pierce and John C. Breckinridge was elected vice president.

The Colfaxes were invited to attend dinners and other social events from time to time. Evelyn Colfax also attended many prayer meetings. She wrote a friend in Indiana that the churches in Washington were "having a great many prayer meetings now, and I hope much good is being done here in this wicked city."

Reelected as a representative in 1858, Colfax voted for the admission of the state of Oregon to the United States in 1859, even though most of his Republican friends did not. Colfax believed the Northwest Territory was ready for statehood, and his friends only opposed the admission because they were afraid the citizens would be Democrats.

President Abraham Lincoln faced a nation already breaking apart when he took office on March 4, 1861. President Buchanan had done little to prevent secession by Southern states, although any efforts made would probably not have prevented the Civil War.

Representative Colfax could not serve as the active editor of his newspaper while he was in Congress, but the paper was still under his care and control. The

Register published an editorial which stated an opinion that President Lincoln was bound by law to enforce federal statutes in all states and that no state could secede legally.

When the Civil War hostilities began, Schuyler Colfax and other men in government did not believe it would be a long war. Colfax proceeded with plans to prepare Indiana for battle, but he did not join the army himself. That fact would be used against him in future political campaigns.

Representative Colfax became irritated by President Lincoln's careful and thoughtful approach to emancipation. When Union troops lost a battle, Colfax reminded the president that the soldiers were forced to be away from their homes and families, living in squalid conditions and causing deprivation to their families back home with no bread-winner in the homes. The war should be prosecuted fully and finished as rapidly as possible, Colfax told the president.

Evelyn Colfax had been in failing health for several years, and in March 1863, she was too ill to leave Washington to return to South Bend for the summer, as was their custom.

Schuyler took her to Newport, Rhode Island, for the summer in an attempt to improve her condition, but she died on July 10 that year and was returned to South Bend for burial. They had no children, so Schuyler was left with only memories of their happy life together.

In December 1863, Colfax was elected Speaker of the House. Mr. and Mrs. Matthews and their daughter Carrie had come to Washington to live with Colfax after his wife died, and his mother now served as his hostess at receptions which she wrote proudly to a friend in Indiana were attended by hundreds of people. She claimed they rivaled receptions held by First Lady Mary Lincoln.

Colfax and his whole family were strict teetotalers, and no alcoholic beverages were ever served at his receptions. Refreshments served were cake, ice cream, and coffee.

Speaker Colfax talked with President Lincoln shortly before he and Mrs. Lincoln left to attend Ford's Theater on the fateful night of April 14, 1865. He was deeply shocked and saddened when he heard the president had been shot, and he joined other friends at Lincoln's bedside.

Colfax attended the president's funeral in Springfield, Illinois, and went on to South Bend to prepare a tribute to the fallen executive for his newspaper. While there, he sold his interest in the paper to Alfred Wheeler, who had been serving as editor since 1855. Colfax had bought the paper to have a forum for his political opinions and his views about the evils of slavery. With slavery now ended and the war over, he thought he did not need this platform any longer.

In the summer of 1865, Speaker Colfax took a train trip through the western United States. He had talked about going for four years, but conditions had never been right.

One of the highlights of the trip was a Chinese banquet held in his honor in

San Francisco. There were dried shark fins, stewed pigeon with bamboo soup, stewed seaweed, reindeer sinews, scorpion eggs, and other exotic dishes offered to the diners, as well as stewed chicken, ducks, and mutton.

When Colfax returned to Washington, he found himself in sharp disagreement with President Andrew Johnson's reconstruction policies. President Johnson pursued Lincoln's moderate approach, while the radicals in government such as Colfax wanted Southerners to be punished and humiliated. The Civil Rights Bill was passed over President Johnson's veto.

Colfax was reelected as Speaker of the House by 139 votes to 36 for his opponent, James Brooks of New York. Colfax insisted that freed black men should be allowed to vote, saying that without voting rights, their freedom was a "mockery." Other Republicans feared their party would split apart over the issue, however, and the measure was defeated.

The differing opinions about Reconstruction led to a move to impeach President Johnson, but the votes were not there and he stayed in office.

Despite much urging by his supporters, Representative Colfax refused to run for either the United States Senate or for governor of Indiana. He had been Speaker of the House for three terms, and he wanted to move on, but not to either of those offices. He wanted to be nominated as vice president. General Ulysses S. Grant was almost certain to be the nominee for president.

Both men were nominated, as predicted by political analysts, and they won the election. Colfax was in Washington presiding over the Senate during the Republican Convention and could not attend, but telegraph wires hummed with frequent messages to keep him informed on events there.

The year of 1868 was one of the most important years in Colfax's life. He was elected vice president, and he remarried. His new wife was Nellie Wade of Ohio, a niece of Senator Benjamin F. Wade, who had been Colfax's leading opponent for vice president.

Nellie Wade and Schuyler Colfax were married in her mother's home in Andover, Ohio, on November 18, 1868, after the election.

In his new office as vice president, Colfax was not as busy as he had been as Speaker of the House. He had time to make speeches to various groups and was much in demand. He did not use politics as his only topic; he was also an avid crusader for the temperance movement.

One speech Vice President Colfax enjoyed making was at Promontory, Utah, on May 10, 1869, when the Union Pacific rail lines were connected with the tracks of the Central Pacific. A few months later he, his wife, and her sister Marcia traveled with some friends through the West on the new railway, marveling that they had made the scenic trip in only a few days, when it would have formerly required weeks.

In the campaign of 1870, Vice President Colfax assured the voters that "the scandals which previously dishonored the [Johnson] administration have ceased." These words would later seem ironic.

In April 1870, the Colfaxes' only child, a son named Schuyler Colfax III, was born. When Vice President Colfax insisted he planned to retire at the end of his term, many thought he wanted to spend more time with his family. His mother was living with them also, and her health was poor.

Plans got underway to nominate Senator Henry Wilson for vice president, and there was no opposition from President Grant. A coolness had developed between Grant and Colfax, which may have been caused by a suspicion on the president's part that Colfax planned to oppose him for the nomination for president.

It was just as well that Colfax was not nominated to run for vice president again with President Grant, as he would have probably caused Grant to be defeated. Early in 1872, Colfax was accused of accepting stock shares at cut-rate prices from the contracting company Credit Mobilier, which had been involved in the railroad connection in Utah. The company had sold shares to various government officials in an attempt to prevent an investigation of its corrupt practices.

Vice President Colfax denied the charges vehemently, but when Congressman Oakes Ames of Massachusetts, one of the owners of Credit Mobilier, insisted Colfax had received a dividend payment of $1,200 from the stock, Colfax left office in disgrace.

In a later congressional hearing, Representative Ames could not show a receipt from Colfax for the money, and he admitted the stock shares had never been transferred or given to Colfax. The investigation was dropped for lack of evidence.

President Grant believed Colfax had been accused falsely, and he wrote his former vice president: "I sympathize with you in the recent Congressional investigation. . . . I am satisfied of your integrity and patriotism."

The damage was done, however, and Schuyler Colfax never held public office again. Some of his supporters urged him to run for Congress again, but he declined. He made campaign speeches for other candidates and watched the political maneuvers, but he did not want to be a candidate again.

Instead, Colfax became a professional public speaker in his last years, which kept him pleasantly busy. His investments in local businesses provided income, and he enjoyed his later years as much as the period when he was holding political offices.

On July 17, 1875, Colfax wrote a friend, John G. Nicolay: "I have had the jolliest and most independent and most money-making winter of my life—have had over six hundred invitations [to speak]." He had only accepted about one hundred and twenty, but that was still an average of one every third day—a lot of speeches.

In 1883, Schuyler Colfax and his wife traveled by rail to the West Coast again at the invitation of Henry Villard, president of the Northern Pacific Railroad, which had just been completed. "It was a royal trip, the grandest and most delightful of my life, and the hospitality princely," Colfax wrote to Villard after their return home.

On January 13, 1885, Colfax took a train to a speaking engagement in northwestern Iowa, and he had to change trains in Mankato, Minnesota, where the temperature was 30 degrees below zero. To reach the other train station, Colfax had to walk about three-quarters of a mile, and he collapsed and died from a heart attack while walking. He was identified by the papers he carried with him.

Schuyler Colfax's funeral was held in the Reformed Church in South Bend, a church he had helped establish some years before. Burial was also in South Bend in the city cemetery.

Bibliography

Sievers, Harry J. *Benjamin Harrison: Hoosier Statesman.* New York: University Publications, 1959.

Smith, Willard H. *Schuyler Colfax: The Changing Fortunes of a Political Idol.* Indianapolis: Indiana Historical Bureau, 1952.

18. Henry Wilson

Henry Wilson rendered an important, vital service to the United States when he served as chairman of military affairs during the Civil War. His duties included helping to organize the army and equip the soldiers to enable them to defend the Union.

Henry Wilson was the son of Abigail and Winthrop Colbath. At birth he was given the name Jeremiah Jones Colbath. He was born on February 16, 1812, near Farmington, New Hampshire, to a practically destitute couple. His mother, the former Abigail Witham, performed household chores for neighbors, and Winthrop Colbath worked sporadically in a sawmill. Winthrop lacked ambition and also considered whiskey a necessity of life, which did not improve matters.

Little Jeremiah attended the village school, and when he was about eight years old, a neighbor, Mrs. Anstress Eastman, took an interest in him. Because Jeremiah's mother worked for Mrs. Eastman occasionally, the latter knew Jeremiah, but her interest was piqued when she saw him fighting with another boy. She stopped the fight and asked Jeremiah to go home with her.

Mrs. Eastman believed an idle mind was not desirable, and she asked Jeremiah if he could read. He said he could, so she told him he could come to visit her anytime he wished and could read the books in her husband's library. He accepted the offer, and she gave him a Bible, the first book he had ever owned. She also began passing clothes to him which her relatives had outgrown.

At age sixteen, Jeremiah was apprenticed to a farmer, for whom he worked for the next four years. The farmer, William Knight, was a hard worker himself, and he taught his apprentice to work. The boy had enough food to eat and good clothes to wear for the first time in his life, but he only had time to attend school occasionally.

It was a hard, lonely, and confining life for a young boy, and he escaped by reading. He read hundreds of books on assorted subjects and developed a strong interest in history and literature in particular.

When Jeremiah reached the age of twenty-one on February 16, 1833, his years of indentured service ended. Knight gave him six sheep and two oxen to help him get started in life. Jeremiah sold the livestock for a total of eighty-four dollars, a considerable amount for the time.

Henry Wilson. Reproduced from the collections of the Library of Congress.

In June of that year, Jeremiah had a petition introduced in the New Hampshire House of Representatives to change his name legally to Henry Wilson. The reason is unclear, but his request was approved by the governor in July.

Henry Wilson may have wanted to rid himself of the stigma of being the son of a drunkard father. He never gave an explanation of why he changed his name or why he chose that particular name. His four brothers kept their last name of Colbath.

In December 1833, Wilson decided to go to Massachusetts, where he had heard a man could earn a good living as a cobbler. He went to Natick and learned the trade from a shoemaker named William Legro, after which he opened his own shoe shop.

Wilson boarded with Deacon William Coolidge and his family, where again he had access to a diverse library. He continued to read many more books during the three years he was there and worked long hours in his shoe shop during day-time hours.

The more Wilson moved around, the more he felt the need for an educa-tion. He saved his money and attended two academies in Natick in 1836 and 1837. After he left school, there was no other employment available, so he went back to making shoes.

Apparently, Wilson was a good cobbler, and his business grew. He began selling shoes to wholesale merchants, and by 1839 he had eighteen employees and his total income that year was seventeen thousand dollars, a fortune during that period in history.

Debating was then a popular pastime. Reverend Erasmus Moore in Natick organized a debating club for the young men in town, and Wilson joined. At first he was hesitant about speaking to an audience, but he gained confidence gradu-ally and became an adept debater.

The ability proved valuable in Wilson's campaign to be elected by the Whigs as a representative from Natick to the General Court of Massachusetts. During the frenzied campaign, he took time to woo and win a sixteen-year-old bride named Harriet Malvina Howe. They were married on October 20, 1840, in the Natick Congregational Church.

Henry Wilson also won the election and served two terms as a representa-tive before going back to shoemaking in Natick. He accepted an offer to run for the Massachusetts Senate, but he did not win that election.

Wilson joined the Massachusetts Volunteer Militia, where he was commis-sioned a major. He reentered politics in 1844 and was elected to serve in the Massachusetts Senate. He openly opposed the admission of Texas to the Union if it meant slavery would be allowed there because he was adamantly opposed to slavery.

In December 1845, Wilson and John Greenleaf Whittier, the poet, went to Washington to present a petition of protest of the annexation of Texas to the United States Congress. They failed in their mission, however, and Texas was ad-mitted to the United States.

In June 1846, Wilson was promoted to colonel of his militia regiment, and six weeks later he became a brigadier general of the Third Brigade.

Henry Wilson was a successful man. He had a comfortable home on Central Street in Natick, fifty-two employees in his shoe factory, and on November 11, 1846, the Wilsons' first child was born, a son they named Hamilton.

Becoming dissatisfied with the Whig party because of its lack of effort to get slavery abolished, Wilson helped found the Free Soil party in 1848. He bought a newspaper publishing company to promote his views, but the venture failed. *The Republican* ceased publication in January 1851; Wilson lost about seven thousand dollars in the venture.

The Free Soilers and Democrats formed a coalition in 1851, with Henry Wilson one of the leading proponents of the move. Wilson supported Charles Sumner in his campaign for the Senate, and Sumner won.

In 1853, Henry Wilson ran for governor of Massachusetts, but he lost even though Senator Sumner helped him campaign. The coalition of the two groups was called the Know-Nothing party in derision.

The next year Wilson ran for a seat in the United States Senate, and he took office on February 10, 1855. He served in the Senate continuously for the next eighteen years.

As civil war loomed on the horizon, Senator Wilson did not conceal his distaste for slavery, but he believed the slaves should gain their freedom gradually, so there would not be any disruption or disorder in the nation.

Wilson was furious when he heard of the John Brown raid at Harpers Ferry and said that while he deplored slavery, he thought Brown and his companions should be hanged. He thought John Brown was a criminal who exerted his will by force and was not a true friend of black people. On the other hand, in April 1860 Wilson introduced a bill to provide $25,000 to educate all children, regardless of race, who lived in Washington.

When Senator Jefferson Davis left his Senate office to "go South" to join the Confederate forces, Senator Wilson was named chairman of the Military Affairs Committee.

Many wives of government officials left Washington in 1860 before more trouble developed, but Harriet Wilson remained in the Washington hotel, where she and Henry lived. Their son, now fourteen years old, was staying with relatives in Massachusetts, and she considered it unlikely war would be waged there. Her own health was not good, and she preferred to stay by her husband's side during the trying times.

The regular United States Army was a skeleton force totaling only eighteen thousand men when the Civil War began. Senator Wilson worked at a frantic pace to improve their capability. Within four months, there were almost five hundred thousand men in uniform for the Union.

The soldiers had to be supplied with food, tents, guns, medicine, clothes, and transport, and all of these were obtained because of Senator Wilson's insistence that money be appropriated from month to month for such purchases, usually accompanied by loud objections from members of both houses of Congress.

These legislators were prone to argue and add amendments, until Senator Wilson remarked in exasperation, "I believe if we introduced the Lord's Prayer here, there would be a large number of amendments proposed to be added to it."

It was the fault of Congress that the army was so weak anyway. Congressmen had not been able to see the need to build and maintain a defense force and had pinched pennies for years.

As the war continued, Senator Wilson had army hospital facilities improved and regulated. He instituted the custom of prompt payment of their salary to the soldiers, many of whom had families back home that had become destitute for a lack of income. Wilson suggested a draft to keep fresh soldiers coming into duty, but he ran into a fierce battle on that proposal. It finally passed, but men were allowed to hire substitutes to serve in their stead, and many did so.

Senator Wilson was a good friend of President Lincoln when the president needed one most, but he became impatient with Lincoln for not issuing a proclamation to free the slaves. In September 1862, the Emancipation Proclamation was finally issued, but President Lincoln had always been a strong supporter of gradual abolition, with owners of slaves being paid to give them their freedom.

Hamilton Wilson, Senator Wilson's son, joined the Union army in 1866 and was commissioned a second lieutenant with the Sixth United States Cavalry. He was stricken with dysentery while stationed in Austin, Texas, and died on December 24, 1867, at age twenty. He had attended a military school in Worcester, Massachusetts, and had attended the United States Naval Academy for one year.

Both Henry and Harriet Wilson were deeply saddened by their child's death, and Henry felt guilty because he had not spent more time with Hamilton in his childhood.

Senator Wilson opposed President Andrew Johnson's reconstruction methods, even though Wilson was not as extreme in his thinking as were some Union citizens. Wilson did support the idea of punishing Confederates.

Some Northerners felt Confederate leaders should be executed. When former Confederate president Jefferson Davis was in danger of being killed, Senator Wilson appealed personally to President Johnson to spare his former fellow senator, and Johnson did.

General Ulysses S. Grant was elected president in 1868, and prior to the election, Henry Wilson had been mentioned by some Republicans as being a good candidate for vice president.

Senator Wilson declined the honor because his wife was dying with cancer, and he wanted to stay with her as much as he could. She died early in 1869, leaving Henry alone in the world. She was buried in Dell Park Cemetery.

Wilson turned his attention back to politics, this time to the railroad being built from Omaha, Nebraska, to California. On May 10, 1869, the final section of the railroad was completed at Promontory, Utah.

Henry Wilson had been a strong supporter of construction of the railroad, and he said: "I give no grudging vote in giving away either money or land. I would spend one hundred million dollars to build the road . . . and think I had done a great thing for my country."

The railroad was the result of joint efforts of both the Union Pacific Railroad Company and the Central Pacific Company. Thomas Durant, president of Union Pacific, chartered a construction company in 1864 to do the actual work, and he named his construction company Credit Mobilier Company of America.

The United States Congress, in a rare burst of generosity, awarded $50 million to finance the project, which would cost less than half that amount. Between 1862 and 1872, over one hundred million acres of land were also given directly to the railroad companies to aid them in construction.

Henry Wilson did not approve of vast land tracts being given to wealthy railway companies. He thought any land donations should be made to men who would cultivate it and who could not afford to buy land of their own. "I think our business is to take care of the interests of the country, and not to take care of the interests of the Union Pacific Railroad or the Central Pacific Railroad," he said.

Following President Grant's election, Senator Wilson urged that laws be passed insuring American Indian rights. He said, "We have emancipated one race and given it the rights of citizenship, and we will now enter upon the policy of taking care of and preserving and civilizing the small remnants of the Indian tribes on this Continent." He asked Congress to settle grievances of Indians who had been illegally deprived of their land and denied payment which had been promised to them under government treaties earlier.

With the aid of the Reverend Samuel Hunt, who had officiated at the Wilsons' marriage, Senator Wilson began writing about laws passed during his years in Congress. The first book was entitled *History of Anti-Slavery Measures of the 37th and 38th Congresses*, and the second was entitled *History of Reconstruction*. The third and last volume, *Rise and Fall of Slave Power in America*, is often referred to in reference notes today.

On June 10, 1872, Senator Henry Wilson was officially nominated to run for vice president with incumbent president Ulysses S. Grant. They were elected, but not before Wilson's aristocratic New England neighbors of his childhood voiced their contempt that a lowly shoemaker could become vice president.

When Credit Mobilier officials were accused of using company stock as bribes to congressmen to get preferential votes, Vice President Wilson was named as one of the men who had benefited.

In the House investigation, it was learned that Wilson had not lied when he said no official of Credit Mobilier had sold him stock at a discounted price. Instead Mrs. Wilson had bought stock in the company several years earlier with money she and her husband had received as a twenty-fifth wedding anniversary gift in 1865.

Less than three months after taking the oath of office on March 3, 1873, Vice President Henry Wilson suffered a stroke while presiding over the Senate. He lived in declining health until his death on November 22, 1875.

Henry Wilson was buried beside his wife.

Bibliography

Abbott, Richard H. *Cobbler in Congress: The Life of Henry Wilson, 1812–1875*. Lexington: University Press of Kentucky, 1972.
McKay, Ernest. *Henry Wilson: Practical Radical*. Port Washington, N.Y.: National University Publications, Kennikat Press, 1971.

19. William Almon Wheeler

William Almon Wheeler was a scrupulously honest government official, when all about him other politicians "fed at the trough," passing such laws as the Act of 1873, which increased the salaries of congressmen by fifty percent. Representative Wheeler returned his increase to the United States Treasury for deposit to pay government expenses.

William Wheeler was born on June 30, 1819, at Malone, New York, to a young lawyer, Almon Wheeler, and his wife, Eliza Woodworth Wheeler.

Almon Wheeler did not have a lucrative law practice, and when he died in 1827, he left no estate for the support of his wife and children.

Eliza Wheeler supported her family by keeping boarding students from Franklin Academy. Young William worked to pay his own expenses at the Academy, and after completing his coursework there, he entered the University of Vermont.

A chronic lack of money and an eye ailment combined to force William Wheeler to leave the university after only one year. He then began studying law with Attorney Asa Hascell in Malone. He was admitted to the New York Bar in 1845, and he married Mary King on September 17 that same year.

Wheeler served as district attorney of Franklin County in New York from 1846 to 1849, having been elected by his fellow Democrats. He was also elected by Whigs to serve in the New York State Assembly from 1850 to 1851. During these years he also managed a local bank.

William Wheeler was perceived to be a capable, honest banker by stockholders and depositors, and in 1853 he was named a trustee for mortgage holders of the Northern Railway System.

Joining the Republican party in 1855, William Wheeler was elected to the New York Senate as the party's nominee, where he served as president pro tem from 1858 to 1860.

Wheeler began his service in the United States House of Representatives in 1861, a turbulent time in American history. He served one term there, supporting any and all attempts to end slavery. As a freshman in Congress, he had little influence, and he returned gladly to his Malone law practice when his term ended.

William A. Wheeler. Reproduced from the collections of the Library of Congress.

In 1869, the Civil War had ended, and William Wheeler was again elected to Congress by the Republicans, where he was named chairman of the Pacific Railroads Committee.

New York Republican party boss Roscoe Conkling told Wheeler, "If you will join us and act with us, there is nothing . . . to which you may not reasonably aspire."

Representative Wheeler told Conkling that there was nothing in the state of New York "which will compensate me for the forfeiture of my own self-respect."

When several high-ranking government officials were accused in the Credit Mobilier scandal in 1873 of accepting railroad stock at reduced rates for favors granted, Wheeler was not involved. He had turned down the stock offer earlier.

Later that same year, congressmen voted a fifty percent increase in their salaries, retroactive for up to five years. Representative Wheeler took the extra money he received, bought government bonds with it, and sent them to the United States Treasury for deposit. He sent the following letter with the bonds:

> New York, March 19, 1873.
> Sir, — The law passed by the late Congress for increased compensation to members of the House of Representative and other officials, gives me for the last two years, after specified deductions, $4,482.40. As this measure was opposed by my vote in all its stages, it does not comport with my views of consistency or propriety to take the above sum to my personal use. I desire, therefore, without giving publicity to the act, to return it to the Treasury.

Representative Wheeler received a receipt for the money from the secretary of the treasury, W. A. Richardson.

It was during this time that Wheeler became concerned about his health and talked of withdrawing from public office. His wife Mary insisted he would be all right, and she thought he should continue to serve in Congress.

In 1874, President U. S. Grant sent Wheeler to Louisiana to try to still political turmoil there resulting from a disputed election. Radical Republicans were in control of the Louisiana government, and military force was necessary to keep them in office.

Representative Wheeler and six other congressmen began working on a compromise agreement with Louisiana officials, but President Grant showed little interest in the proposal. Wheeler stormed out of the White House in an uncharacteristic rage and vowed he would never enter the mansion again until a new president was elected.

When President Grant was advised that Wheeler's plan presented the only feasible option for settlement of the unrest in Louisiana, he told Wheeler: "You are right about this Louisiana affair and the whole power of government shall be exerted to aid you in carrying it through."

Under the terms of Representative Wheeler's plan, the Reconstruction governor Kellogg would complete his present term in office without any threat of impeachment. Democrat state senators who had boycotted the Louisiana legislature would return to the Senate and assist in legislation, and in the final Compromise of 1877, the last of federal troops were withdrawn from the South, ending Reconstruction.

Wheeler had received favorable reports in newspapers about his peacemaking efforts, and it was no surprise when the Republican Convention chose him in 1876 to be its nominee for vice president to run with presidential candidate Rutherford B. Hayes.

William and Mary Wheeler had lived in Mrs. Logan's boarding house with other officials during his years in Congress, where it was well known that William and Mary Wheeler enjoyed a close, loving relationship. They never had any children, however, and when Mary died on March 3, 1876, William was completely alone. His wife had always loyally supported his political activities, and he was deeply saddened that she died before he might be elected to be vice president.

Wheeler and Hayes were elected, and after they took office, Vice President Wheeler often joined the Hayes family for Sunday night dinner and hymn sings, at which Wheeler furnished the song books.

In May 1878, Vice President Wheeler invited First Lady Lucy Hayes and her daughter, Fanny Hayes, to visit him at his home in Malone, located near the Canadian border. Wheeler enjoyed being with the Hayes children, and in Lucy's thank-you note to him for his hospitality, she told him about the children's various activities.

Although the senators considered Vice President Wheeler a good presiding officer, he did not really enjoy the office or the honor. He was miserably lonely without Mary.

When his term as vice president ended, Wheeler returned home to Malone. He was no longer able to pursue either business or political interests due to ill health.

William Wheeler died in Malone on June 4, 1887, and was buried beside his beloved Mary in Morningside Cemetery there.

President Hayes wrote of his vice president: "He was one of the few Vice Presidents who was on cordial terms, intimate and friendly with the President. Our family were heartily fond of him."

Bibliography

Barnard, Harry. *Rutherford B. Hayes and His America*. New York: Russell and Russell, 1967.

Geer, Emily Apt. *First Lady: The Life of Lucy Webb Hayes*. Fremont, Ohio: Kent State University Press, 1984.

Otten, James T. "The Wheeler Adjustment in Louisiana." *Louisiana History*, 13 (Fall 1972).

20. Chester Alan Arthur

Chester Alan Arthur was born on October 5, 1830, in Fairfield, Vermont, to Malvina Stone Arthur and Elder William Arthur, who was a part-time preacher and a part-time educator. The Arthur family moved a total of seven times to various towns in Vermont during Chester's childhood and then to Union Village (now Greenwich) near Saratoga, New York.

For three years, young Chester attended an academy in Saratoga operated by James I. Lowrie. When the Arthurs moved on to Schenectady, Chester enrolled at the Lyceum to prepare for college.

On September 5, 1845, Chester became a sophomore student at Union College because he was so well prepared he was allowed to skip his freshman courses.

After he graduated from Union, Chester Arthur taught school for a few months and then decided to study law. In March 1853, the young man went to work in New York City with the law firm of Culver and Parker. After having been there only a few months, he was admitted to the bar and became a partner in the law firm.

One of the big concerns of the time was enforcement of the fugitive slave law, which was advocated by Southerners. In the North, citizens demanded legal protection for the people who had fled from their slave owners.

Arthur had been reared by an abolitionist father, and he took his father's beliefs about the evils of slavery as his own. Many of his law cases involved these issues.

On October 25, 1859, Arthur married Ellen Lewis Herndon. They met through Ellen's cousin, Dabney Herndon, who lived in Bancroft House, a hotel where Chester Arthur also resided.

The newlyweds went to live with Ellen's mother. Over the years they had two children. Their son Chester Jr. was born in 1864 and their daughter Ellen in 1871.

When the Civil War started in 1861, Arthur was named to the post of assistant quartermaster general of the New York militia. He was assigned the tasks of acquiring food, supplies, and equipment for all the New York regiments — a monumental job which had to be done as rapidly as possible.

Chester A. Arthur. Reproduced from the collections of the Library of Congress.

Chester Arthur was rigidly honest in his dealings with tradesmen and suppliers of merchandise for the troops. He returned with thanks any gifts suppliers sent him to try to insure their firms would be awarded contracts for supplies. When his superior officer reported on Arthur's capability and fairness, he was named quartermaster general when that senior officer retired.

Ellen Arthur, Chester's wife, was a Southern sympathizer because she had many close relatives living in Virginia and other Southern states. The war made life difficult for her.

After the war finally ended, Arthur was hired to be an attorney for the New York City Tax Commission, for which he received a salary of $10,000 a year. In 1871 he was appointed to be the collector of fees of the port of New York City by President Ulysses S. Grant. Arthur worked in that job until 1878, at which time he was discharged by President Rutherford B. Hayes because he had solicited money from employees of the port for use in Republican political campaigns, a violation of the New York State merit system.

President Hayes offered him a post as consul in Paris so his termination as collector would be less obvious, but Arthur chose to return to his law practice of Arthur, Phelps, Knevels, and Ransom in New York City, where he was a senior partner.

In January 1880, Ellen Arthur died after a brief bout with pneumonia. Chester was devastated by his wife's death, partly because he had failed to reach her bedside while she was still conscious. He never remarried and grieved deeply for months.

Arthur entered the political arena that fall to keep his mind occupied, and he was asked by the Republican party leaders to serve as a candidate for vice president with the presidential candidate, James A. Garfield. Roscoe Conkling, New York's Republican party boss, advised Arthur to decline the offer, but he said, "The office of Vice President is a greater honor than I ever dreamed of attaining." Garfield and Arthur were victorious in the election.

The Senate was evenly divided between the two parties after the election, and Arthur's duties as vice president were more important than anyone had expected them to be. With his tie-breaking vote, he could guarantee the Republicans a chance to organize the Senate and name the chairmen of various Senate committees.

Only four months after his March inauguration, President Garfield was shot by an assassin on July 2, 1881, as he walked across the waiting room in the depot of the Baltimore and Potomac Railroad in Washington. The assassin was Charles Guiteau, who claimed he had shot President Garfield so Chester Arthur would become president.

Efforts were made to remove the bullet fragments from the wounded president, but unsterilized instruments were used and Garfield died of blood poisoning on September 19. He had lingered for ten weeks in pain, drifting in and out of consciousness. While President Garfield lay ill, Vice President Arthur flatly refused to assume the office and duties of the presidency.

On September 20, 1881, Arthur took the oath of office as president at his home in New York City. The oath was administered by a Supreme Court justice, John R. Brady.

When Chester Arthur became president, there was no vice president and as yet no Senate president pro tem or Speaker of the House. To protect the government, President Arthur wrote a proclamation which called a special session of the Senate and mailed it to the White House. After he reached Washington safely, he destroyed the letter and called a special session in person.

If President Arthur had died or had also been assassinated before he reached Washington, the letter would have provided the president pro tem of the Senate with the authority to be named president. Otherwise, there was no line of succession.

President Arthur found problems awaiting him in Washington. Since he was known to be a close friend and associate of Boss Roscoe Conkling, President Arthur had to reassure voters that Conkling would not be "the power behind the throne."

When President Arthur inspected the White House where he would be living for a while, he did not like the varied styles of furniture that had accumulated through the years, and he had the mansion redecorated in late Victorian style.

Arthur's sister, Mary Arthur McElroy, a widow, served as the official White House hostess and surrogate mother for ten-year-old Ellen Arthur, who was called "Nell." Chester A. Arthur, Jr. was a student at Princeton University during the period his father was president. After he graduated from Princeton in 1885, he went on to Columbia Law School.

To the surprise of his critics, President Arthur demonstrated real ability to deal with the problems he encountered during his administration and was a good, if not great, chief executive.

Arthur was president when women were starting to demand the right to vote, Clara Barton was organizing the Red Cross in the United States, and Dorothea Dix was waging a campaign to reform hospitals for the mentally ill. It was a period of tremendous social changes.

President Arthur signed into law a bill creating the Federal Civil Service system, ending the old spoils system under which newly elected officials could sweep out employees in government jobs and put their cronies into key jobs. The new law required competitive tests for all applicants for government jobs and selections for jobs to be made on the basis of test scores rather than political affiliation.

The trial of President Garfield's assassin was the news sensation of the period. Guiteau was found guilty and was hanged on June 30, 1882.

Another problem President Arthur faced was a surplus in the Treasury, a problem today's politicians would welcome. The surplus led to spending on "pork-barrel" projects and outright waste in some areas.

President Arthur advocated using the money to bolster defense, improve education, and reduce the national debt, but when he vetoed an appropriation of $18,700,000 to improve harbors and waterways, his veto was overridden. He did manage to get a substantial amount applied to reducing the debt.

Chester Arthur was not nominated as a presidential candidate in his own right because he had angered politicians by ignoring their instructions and using his own judgment.

When Arthur's term ended, he went back to his law firm in New York City and resumed the practice of law once again. He was not as active as he had been formerly because of failing health, however. He had developed Bright's Disease, a kidney ailment, while he was president.

On November 16, 1886, Arthur suffered a stroke during the night, and he died on November 18, only twenty months after he left the White House.

Arthur's funeral was held at the Church of Heavenly Rest in New York City, and pallbearers included President Lincoln's son Robert, Charles L. Tiffany, and Cornelius Vanderbilt. Arthur was buried beside his wife in Rural Cemetery in Albany, New York.

Bibliography

Howe, George Frederick. *Chester A. Arthur*. New York: Frederick Ungar, 1957.
Reeves, Thomas. *Gentleman Boss: The Life of Chester A. Arthur*. New York City: Knopf, 1975.

21. *Thomas Andrews Hendricks*

The Civil War in America caused dissension and division even in family groups in Indiana, as it did in other areas of the nation. Thomas Andrews Hendricks, who was elected governor of Indiana in 1872, helped restore unity and agreement between various political factions by supporting the continuation of the Union, but opposing abolitionists' harsh Reconstruction measures in Southern states.

Thomas Hendricks was born near Zanesville, Ohio, on September 7, 1819, to John and Jane Thomson Hendricks. John Hendricks was a farmer, and the family moved frequently to seek better opportunities. When Thomas was one year old, they moved to Madison, Indiana.

In 1822, John Hendricks bought some land of his own in Shelby County, Indiana, and this last location became their permanent home.

Thomas attended the Shelby County Seminary and the Greenburg Academy in his early school years. In 1836 he went to Hanover College in Madison, Indiana, for college preparatory courses and entered the freshman class there the next year.

Thomas Hendricks proved to be an able debater in college, and after graduating from Hanover in 1841, he decided to study law. He read law for a year in Shelbyville with Judge Stephen Major and went on to Chambersburg, Pennsylvania, in 1843 to attend law school for eight months. He was admitted to the Indiana bar later that same year.

Hendricks started his own law practice in Shelbyville, and it was a success from the beginning. On September 26, 1845, he married Eliza C. Morgan from North Bend, Ohio. Thomas had met Eliza some months earlier when she visited relatives near his home.

The couple's only child, a son named Morgan, was born three years later in 1848, the same year Thomas Hendricks entered politics. That year he was elected to the Indiana House of Representatives, where he served until 1852, at which time the Democrats elected him to the United States House of Representatives.

Little Morgan Hendricks died in 1851 while his father was campaigning for the House seat to represent Indiana. Hendricks served two terms in the House

Thomas A. Hendricks. Reproduced from the collections of the Library of Congress.

before leaving to accept a position as commissioner of the General Land Office in President Franklin Pierce's administration.

Plainly, Hendricks was needed in the office, as a backlog of four years of work had piled up as a result of the opening of western lands for sale and settlement and the granting of land parcels to former soldiers by the federal government.

Thomas Hendricks went to work with zeal, and during the years he served as commissioner, 400,000 land surveys were made and recorded. Also 20,000 law suits involving contested ownership of land were resolved.

After President James Buchanan took office, Hendricks became increasingly dissatisfied with the job and was possibly suffering job burnout. The president also wanted to use jobs in the land office as patronage awards, and he opposed a homestead bill Hendricks favored.

Hendricks resigned in 1859, and he and his wife left Washington. They returned to Shelbyville, but soon moved to Indianapolis, where Thomas opened a highly successful law practice in partnership with Oscar B. Hord.

In January 1863, Hendricks was elected to serve in the United States Senate by the Democrat-controlled Indiana legislature and served there until 1869. In the Senate, Hendricks approved the buying of war supplies and voted money for the purchases, but he did not agree with the draft and heavy taxes imposed nor with President Lincoln's suspension of the writ of habeas corpus during the Civil War.

After the war finally ended, Senator Hendricks, leader of the Democratic minority, agreed with President Andrew Johnson's contention that Southern states had never successfully left the Union and they were entitled to have representatives in Congress.

Senator Hendricks did not vote for the Fourteenth Amendment because Southern states had no representatives present to vote for ratification. He insisted the United States Constitution should only be amended when "the public should be in a cool, deliberative frame of mind." He also refused to vote to impeach President Johnson, and he did not vote for the Fifteenth Amendment, which gave the right to vote to all male United States citizens.

In the early 1860s, fellow Indiana lawyer Lamben K. Milligan joined a Peace Democrat political group that opposed the Civil War. The members of the group believed the Union would be preserved by making concessions to the states in the South rather than going to war with Southerners.

Milligan was arrested after the Civil War began, tried for treason, and sentenced to hang. He hired Thomas Hendricks to represent him on his appeal of his sentence in 1871.

Former senator Hendricks had opposed the war also in principle, and he had no qualms in accepting Milligan as a client. Future president Benjamin Harrison was the lawyer for the federal government at the trial. Milligan was ultimately cleared of all charges against him.

In 1872, Thomas Hendricks was elected governor of Indiana, one of the first Democrats elected in a Northern state after the end of the war.

Hendricks was chosen to be the Democrat nominee for vice president in 1876 on a ticket with Samuel J. Tilden, the presidential candidate. They lost the bitterly contested election to Republicans Rutherford B. Hayes and William A. Wheeler.

Electoral votes in South Carolina, Louisiana, and Florida, plus one of Oregon's votes, were disputed. The disputed votes were eventually awarded to the Republicans by the Electoral Commission, which was composed of five members from the United States House of Representatives, five United States senators, and five Supreme Court justices.

President Hayes won the election by receiving 185 electoral votes to Tilden's 184, but Tilden had received 51% of the total popular vote to Hayes's 48%.

When the 1880 election approached, Thomas Hendricks hoped he would be chosen as the nominee for president at the Democratic convention, but General Winfield S. Hancock was nominated instead. As it turned out, James A. Garfield won the election as president.

Thomas Hendricks turned his attention back to his law practice. That year he had a grave marker shaft erected in the Crown Hill Cemetery in Indianapolis to mark his own future gravesite, and he had his little son's body removed from Shelbyville and reinterred in Crown Hill.

In 1884, Indiana Democrats hoped Hendricks would be nominated for president at last, but Grover Cleveland was chosen, with Hendricks receiving a unanimous nomination for vice president. Hendricks was a favorite with Indiana voters, and if Cleveland could carry Indiana, he had an excellent chance to be the first Democratic president elected since the Civil War.

James G. Blaine, who had served in the United States Senate, as Speaker of the House of Representatives, and as secretary of state for President Garfield, was chosen as the Republican candidate for president. Blaine had been accused of graft earlier in the sale of railroad stocks and bonds, however, and this caused some prominent Republicans to bolt the party.

Believing this might be an ominous sign for Blaine's campaign, his managers decided to publicize a story about Grover Cleveland's illegitimate son that had made the rounds years earlier.

Cleveland had admitted paternity and had paid child support, but in an effort to smear his reputation in order to promote Blaine's campaign, the latter's managers also tried to get ministers involved in the morality issue of Cleveland's past. They told Thomas Hendricks if he would tell them what he knew about Grover Cleveland, he might be named to be the candidate for president when Cleveland was removed from the ticket.

Thomas Hendricks replied with the following letter:

Indianapolis, August 21, 1884.
I have your letter of the 19th inst. I cannot consider with favor your suggestions of a change in the national ticket. The actions of the Convention cannot now be reconsidered; it must stand, and I think it ought to stand. I do not agree with you in respect to the probable result. I think the probabilities are favorable to the success of our ticket. The Cleveland scandal will not have weight with the people, and ought not to have weight. . . .
Whatever there may have been of the scandal existing before, it is not just either

to him or the people now to revive it. The public welfare requires that he be judged by his public record, his capability and fitness for the discharge of responsible and important public duties, and not by old and exploded private scandals.

Very respectfully yours, etc.
T. A. Hendricks

Hendricks worked long hours during the campaign, making speeches in various states. He was involved in a train wreck in Illinois during his travels, but was not injured.

When the election was held, Grover Cleveland was elected president, receiving 49% of the popular vote and 219 electoral votes to Blaine's 48% of the popular vote and 182 electoral votes.

Thomas Hendricks was given much credit for Cleveland's success. Cleveland had carried New York, Connecticut, and New Jersey, while Hendricks had captured the Indiana votes for the ticket. Southern and border states voted for Democrats as usual.

Sadly, Vice President Hendricks died on November 25, 1885, in Indianapolis after suffering a stroke less than a year after he was elected. He was sixty-six years old.

Hendricks's funeral was held in Indianapolis, and he was laid to rest beside his son. Eliza Hendricks requested President Cleveland to stay away from the funeral because of a possible accident or assassination attempt. There was no elected successor to the presidency.

Under the Presidential Succession Act passed in 1792 by the Second Congress, in the event there was no longer either a president or vice president, the president pro tem of the Senate, and after him the Speaker of the House would "act as president . . . until a president be elected."

Vice President Hendricks's death required Democratic officials to place a Republican president pro tem of the Senate in direct succession to the presidency if President Cleveland died. In 1886 Congress changed the succession law to run down through the president's cabinet, beginning with the secretary of state.

Bibliography

Nevins, Allan. *Grover Cleveland: A Study in Courage.* New York: Dodd, Mead, 1932.
Sievers, Harry J. *Benjamin Harrison: Hoosier Statesman.* New York: University Publications, 1959.

22. Levi Parsons Morton

Either Levi Parsons Morton had the Midas touch, or he had a talent for financial matters and understood them completely.

Levi Morton was born on May 16, 1824, in Shoreham, Vermont. His father, the Reverend Daniel Oliver Morton, was pastor of the Congregational church in Shoreham, and his mother, the former Lucretia Parsons, had a religious background. She named her new son for an ancestor who was the first missionary to Palestine from America.

Little Levi had an older brother, Daniel Jr., who became a lawyer and an older sister, Lucretia, who graduated with a bachelor of arts degree from Mount Holyoke. By the time Levi was ready to go to school, there was no money for higher education. He had to be satisfied with the education he received at Shoreham Academy, and later at the Select School when his family moved to Springfield, Vermont.

After completing whatever education was available to him in district schools, Levi Morton went to work in Enfield, New Hampshire as a clerk in a general store when he was only fourteen hears old. He earned fifty dollars a year and was asked to live with the family of the store's proprietor, Ezra Corey.

After working for two years as a store clerk, Levi Morton decided that if he could teach school, he would have more free time to pursue his own interests. He tried teaching for one year, but that was enough. He got another job as a clerk in a general store in Concord, New Hampshire.

Morton's salary in his new job was two hundred dollars a year, a significant improvement over his first job, and he lived with the store owner, W. W. Estabrook, as a member of the family.

In 1843, Estabrook decided to open a second store in Hanover, New Hampshire, and he put Morton in charge as manager. There Morton got room and board in the home of a Latin professor at Dartmouth College who was named Edward David Sanborn. It was in the Sanborn home that Morton first met Lucy Young Kimball of Long Island, New York, whom he would later marry.

The store in Concord failed, and Estabrook's chief creditor, James M. Beebe of Boston, ordered it closed. When Beebe checked the financial affairs of the Hanover store, he found it was prospering under Levi Morton's management.

Levi P. Morton. Reproduced from the collections of the Library of Congress.

There was no reason to close the store in Hanover, so it remained open for business. The next year Morton bought out Beebe's interest and became the owner and operator of his own business at age twenty-one.

Levi Morton discovered he enjoyed financial dealings more than any other intellectual pursuit, and he began to expand his business activities. His father became alarmed by what he perceived to be reckless fiscal behavior by his son and cautioned him in a letter: "We are not without our fears that you may undertake too much business. You have now a great business on hand, and if you can manage it honorably and successfully, you will certainly deserve credit. I hope you will avoid speculations and purchases which involve much risk; it cannot be necessary."

In 1849, James M. Beebe and Company offered Morton a job with the firm in Boston, which he accepted. In 1851 he became a junior partner in the company. In 1854 he was sent to New York City to establish and manage a new branch office of the Beebe Company.

Levi Morton had been saving his money, making investments, and watching for a better opportunity. When George Bird and Company, a Beebe competitor, offered him a senior partnership and management of the company in 1854, he accepted.

On January 1, 1855, Morton began working at his new job. He had invested one hundred thousand dollars of his own capital in the wholesale dry goods establishment, and he worked as diligently to make it a success as if it were entirely his own company.

Lucy Young Kimball reappeared in his life, and she and Levi were married at Flatbush, Long Island, on October 15, 1856. Her father was a man of influence and respected by his peers, but he was not wealthy by New York City standards. Lucy's mother also had good social connections. The bride had spent some time in Portugal, where her uncle, C. B. Haddock, was serving as the American minister to that country.

When the Civil War began, Levi Morton could not collect money due his company from customers in the South because the people there were being attacked on many fronts by Union forces. His company was bankrupted by events, but later that year he managed to restore the company's solvency and started business dealings again.

"In 1863 I commenced a banking business at 30 Wall Street with Mr. Walter H. Burns and H. Cruger Oakley as partners," Morton noted in his *Personal Memorandum*. The L. P. Morton Company was almost immediately successful, and it continued to prosper all during the war.

After the end of the war, Morton repaid in full all the people to whom he owed money because of the earlier bankruptcy, although none of them had any legal claim against him.

When Oakley retired in 1869, Morton took in a new partner named George Bliss. Bliss invested $2,500,000 in the company, and they opened a branch in London. The name of the company became Morton, Bliss, and Company.

Levi's wife, Lucy, died on July 11, 1871, in Newport, Rhode Island. After donating a large financial memorial to the Grace Church, Morton tried to find solace in hard work.

Two years later Morton entered politics, and on February 12, 1873, he married his second wife, Anna Livingston Reede Street, twenty-seven, of Poughkeepsie and New York City. The new Mrs. Morton also had good social and political connections in New York State. Over the next several years, they would have six children, with three daughters reaching adulthood.

In 1879, Levi Morton took his seat in the United States Congress to represent New York. The next year he was asked to accept nomination as vice president on the Republican ticket with presidential candidate James Garfield.

The Republican party boss in New York, Roscoe Conkling, advised Morton not to accept because he believed Garfield could not win the election. Morton trusted his adviser and rejected the nomination. Instead Chester Arthur was nominated vice president and became president after Garfield was assassinated. Morton was reelected to the House of Representatives.

In 1881, Morton was named minister to France by President Garfield, and he resigned his House seat. He and his family were preparing for their move to France when he received notice that President Garfield had been shot. They went on to France and were living there when President Garfield died in September. If he had ignored Conkling's bad advice and run for vice president, Morton would have been the new president.

With his wealth, neither Morton nor his wife could bear living in the two-room, third-story apartment over a Parisian grocery shop which had been the home of former ministers sent from America to service in France. Instead they rented a house near the Trocadero Palace off the Champs Elysées. While it was being refurbished for their use, they went to stay in a summer home in Poissy in the country.

It was a new day for American representation in France. Levi and Anna Morton were hospitable and friendly people. Their home in Paris at 6 Place des Etats Unis became a social center for all Americans in France, regardless of their political affiliation.

Morton and Jules Grevy, president of France, became friends, and Morton was a favorite with other government officials too, who conversed with him about legislative and business affairs in the two countries.

One French official who became Morton's friend was Edouard René Lefebvre de Laboulaye, president of the Franco-American Union. It was M. de Laboulaye's group that began a movement to present a lasting monument to the United States as a token of enduring friendship. Their choice was the Statue of Liberty by Bartholdi, which still stands at the entrance of the harbor of New York. The statue was originally called "Liberty Enlightening the World."

Ambassador Morton accepted the statue officially for the United States government on July 4, 1884. Sadly, M. de Laboulaye died before the official presentation. Morton attended his funeral and was honored by being seated with members of the family.

Morton obtained better legal status for American companies engaged in business in France as one of his accomplishments in France. Before his efforts to improve the situation, American companies paid taxes to France and were subject to lawsuits in the courts. Judgments rendered against them were enforced, but if the ruling was in favor of Americans, they had no right to recover losses.

Another of Morton's accomplishments was having French markets opened to pork from America. Protectionists in France delayed abolishment of the ban against pork until December 11, 1891, six years after Morton had returned home. He was given credit for the change, however.

Other controversies concerned the citizenship status of Americans living in France and that of French people living in America, all of which had been resolved by the time the Mortons left Paris.

Upon his return home, Morton ran for a Senate seat in 1885 and again in 1887, but he was defeated each time. In 1888 the Republican National Convention nominated him for vice president to run with presidential candidate Benjamin Harrison. Morton accepted the honor this time.

Harrison and Morton were elected when President Grover Cleveland, the incumbent, failed to carry his own home state of New York with its thirty-six electoral votes.

After their return from Paris, the Mortons established a country estate on the Hudson River they called "Ellerslie." When he took office as vice president, Morton bought a house on Scott Circle in Washington, and he and his family became active members in Washington society.

Vice President Morton and President Harrison had a congenial relationship during the next four years. When Harrison married his deceased wife's niece, Mary Scott Dimmick, in 1896, Morton was one of the thirty-six guests attending the wedding.

In 1892 the Republicans were defeated, and the Mortons went back to live in New York. He was elected governor of New York in 1894, but did not realize his hopes to be the nominee for president in 1896. He campaigned for the ticket the Republicans chose — William McKinley for president and Garret Hobart for vice president, and they were elected.

In 1899, Morton founded the Morton Trust Company in New York, and the marble mansion in which he and his family had lived in Washington became the new Russian embassy.

The Mortons' three daughters, now young ladies, began marrying. Edith married William Corcoran Eustis in April 1900, Helen married the Duke de Valencery in London in October 1901, and Alice married Winthrop Rutherfurd of South Carolina in February 1902.

Anna Morton died in 1918 in their home on the Hudson, and Levi survived her by two years, dying on his birthday on May 16, 1920, at age ninety-six. His children and their families were visiting him in honor of his birthday when he was stricken with his final illness.

Interment was in the Rhinebeck Cemetery in Duchess County, New York.

Bibliography

Brough, James. *Princess Alice: A Biography of Alice Roosevelt Longworth.* Boston: Little Brown, 1975.

McElroy, Robert McNutt. *Wall Street and the Security Markets.* New York: Putnam, 1930.

Taylor, John M. *Garfield of Ohio.* New York: W. W. Norton, 1970.

23. Adlai Ewing Stevenson

The first Adlai Stevenson started a political dynasty in Illinois when he began his career as a representative in the United States Congress. Later he was elected vice president to serve with President Grover Cleveland. His son, Lewis Green Stevenson, was secretary of state for Illinois at the time of his father's death. Lewis's son, Adlai II, served as governor of Illinois from 1949 to 1953 and was the Democratic presidential nominee in 1952 and 1956, but he was defeated both times by Republican Dwight D. Eisenhower.

The founder of the dynasty was born in Christian County, Kentucky, on October 23, 1835, to a planter named John Turner Stevenson and his wife, the former Eliza Ewing.

Young Adlai's first name came from 1 Chronicles 27:29 in the Bible. A Presbyterian minister, Reverend Richard Paul Graebel, pastor of the First Presbyterian Church in Springfield, Illinois, told Adlai II his name meant "my witness" in ancient Hebrew.

The first Adlai Stevenson attended a school operated by Presbyterian church workers in his early years. When he was sixteen, his father's tobacco crop was ruined by frost, and John Stevenson moved his family to Bloomington, Illinois, where he started a sawmill. Adlai worked in the mill for him to earn money for college.

Adlai Stevenson entered Centre College in Danville, Kentucky, in 1854, where he met and fell in love with the daughter of the college president, Dr. Lewis W. Green. Stevenson's heart was captured by beautiful Letitia, and he wanted to marry her. Unfortunately, the fathers of both the young people died two years later. Stevenson had to return to Illinois to support his widowed mother and his younger brothers and sisters.

Deprived of a chance to complete his college studies, Stevenson began reading law in June 1857 with the Honorable Robert E. Williams, senior partner in the law firm of Williams, Cord, and Dent. He studied there for over a year and was admitted to the Illinois bar late in 1858.

Adlai Stevenson practiced law in the general county court in Metamora, Illinois, for ten years. During this time he served from 1860 to 1864 as master in chancery of the circuit court and from 1865 to 1869 as district attorney.

Adlai E. Stevenson. Reproduced from the collections of the Library of Congress.

After Dr. Green's death, his widow and daughter Letitia moved to Chenoa, Illinois, which was only a few miles from Bloomington. On a visit to his family there, Stevenson encountered Letitia at church and their romance was rekindled. They were married in December 1866, even though Letitia's mother believed that Adlai was unsuitable for her daughter. They went to live in Metamora, where Adlai was still serving as district attorney.

When Adlai Stevenson's term as district attorney ended in 1869, the couple moved to Bloomington, where Adlai formed a law partnership with his cousin, James S. Ewing.

In 1874, Stevenson ran for a seat in the United States House of Representatives on the Democratic ticket and was elected, although his home county was a Republican stronghold. He served one term but was defeated in his bid for reelection. In 1878 he was elected as a representative for a second time with Greenback support and served until 1881.

Stevenson returned to his Bloomington law practice between terms in political office. In 1885, newly elected President Grover Cleveland named him to be the first assistant postmaster general.

It was an honor to be chosen, but it was a thankless job. The Democrats were eager to replace Republican office holders with loyal Democrats, and it was Stevenson's responsibility to name or replace postmasters in fourth class post offices. President Cleveland believed Stevenson was tactful and pleasant enough in demeanor to accomplish the task with a minimum of hurt feelings.

Stevenson replaced forty thousand postmasters throughout the country, and in the process critics dubbed him the "Headsman." He had many grateful Democrats thanking him for their new government jobs, but many Republicans hated him.

After Stevenson staffed the post offices, President Cleveland appointed him to be a federal judge. The appointment had to be confirmed by Congress, however, and Republican members blocked it.

Stevenson returned to Bloomington and his law practice when President Cleveland's term ended in 1889 and Benjamin Harrison became president.

To Stevenson's surprise, he was nominated to be the vice presidential candidate with Cleveland in 1892. Stevenson was the leader of the Illinois delegation to the Democratic Convention, and the delegates cast all their votes for Cleveland. Because Illinois was crucial to Cleveland's reelection and Stevenson was a popular man in Illinois, Cleveland favored his nomination.

Adlai Stevenson was honored to be chosen, and he believed the office of vice president was one of "great dignity." He took pride in achieving such a high honor when they were elected.

Letitia and their three children went to live in Washington with Adlai. Their son Lewis served as his father's secretary, and their two daughters, Letitia and Julia, were belles in Washington society.

Letitia Stevenson decided to help establish a historical organization for women to be known as the Daughters of the American Revolution. She was elected to be the second president general of the group, succeeding former first lady Caroline Harrison. The founders hoped women in both the North and South could establish lasting bonds of friendship through their mutual interest in the nation's history.

Letitia Stevenson also worked with the National Congress of Mothers organization in Washington, the forerunner of present day Parent-Teacher Associations and other similar groups.

Vice President Stevenson had found his niche in presiding over the Senate.

He was an affable man, slow to anger, and he bore no ill will toward the senators who had blocked his appointment to the federal bench years before.

Stevenson did not agree with President Cleveland that the monetary system of the United States should be on a gold standard, but he never made his objections public on any subject during their four-year term in office.

President Cleveland had a dynamic personality, and his fellow Democrats trusted him to prevent a turn to silver as a standard for the nation's money. If a silver standard were adopted, it would devalue dollars issued on the gold standard by fifty percent.

When a malignant tumor was discovered in President Cleveland's mouth on June 18, 1893, he was afraid to enter a hospital for treatment because he feared Vice President Stevenson would sway the vote to adopt the silver standard. Even though they never had a close relationship, Cleveland was well aware of his vice president's views.

President Cleveland and his doctors went on board a ship, where the operation was done secretly without the public knowing of his illness. Stevenson knew some of the medical diagnosis, but he never revealed it to anyone.

When Adlai's term as vice president ended, the Stevensons, except for Lewis, went home to Bloomington. Lewis got a job with the widow of William Randolph Hearst as manager of her mining properties in Arizona and New Mexico. He married a few months later, and he and his wife were the parents of Adlai Ewing Stevenson II, who would be the future unsuccessful candidate for president in 1952 and 1956.

In 1900, President William McKinley appointed Stevenson to serve on the Monetary Commission. Letitia traveled with him when he visited various European nations in promoting the commission.

Later that year Stevenson ran for vice president again with the Democratic presidential nominee, William Jennings Bryan, but they were defeated. Stevenson suffered another political defeat when he ran for governor of Illinois in 1908.

In 1909, Stevenson began writing his memoirs, and he also wrote *Something of Men I Have Known*.

Letitia Green Stevenson died during the Christmas season in 1913. Even though she always called her husband "Mr. Stevenson" and he called her "Mrs. Stevenson," they had a close, loving relationship and a happy marriage. He wrote a history of the Daughters of the American Revolution as a tribute to her after her death.

Adlai Stevenson survived his wife by only about six months, dying on June 14, 1914, in Bloomington. They lie side by side in Bloomington Cemetery.

Their son Lewis had recently become secretary of state in Illinois. Julia Stevenson married a Presbyterian minister, Martin D. Hardin, and they lived in Chicago. Young Letitia Stevenson never married.

Bibliography

Cook, John W. "Life and Labors of Honorable Adlai Ewing Stevenson." *Journal of the Illinois State Historical Society*, 8 (July 1915).

Ewing, James S. "Mr. Stevenson: The Democrat Candidate for Vice President." *American Monthly Review of Reviews* (October 1900).

McKeever, Porter. *Adlai Stevenson: His Life and Legacy*. New York: William Morrow, 1989.

24. Garret Augustus Hobart

From the moment Garret Augustus Hobart was inaugurated as President William McKinley's vice president, he worked diligently to expand the duties of his office. By paying close attention to the details of laws approved and those still pending, Vice President Hobart brought a new level of efficiency to the office and improved public esteem for the post.

Garret was the son of Addison Willard Hobart, a schoolteacher in Marlboro, New Jersey. Addison married Sophia Vanderveer a short time after he began teaching. He met Sophia through his acquaintance with her sister, who taught in the same school with him.

Garret Hobart was born on June 3, 1844, the second child in the family. By the time of his birth, his parents and brother had moved to Long Branch to live, and Garret was born there. Addison Hobart had established a school of his own in Long Branch, and young Garret began attending this school part-time when he was five years old.

In 1852, Addison Hobart returned to Marlboro to farm and to work as a storekeeper. Garret went to the village school there for several years and then went on to a boarding school in Matawan that was operated by James W. Schermerhorn.

By the time young Garret was fifteen, he had received sufficient education to qualify him for college. Because of his youth, he helped his father by working in the store for a year and then entered Rutgers College as a sophomore at age sixteen.

Garret Hobart was an attentive, studious scholar, and when he graduated from Rutgers three years later, he was third best in his class and won prizes in mathematics and public speaking.

Hobart needed to find a job immediately to pay back loans he had received for his education, so he accepted an offer to teach school in a parochial academy near his home, to which he rode on horseback each day. He was paid one dollar a month for each of his students, and he soon saved enough money to pay his debt. Hobart then went to Paterson, New Jersey, to study law with a longtime friend of his father's, Socrates Tuttle. He received his law license on June 7, 1866, and became a master in chancery in 1872.

Garret A. Hobart. Reproduced from the collections of the Library of Congress.

Law was not the only attraction in Paterson for Hobart. Tuttle had a pretty daughter named Jennie, and she and Garret were married on July 21, 1869, in the Tuttle home.

In 1871, when his father-in-law became the mayor of Paterson, Hobart was selected to be the city attorney. The next year he was elected to serve in the New Jersey Assembly, the lower legislative body, and he became Speaker of the House in 1874. His ability was recognized, and in 1876, he was elected to serve in the New Jersey Senate. During the 1881–82 session, he served as president of the Senate.

All Hobart's achievements in legislative matters improved his law practice, and he became a receiver for various railroad companies in financial trouble. He worked hard and soon had their affairs in good financial condition. He was also named president of two large water companies, one of which furnished water to the city of Newark, New Jersey.

As the election of 1896 neared, friends of Hobart told him they expected him to be nominated as vice president. To spend some time together before the election, the Hobarts took their daughter Fannie and their son Augustus Jr. on a vacation trip to Europe.

After visiting Venice, the Hobarts went to Bellagio, also in Italy, to rest for a few days. Young Fannie Hobart was stricken with diphtheria shortly after their arrival, and she died on June 27, 1895.

Because Fannie had died of an infectious disease, her parents had to allow her burial in Italy, as Italian law required. They returned home with heavy hearts and with scant interest in politics.

When Hobart was nominated by the Republicans as their vice presidential candidate, he was ambivalent about whether he wanted the job, if elected. He was congratulated heartily by prominent people on his nomination, and crowds gathered to hear him speak and cheer for him at railroad stations.

President William McKinley was elected by 52% of the popular vote, and Garret Hobart found himself the new vice president. He had not been introduced to President McKinley prior to their election, but they soon became good friends.

In his acceptance speech at the inauguration, Vice President Hobart reiterated his firm conviction that currency in the United States should remain on the gold standard, saying, "An honest dollar worth one hundred cents everywhere, cannot be coined out of fifty-three cents of silver plus a legislative fiat."

As vice president, Garret Hobart was faithful in his duties as he listened respectfully to Senate speeches, and he demonstrated an awe-inspiring memory regarding the status of various bills before the Senate. He was familiar with parliamentary procedures from his years of service in the New Jersey legislature. He also began expanding the duties of the vice presidency. Instead of asking for Senate approval or disapproval on rules of order, Vice President Hobart made rulings himself as the presiding officer.

President McKinley consulted his vice president frequently on questions of general policy, and Hobart believed he was helping govern. He cast the tie-breaking vote in support of President McKinley's decision to maintain control of the Philippine Islands after the Spanish-American War ended.

First Lady Ida McKinley suffered from epilepsy, and she was almost a complete invalid. Jennie Hobart knew Ida McKinley was spending lonely hours since her husband had become president, and she made a regular habit of visiting with her almost every day. She became one of Ida McKinley's cherished friends.

Due to the first lady's health problems, Jennie Hobart, who termed herself "second lady," had to assist the president with social events. At White House dinners or receptions, if Ida McKinley faltered in responding to a guest, Jennie Hobart stepped forward and answered for her. She often took Ida McKinley's place at the president's side when Ida was not able to attend a state function.

The Hobarts rented a large mansion-type house on Lafayette Street near the White House when they moved to Washington, and they entertained frequently. Jennie Hobart usually asked six young women to join her to mingle with guests, and often she spent four days a week issuing invitations, arranging dinners, and replying to invitations.

One dinner hosted by the Hobarts was especially appreciated by President McKinley. The vice president and his wife invited all the senators and the president to meet and get acquainted on a social level. President McKinley believed the party aided him in getting votes for bills he favored when they were presented in the Senate.

Vice President Hobart developed a serious heart condition, and his doctor ordered him to take a complete rest in the summer of 1899. He had never recovered completely from the shock of his young daughter's untimely death in Italy, although they were allowed to return her body to the United States for burial in 1896.

At first his doctors were hopeful the vice president would soon be able to return to his duties in Washington, but his condition worsened gradually, and he died in Paterson on November 21, 1899, with Jennie and their son by his bedside.

Garret Hobart was interred in a mausoleum in Cedar Lawn Cemetery in Paterson in the family plot where his daughter Fannie was buried. A bronze statue of Vice President Hobart was erected on the plaza of the Paterson City Hall in 1903.

Bibliography

Magie, David. *Life of Garret Augustus Hobart.* New York: G. P. Putnam and Sons, 1910.
Olcott, Charles S. *The Life of William H. McKinley.* 2 vols. Boston: Houghton Mifflin, 1916.

25. Theodore Roosevelt

Theodore Roosevelt served as vice president with President William McKinley and became president of the United States at age forty-two when McKinley was assassinated on September 6, 1901. Roosevelt was subsequently elected to serve a second term in his own right.

Theodore Roosevelt was born on October 27, 1858, to Martha (Mittie) Bulloch Roosevelt and her husband, Theodore Roosevelt, Sr., in New York City; he was the second of their four children.

At age three little Theodore developed bronchial asthma which plagued him for the rest of his life. Because of his illness, young Theodore was an avid reader, but his father urged him to partake in active sports to build his stamina. His father enjoyed outdoor activities, and his young son developed a liking for them also.

After Theodore had suffered a particularly severe attack of asthma, his father had a gymnasium installed in their home so he could get more exercise. Theodore realized he had to be strong if he wanted to experience heroic adventures like the ones he read about, and he began an arduous regime of bodybuilding on his own.

Following a humiliating experience at summer camp when he was fourteen during which two fellow campers taunted him about his spindly limbs and thick lens in his eyeglasses, Theodore begged his father to let him take boxing lessons.

Mr. Roosevelt agreed, and Theodore continued boxing for many years. After he became president, a military aide landed a blow to Theodore's left eye that permanently blinded him in that eye. To spare the young man's feelings, the president did not publicize the injury.

Theodore's parents took their four children to Europe, Egypt, and other exotic locales as they grew up. Theodore became a naturalist during their visit to the Nile River in Egypt, and the hot desert sun seemed to improve his overall health. He did not have an attack of asthma during the two months they spent there.

Theodore had several girl friends during his teen years, a favorite being Edith Carow. They attended dancing class together, and Edith enjoyed outdoor activities as much as Theodore. They went for walks in the woods, and he named his rowboat *Edie*; both enjoyed rowing.

Theodore Roosevelt. Reproduced from the collections of the Library of Congress.

Mr. Roosevelt wanted Teddy, as Theodore was called by his family and friends, to go to Harvard University to complete his education, and he hired a tutor named Arthur Cutler to tutor his son to insure his passage of the entrance examinations. Teddy had missed school frequently because of health problems, but with the tutoring he received he passed easily. His health had improved by this time also.

Teddy Roosevelt was a novelty to the other Harvard students because of his boundless energy and enthusiasm. The style of the time was to view life as a crashing bore, and almost to a man the students were langorous and slow-moving. Teddy did not conform to their customs because he enjoyed feeling better than he had as a child.

Roosevelt's life changed drastically on October 18, 1878, when he fell in love. He was visiting friends when he was introduced to a young girl named Alice Hathaway Lee. "I loved her as soon as I saw her sweet, fair, young face," he wrote in an article in her memory. They were married in late October 1880.

Theodore and Edith Carow had quarreled the year before and their friend-ship had suffered, but she attended his wedding to Alice in the Brookline Unitar-ian Church and "danced the soles off her shoes," as she said, at the reception.

Teddy and Alice went to live with his recently widowed mother, and he en-tered Columbia Law School. He was not as interested in the study of law as he had thought he would be, but he did develop an intense interest in politics at Co-lumbia. He joined the Republican party.

After their wedding, Teddy and his bride took a trip to Europe, and Teddy enjoyed showing Alice points of interest. Shortly after their return, he was elected to serve as an assemblyman for New York State.

Roosevelt immediately introduced bills aimed at improving efficiency in New York City government. Only one passed, but his efforts and energy attracted the attention of other politicians.

During this period of activity, Roosevelt also wrote a book entitled *The Naval War of 1812*. It was published in March 1883 and became a textbook for the Naval War College.

In late autumn 1883, Roosevelt decided to go on a buffalo hunt out West. Alice was four months pregnant and could not go with him. He was away until February 1884, while their first child, a girl named Alice, was born on Feb-ruary 12, 1884.

On his return, Roosevelt went on to Albany where a telegram informed him of his daughter's birth. A short time later he received another telegram telling him to come home at once because both Alice and his mother were seri-ously ill.

Teddy Roosevelt left Albany on a train, but when he reached his wife and mother's bedsides, his sister told him Alice was dying with Bright's Disease, a kidney ailment, and their mother was dying from typhoid fever. Both women died on February 14.

Roosevelt's sister Bamie took little Alice Lee to care for and he returned to Albany a few days later.

When the election results that year did not suit him, Roosevelt decided to go back to the West and operate a ranch he had bought there earlier in the Dakota Territory. Beef was becoming more and more popular with Eastern din-ers, and he made a success with his ranching over the next several years.

In September 1885, Roosevelt returned to New York City to see his baby daughter and other relatives. While there, he encountered Edith Carow by acci-dent, and they resumed their former friendship.

After he returned to Dakota, Roosevelt wrote a biography of Senator Thomas Hart Benton, which sold well. He also continued to keep in touch with Edith Carow, who had gone to London with her mother. Their correspondence was frequent, and in August 1886, the *New York Times* carried an announcement of their engagement.

A week later a notice appeared in the same newspaper retracting the

announcement. This notice was submitted by Teddy's sisters, who could not believe the engagement was true, but Teddy convinced them he and Edith were really engaged.

Leaving the care of his ranch in the hands of two of his ranchhands, Roosevelt traveled to England to marry Edith on December 2, 1886, in St. George's
Church, which was located on Hanover Square in London. The ceremony took
place in England so that her mother could attend.

The newlyweds went on a honeymoon trip to Europe, where Teddy was
careful to avoid places he had visited years before with his beloved Alice. When
they returned to New York, Edith insisted his daughter Alice should live with
them, and Alice left her Aunt Bamie's home.

During 1887, Roosevelt stayed home, got acquainted with his young daughter, wrote a biography of Gouverneur Morris, who served as American minister
to France during the French Revolution, and awaited the birth of his and Edith's
first child.

Young Ted arrived on September 12, and Little Alice was enchanted by her
baby brother. She adored the baby, as she loved the later arrivals — Kermit in
1889, Ethel in 1891, Archibald in 1894, and Quentin in 1897.

Following little Ted's birth, Roosevelt began writing a multivolume series of
books entitled *The Winning of the West*, but only four were completed because of
his appointment as United States Civil Service commissioner. His political life
had begun.

Roosevelt served six years with the Civil Service and two more years as
president of the New York Police Board. He began his duties with the Police
Board on May 5, 1895, and he went to work improving law enforcement and reforming the system. It had been a custom among the politicians in New York to
sell high-ranking positions in the Police Department. A captaincy sold for ten
thousand dollars.

To guarantee new policemen would be hired on merit, Roosevelt set up an
examining board, and the new recruits received intensive training.

When President William McKinley was elected in 1897, Roosevelt mentioned to various influential political friends that he would like to be appointed
assistant secretary of the navy. President McKinley listened to his friends' arguments on Roosevelt's behalf, but he hesitated to make the appointment because
he explained: "I want peace, and I am told that your friend Theodore . . . is always getting into rows with everybody. I am afraid he is too pugnacious."

Political pressure was brought to bear, however, and Roosevelt's name was
submitted to the Senate for confirmation on April 5, 1897. He went to work as
the new assistant secretary of the navy on April 19, 1897.

John D. Long, a former governor of Massachusetts, was the secretary of the
navy, and he feared Roosevelt would try to take over the Navy Department and
run it. His fears were justified. Roosevelt began an aggressive campaign shortly
after his appointment to add more ships to the navy. He publicly defended the

right of the United States government to annex Hawaii when Japan protested the annexation. As assistant secretary of the navy, he should not have made his views known to the public.

For these and other reasons, Secretary Long soon felt a need to take a long vacation in Massachusetts, which lasted for a month. He left Roosevelt in charge of the department, and Roosevelt wrote him to enjoy his stay — nothing much was happening in Washington.

The *New York Sun* published an article in mid-August 1897, however, which said: "The liveliest spot in Washington at present is the Navy Department. The decks are cleared for action. Acting Secretary Roosevelt, in the absence of Secretary Long, has the whole Navy bordering on a war footing. It remains only to sand down the decks and pipe the quarters for action."

The action anticipated was war with Spain, which President McKinley hoped to prevent. Spanish officials believed the United States would try to annex Cuba after annexing Hawaii, but President McKinley assured them the United States had no such plans.

Meanwhile, Assistant Secretary Roosevelt kept insisting the United States Navy should be put on a war footing, but his advice was ignored.

On January 24, 1898, the United States battleship the *Maine* was sent to Havana on a "courtesy visit." Less than a month later, on February 15, the *Maine* was blown up and two hundred sixty-six crewmen and officers were killed in the explosion. Only eighty-eight survived the attack.

On April 19, 1898, Congress approved a resolution, which was, in effect, a declaration of war. Roosevelt had been in office exactly one year.

Roosevelt was determined to go into battle himself, and he received a commission as a lieutenant colonel to lead a regiment of volunteers known as the Rough Riders. Edith supported his decision, even though he was forty years old, had six children, and was nearly blind without his glasses.

His friends and acquaintances seriously questioned his sanity. Secretary of Navy Long wrote: "He has lost his head . . . running off to ride a horse. . . . He is acting like a fool!"

The Rough Riders trained in Texas, and as they rode by rail to Florida before sailing on to Cuba, they were cheered lustily across the southern United States. When they got near Cuban shores, Roosevelt persuaded one of his former aides to bring their transport ship closer to shore than the other ships so they would be first to land.

After leading a charge by his men up San Juan Hill, Theodore Roosevelt was a certified national hero. He and his men returned to Montauk on August 15, 1898. He greeted Edith, who was waiting for him on the dock, by saying, "Oh, but we have had a bully fight!"

Later that same year Roosevelt was elected governor of New York, and he was inaugurated on January 2, 1899. Republican party boss Thomas C. Platt tried to dictate policy to Roosevelt, but it was a lost cause — he made his own decisions.

When Vice President Garret Hobart died in office, Platt urged the nomination of Roosevelt as vice president in an effort to get him out of New York politics.

President McKinley had no objections, and Roosevelt campaigned enthusiastically for the ticket while McKinley did little. They won election, and Roosevelt was inaugurated as vice president on March 4, 1901, for McKinley's second term.

Roosevelt's duties of presiding over the Senate lasted for four days, after which that distinguished group adjourned for the summer. The new vice president returned to his home on Sagamore Hill to spend a restful summer with his family before he returned to Washington.

In September both President McKinley and Roosevelt began speaking tours in various states to let voters meet them. On September 6, President McKinley was at the Pan American Exposition in Buffalo, New York, and Roosevelt was planning to attend a meeting of the Vermont Fish and Game League on Lake Champlain.

While President McKinley was shaking hands with voters at the exposition, a young man named Leon Czolgosz came toward him, as had many others. This man, however, shot the president with a revolver concealed in a bandage on his hand.

Before Roosevelt left for his own meeting, a telephone caller told him to come to Buffalo at once. President McKinley lived for seven days after receiving severe wounds, but on September 14, 1901, he died.

A few hours later, forty-two-year-old Theodore Roosevelt was sworn in as the youngest president in United States history to that time. He served during a period when a reform movement called the "Progressive Movement" held sway in the country. Excesses and graft in government were exposed, immoral and sinful behavior was deplored, and labor unions were suspect.

First Lady Edith Roosevelt went to work refurbishing the White House. She directed placement of furniture, ordered new curtains and drapes, had walls painted and new carpets installed.

Kermit Roosevelt, then twelve years old, and his brother Archie, age seven, enrolled in public school, and their sister Ethel was sent to the Cathedral School, a nearby private school. Alice Roosevelt, now seventeen, was expected to join Ethel there, but Alice remained with her Aunt Bamie for several months. Young Ted, now fourteen, was a student at Groton. Little Quentin at age four was too young to go to school.

During his first administration, Roosevelt was a leader in acquiring rights to construct the Panama Canal, which aided American ships in traveling between Atlantic and Pacific ports. He also got British officials to work with the United States in establishing permanent boundaries between Canada and Alaska.

In 1904, Roosevelt was elected to the presidency in his own right, and during his second term, he signed the Pure Food and Drug Act into law. He also effected an open-door compromise with Japan on immigration and trade.

Roosevelt's daughter, Alice, was married to Nicholas Longworth in a glittering White House wedding on February 17, 1906, with five hundred guests in attendance. Longworth was a New York representative in the United States House, where he was elected Speaker during President Coolidge's administration.

President Roosevelt announced he would not seek a third term, and in the election of 1908, he promoted his friend William Howard Taft to be his successor. Taft was elected president, but when he refused to continue some of Roosevelt's policies, the old friends became enemies.

After President Taft was nominated by the Republicans to run for a second term in 1912, Roosevelt left the Republican party and accepted the nomination of the Progressive party to run for president again.

The campaign was bitter and vitriolic. Roosevelt said President Taft was "a fathead with brains less than a guinea pig," and Taft described Theodore as "a man who can't tell the truth."

Roosevelt beat Taft in the popular votes, receiving 4,126,020 votes to Taft's 3,483,922 votes. The Democratic nominee, Woodrow Wilson, defeated both of them, however, by receiving 6,286,820 votes, or 42% of the popular vote.

In 1909, between campaigns, Roosevelt had gone to Africa for a year-long safari with his son Kermit and naturalists from the Smithsonian Institution. Following his defeat by Wilson, Roosevelt went on a Brazilian exploration and specimen-collecting trip for seven months. He contracted malaria in Brazil, which recurred intermittently for the rest of his life.

Both Theodore and Edith Roosevelt were deeply grieved by the death of their son Quentin, who was serving as a pilot of a fighter plane in World War I when his plane was shot down in July 1918, and he was killed.

Roosevelt never recovered completely from the shock and grief he suffered, and he resumed writing books about his travels and political affairs to occupy his mind. He died in his sleep at Sagamore Hill on January 6, 1919. He had written a total of twenty-one books by the time of his death.

Theodore Roosevelt was buried in Young's Memorial Cemetery in Oyster Bay, New York, near his home.

Bibliography

Hagedorn, Hermann. *The Roosevelt Family of Sagamore Hill.* New York: Macmillan, 1954.

Harbaugh, William H. *The Life and Times of Theodore Roosevelt.* New York: Oxford University Press, 1975.

Miller, Nathan. *Theodore Roosevelt: A Life.* New York: William Morrow, 1992.

Pringle, Henry F. *Theodore Roosevelt.* New York: Harcourt, Brace, and World, 1956.

26. *Charles Warren Fairbanks*

It is difficult to understand why a successful railroad financier like Charles Fairbanks, with interests in both North America and South America, would want to become vice president of the United States. Fairbanks had proven his competence as a businessman years before he entered politics; perhaps he welcomed a new challenge.

Charles Fairbanks was born on May 11, 1852, in Union County, Ohio, to Loriston Monroe Fairbanks and his wife, the former Mary Adelaide Smith. The family lived in a log cabin on the farm they owned, and Charles had the distinction of being one of the last major American politicians to be born in a log cabin.

The boy grew up working in the fields with his father, and he attended local neighborhood schools. His parents were Methodists and passionate abolitionists. They provided food, shelter, and comfort to any runaway slaves who came to their door.

When he was fifteen, Charles entered Ohio Wesleyan University at Delaware, Ohio, from which he graduated in 1872. He had to work at the college to pay his expenses, but as he neared graduation, he began buying law books with the plan of studying to become a lawyer.

After leaving college, young Fairbanks's first job was working as a news reporter for the Western Associated Press, which was managed by his uncle, William Henry Smith. Fairbanks attended law school at night.

In 1874, Fairbanks married his college sweetheart, Cornelia Cole, and he qualified as a member of the Ohio bar the same year. Cornelia was the daughter of Judge P. B. Cole of Marysville, Ohio, and she had worked with Charles on the college newspaper at Ohio Wesleyan. She was a beautiful young woman who admired the tall, lanky, serious-minded Charles. Believing he would have a better opportunity to build a profitable law practice in Indiana, Charles and Cornelia moved to Indianapolis a few weeks after their wedding.

Charles Fairbanks began practicing law at a propitious time in history. Railroads were being built in all parts of the country, and law suits always abound in big businesses. When Attorney Fairbanks handled the affairs of a bankrupt railroad in a very competent way, other railway officials turned to him for assistance with their problems too.

Charles W. Fairbanks. Reproduced from the collections of the Library of Congress.

Fairbanks did not have to worry about collecting fees from his clients, as they always paid on time, and he soon became a wealthy man. His practice extended from Indianapolis into Ohio and Illinois, and eventually into New York.

For twenty-three years, Fairbanks practiced law in Indianapolis. He became a rich man, but he and Cornelia continued to live simply in their two-story frame house and never paraded their wealth in their life-style. They were active members of the Meriden Street Methodist Episcopal Church, and Charles was named a trustee of Ohio Wesleyan University.

Charles and Cornelia had a total of five children. Son Warren and daughter Adelaide both graduated from Ohio Wesleyan, son Frederick was educated at Princeton University and Columbia Law School, son Richard graduated from Yale, and their youngest son, Robert, also graduated from Princeton.

Wealth and politics are often linked, and for a time Fairbanks was content to speak for various Republican candidates for office and contribute money to their campaigns. After a while he decided to seek office as a senator from Indiana, and he was elected in 1897 to the United States Senate.

Charles and Cornelia Fairbanks lived in the Van Wyck house near DuPont Circle in Washington while he served in the Senate. Cornelia Fairbanks was elected president-general of the Daughters of the American Revolution, and their family home was the scene of social gatherings both for her organization and his political friends.

In his role as senator, Fairbanks supported President William McKinley's policies, even during the Spanish-American War. They became good friends.

Fairbanks served on the Foreign Relations Committee. He strongly advocated internal improvements in the nation, especially to the waterways, and was named the United States chairman of the commission to resolve controversies between the United States and Canada.

This commission failed to settle the problems with England and Canada that had arisen from a bitter dispute about the Alaskan boundary. Because of Fairbanks's efforts, however, the city of Fairbanks in Alaska bears his name.

In 1903, Senator Fairbanks was reelected to the Senate, but later that year he was nominated to run for vice president with incumbent President Theodore Roosevelt, who had become chief executive after President McKinley was killed.

Fairbanks had hoped he might be nominated for president, but President Roosevelt was favored. They were elected, and even though each represented different factions in the Republican party, they maintained cordiality. Fairbanks had campaigned vigorously, and the president included him in the formulation of his administration's legislative agenda, before their election.

President Roosevelt feared his ultraconservative vice president would oppose his progressive policies, however, and their friendship ended on election day. Vice President Fairbanks did disagree with Roosevelt's liberal views and had voted often with conservatives when he was a senator, even against some of the bills sponsored by Roosevelt.

Fairbanks was a good friend of Senator Mark Hanna and other Republican supporters of big business interests. Some of these men questioned the president's sanity when he promoted antitrust and prolabor legislation.

On Memorial Day, 1907, President Roosevelt came to Indianapolis to speak, and Vice President Fairbanks and his wife hosted a luncheon and lawn party in his honor.

The Fairbankses had always been strict abstainers from alcoholic beverages and were astounded when Manhattan cocktails were served to their guests. Charles Fairbanks had campaigned on his record as a teetotaler and had been widely supported by temperance groups. The newspapers had a field day with the story of teetotaler Fairbanks serving alcohol at the luncheon, and Fairbanks was ruined politically.

Later, Fairbanks wondered if President Roosevelt or some of his staff had ordered the drinks served to discredit him. President Roosevelt had made jokes about Fairbanks for years, and he made it clear when he announced he would not seek reelection that Secretary of War William H. Taft was his chosen successor. James S. Sherman was nominated vice president to serve with Taft.

Charles and Cornelia Fairbanks returned to their home in Indianapolis in March 1909, and he continued his interest in politics. He never held any public office again, although he was nominated for vice president on the Republican ticket with presidential candidate Charles Evans Hughes in 1916. They were defeated by Democrats Woodrow Wilson and Thomas R. Marshall.

Cornelia Fairbanks died in 1913, and Charles turned to work as a solution for his loneliness. He stayed busy with the supervision of his farms in Illinois and his positions as trustee for various education and religious organizations, and he developed a deep interest in forestry and conservation before his death on June 4, 1918.

Bibliography

Dictionary of American Biography. Vol. 3.
Gould, Lewis L. "Charles Warren Fairbanks and the Republican National Convention of 1900: A Memoir." *Indiana Magazine of History* 77 (1981).
Harris, Addison C. "Charles Warren Fairbanks." *North American Review* 188, no. 630 (May 1908).
Shipp, Thomas R. "Charles Warren Fairbanks: Republican Candidate for Vice President." *American Monthly Review of Reviews* (August 1904).

27. James Schoolcraft Sherman

James Schoolcraft Sherman had years of experience as a business executive before he was elected vice president when William Taft was elected president. Sherman's background made him a particularly effective presiding officer over the United States Senate.

James Sherman was born on October 24, 1855, in Utica, New York, to Richard Updike and Mary Frances Sherman. Richard Sherman was a newspaper editor and a strong supporter of the Democratic party and its policies.

Young James attended public schools in Utica, and later he went to Whitestown Seminary. He completed his education at Hamilton College, where he met the requirements for an L.L.B. degree in 1879; he was admitted to the bar later that year.

The next year Sherman went into a law practice in Utica with his brother-in-law, Henry J. Cookinham. He confined his practice almost entirely to advising clients about business matters.

Sherman married Carrie Babcock, daughter of another Utica attorney, on January 26, 1881. During the next five years, they had three sons — Sherrill, Richard, and Thomas. They bought a house in a pleasant neighborhood and appeared to be settled in Utica for their lifetimes.

James Sherman was a strong conservative, and he registered to vote with the Republican party. His strongly Democratic father was surprised, and a little disappointed, but he accepted the fact after James was elected mayor of Utica in 1884.

In 1887, Sherman was elected a member of the United States House of Representatives, where he served until 1901, except for a period in 1892–93 when he was not elected.

In 1895, Richard Sherman died, and James took over his position as president of the New Hartford Canning Company; later he served as president of the Utica Trust and Deposit Company.

James Sherman was an amiable, friendly man, and his friends referred to him as "Smiling Jim." He usually voted with the other Republicans in Congress, where he served as chairman of the Indian Affairs Committee and as a member of the Committee on Interstate and Foreign Commerce.

James S. Sherman. Reproduced from the collections of the Library of Congress.

In the latter post, Sherman promoted construction of a canal across Nicaragua, but when the Isthmus of Panama appeared to offer a better location for a canal, he supported the change.

Sherman had an excellent record on the Indian Affairs Committee, where he presented and fought for laws to improve living conditions for native Americans, whose numbers under United States control increased when New Mexico and Arizona were admitted to the Union in 1912.

Representative Sherman and his family traveled extensively in the United States and went to Europe in 1904.

William Howard Taft, a friend of President Theodore Roosevelt, was handpicked by the president to succeed him in the 1908 election. Because some Republicans at the convention resented Roosevelt's actions, they insisted on nominating their own choice for vice president, James Sherman.

President Taft and Vice President Sherman won the election and took the oath of office on March 4, 1909. They became friends and were golfing partners for the first fifteen months of the administration, but in 1910 the vice president and former president Roosevelt got into a rivalry for the chairmanship of the New York State Republican Convention, and Sherman won.

President Taft was irritated by his vice president's actions because Roosevelt blamed Taft for his defeat to be convention chairman. President Taft never invited his vice president to go golfing with him again.

When President Taft asked Vice President Sherman to act as liaison between him and Joe Cannon, Speaker of the House, whom Taft detested, Sherman refused. He said, "I am the Vice President, and acting as a messenger boy is not part of the duties of a Vice President."

President Taft was stunned when he learned that his longtime friend Roosevelt planned to seek the nomination for president again in 1912. Taft planned to run for reelection, and he could not believe Roosevelt would become a rival for the office.

Roosevelt was annoyed with President Taft because he did not follow Roosevelt's agenda when he became president. Roosevelt considered Taft to be too conservative.

Regardless of the former president's opinion, both President Taft and Vice President Sherman were renominated. Theodore Roosevelt was so outraged by his failure to be nominated that he and his supporters entered him in the race on a third party ticket, representing a group known as the Bull Moose party.

All the controversy was for naught when Democrat Woodrow Wilson defeated both men and was elected president.

On October 30, 1912, a few days before the election, James S. Sherman died in Utica. He had suffered with Bright's Disease, a kidney ailment, for several years. Even though he had died, he and Taft received almost three million five hundred thousand votes in the election, or 23% of the popular vote.

Sherman was buried in Forest Hill Cemetery in Utica. The Shermans' sons were all successful in their chosen fields of work at the time of their father's death. Sherrill was an officer in a Utica bank, Richard was a mathematics professor at Hamilton College, and Thomas was operating a business of his own.

Bibliography

Biographical Directory of American Congress. 1928.

"Men We Are Watching." *Independent* (Utica, New York) May 28, 1908.

Weed, William E. "James S. Sherman: Republican Candidate for Vice President." *American Review of Reviews* (August 1908).

28. Thomas Riley Marshall

Vice President Thomas Riley Marshall found himself embroiled in a raging controversy when President Woodrow Wilson was disabled by a stroke. Some government officials believed Vice President Marshall should assume the full duties and responsibilities of president during Wilson's illness, while others, especially First Lady Edith Wilson, were emphatically opposed to any changes being made.

Although Vice President Marshall was noted for making humorous remarks, he was probably completely serious and sincere when he in later years wired Calvin Coolidge, who had just been elected vice president, "Please accept my sincere sympathy."

Thomas Marshall was born in North Manchester, Indiana, on March 14, 1854, the son of Daniel M. and Martha Patterson Marshall. Daniel Marshall was a country doctor.

Young Thomas attended the North Manchester public schools and graduated in 1873 from Wabash College in Crawfordsville, where he was selected to be a member of Phi Beta Kappa. After studying law with Attorney Walter Olds, Thomas Marshall was admitted to the Indiana bar in 1875. He and William F. McNagny set up a law partnership in Columbia City and were later joined by attorney P. H. Clugston.

Marshall was a lawyer who involved himself totally in his profession. There was no outside activity for him such as selling stocks and bonds and organizing businesses. He devoted all his attention to his clients and their interests.

Thomas Marshall married Lois I. Kinsey of Salem Center in 1895. Her father was clerk of court in Steuben County, and she was working as a deputy clerk in her father's office when Thomas met her. He had gone to Steuben County to represent a client in circuit court there. Lois Kinsey thought she was marrying a small-town lawyer, who might with luck be able to gain election as a judge at some future date.

Thomas and Lois were on vacation in northern Michigan in the summer of 1908 when they learned Louis Ludlow, a United States representative from Indiana had suggested Thomas Marshall would be a good candidate for governor of Indiana.

Thomas R. Marshall. Reproduced from the collections of the Library of Congress.

Since Marshall had never held any elective office, even at the local level, there was stunned surprise on the part of the prospective candidate. The couple hurried back home to find, as Marshall said:

> My law office was about to be turned into political headquarters. My partners had searched in vain for anything in my life that distinguished me from the common run of men, so they had ventured into the field of fiction. . . . They had printed an eight-page pamphlet reviewing the history of the Marshall family . . . to the year 1907. . . .
> I asked them what they were going to do with it. They told me I was now a full-fledged candidate for the Democratic nomination for governor. . . . I told them very frankly that I could not let my wife read it and ever again look her in the face!

Thomas Marshall's partner, William McNagny, told Marshall he was an unknown except in three or four counties, and that he would have to get some publicity.

Marshall ignored the advice. He did attend a few banquets with other candidates and made speeches there, but he did no other campaigning.

As matters developed, Thomas Marshall was a compromise candidate over two other favorites in the race for governor, and after being nominated, he was elected governor of Indiana in 1908.

Marshall was a good governor. He stopped widespread graft in the state by creating a State Board of Auditors, whose job was to examine financial records of all public offices down to the townships. He worked to reduce the state debt, established prison reforms, and had child labor laws introduced, which were subsequently passed.

Governor Marshall was chosen to be the Democratic vice presidential candidate in 1912 to balance the ticket with presidential candidate Woodrow Wilson, who was governor of New Jersey. They were elected by 42% of the popular vote and 435 electoral votes over William Howard Taft, the Republican candidate, and Theodore Roosevelt, the Bull Moose or Progressive candidate.

President Wilson and Vice President Marshall were sworn into office on March 4, 1913. President Wilson had a thinly veiled contempt for his vice president, referring to Marshall as a "small caliber man."

Marshall walked with a slight limp, was only five feet, four inches tall, and weighed only one hundred twenty-five pounds. He was a giant in integrity and geniality, however.

Vice President Marshall and his wife, Lois, moved into a four-room suite at the new Willard Hotel in Washington, for which they paid eight dollars a day in rent.

Unfortunately, Vice President Marshall had a low opinion of his new job, particularly when it became painfully clear he would have little or no influence in President Wilson's administration. Marshall said being vice president was like being a man in a cataleptic state who is aware of his surroundings but can neither move nor speak.

President Wilson was a former president of Princeton University, and he was dignified and serious. His vice president's humor was not appreciated in the White House; once Marshall sent Wilson a book as a gift and signed the card "From your only vice."

On January 16, 1916, Vice President Marshall and Mrs. Marshall hosted a large dinner at the Willard Hotel in honor of President Wilson and his new bride, Edith Bolling Gault Wilson. That event helped mend the sagging friendship of the two men.

President Wilson asked Marshall to run for vice president with him for a second term in 1916. This time they barely won reelection with only 49% of the popular vote and 277 electoral votes to Republican Charles Evans Hughes's 254. As usual, Marshall was philosophical, saying, "'Tis not so deep as a well, nor so wide as a church door; but 'tis enough, t'will serve."

Vice President Marshall presided over the Senate with fairness and equanimity. As war shadows deepened in Europe, President Wilson struggled with the decision of how much United States involvement there should be.

At first, Marshall was opposed to any involvement of the United States in the war, but when President Wilson proposed a declaration of war on Germany on April 2, 1917, following various attacks by German submarines on United States ships, the vice president supported Wilson's decision loyally.

Lois Marshall was one of the organizers of the Diet Kitchen Welfare Center in Washington to help feed and care for children who were in poor health. A sick baby boy there caught her attention. The child was one of twins, and his twin sister was healthy. Lois persuaded her husband to let her bring the baby into their home so she could care for him. They had a special playroom built for him on a balcony of the hotel. The child's father was employed as a church janitor, and his mother got a job at the Willard Hotel as a chambermaid so she could be near her son.

Thomas Marshall admitted later he had been reluctant to allow his wife to bring the baby to live with them, but he wrote: "He walked into my heart. . . . He came to be the sun and center of Mrs. Marshall's life and of mine."

They did not have an opportunity to adopt the baby because he was fatally ill with a blood ailment and died in February 1920. The Marshalls spent weeks in Arizona later "to get away from the toys."

Vice President Marshall took his duties more seriously during his second term in office and worked diligently to get Senate approval of the Versailles Treaty, which would establish a League of Nations.

The League was a major project for President Wilson, and he was unwilling to compromise with Republican senators who insisted American sovereignty must be preserved in the treaty.

President Wilson led the American delegation to the peace conference in Paris early in 1919. He asked his vice president to preside over cabinet meetings during his absence.

The president returned from Europe more determined than ever to get approval for the United States to join the League. He decided to take the proposal to the voters on a cross-country tour to build public support.

About midway through the tour, on September 25, 1919, President Wilson collapsed from exhaustion in Pueblo, Colorado, and he and Mrs. Wilson were forced to return to Washington.

On October 2, 1919, President Wilson suffered a stroke which completely incapacitated him. He was paralyzed on his left side, could not speak for several days, and could not sign his name for weeks unless Mrs. Wilson held his hand to guide it. She ordered the doctors attending him to withhold any information about his condition from the public.

Secretary of State Robert Lansing called a meeting of the cabinet members to consider invoking the Constitutional rules concerning replacement of a disabled chief executive.

When First Lady Edith Wilson learned of Lansing's actions, she enlisted the aid of both President Wilson's personal physician, Dr. Cary Grayson, and his press secretary, Joseph Tumulty, to counter what she perceived to be treachery against her husband. They assured her they would swear President Wilson was able to continue in office.

Edith Wilson was furious that anyone would try to put Vice President Marshall in the president's place. With such a furor raging, Marshall was caught in the middle. He had no desire to usurp anyone's authority, especially President Wilson's, as he liked and admired him.

First Lady Edith Wilson became madame president in fact, even if unofficially. She defended her actions, saying, "The only decision that was mine was *what was important* and what was not, and the *very* important decision of when to present matters to my husband."

Senator Albert B. Fall from New Mexico told fellow politicians: "We have petticoat government! Mrs. Wilson is President!"

Vice President Marshall refused to take any part in the White House intrigue. He told his wife, "I could throw this country into civil war, but I won't." He went to the White House to confer with President Wilson about the course he should follow, but Mrs. Wilson would not allow him to see the president. Marshall was reduced to asking friends what they knew about Wilson's condition and their advice on any action he should take.

The Marshalls took over official entertaining during this trying period and arranged a ceremonial tour for King Albert and Queen Elizabeth of Belgium when they came to Washington at the end of October 1919. They also entertained other dignitaries, including the British Prince of Wales, who later became Kind Edward VIII. The Marshalls received no money from the Wilsons to pay for the hospitality they furnished to dignitaries, although the White House budget included such funds.

President Wilson continued to be bedfast for weeks, and still no one saw him except for his wife and doctors. The government was adrift with laws passed by Congress that had been neither approved or vetoed by the president. A major steel strike caused violence and deaths in Pennsylvania, and race riots occurred in various cities in both the North and the South.

Secretary of State Lansing assumed control of the cabinet and held twenty-one meetings to conduct necessary business. When the president did recover somewhat, he learned about the meetings and asked Lansing to resign.

President Wilson never fully recovered. It was seven months before he could attend a cabinet meeting. His League of Nations dream languished and died while he refused to accept restrictions proposed by Republicans.

President Wilson hoped the Democrats would nominate him to run for a third term since the matter of the League was unresolved, but James M. Cox of Ohio was nominated instead.

Thomas and Lois Marshall returned to Indianapolis at the end of his second term in 1921, and he resumed practicing law.

Sadly, Thomas died on June 1, 1925, while on a business trip to Washington. He was buried in Crown Hill Cemetery in Indianapolis.

The *New York Times* wrote of the former vice president, "We like him better than we have liked some persons who were greater but were less hospitably human."

Bibliography

Bartholomew, H.S.K. "Thomas R. Marshall." *Indiana Magazine of History* (March 1941).
Heckscher, August. *Woodrow Wilson: A Biography*. New York: Macmillan, 1991.
Montgomery, Keith S. "Thomas R. Marshall's Victory in the Election of 1908." *Indiana Magazine of History* 53 (June 1957).
Thomas, Charles M. *Thomas Riley Marshall: Hoosier Statesman*. Oxford, Ohio: Mississippi Valley Press, 1939.

29. Calvin Coolidge

President Calvin Coolidge was an honest, cautious man who restored public confidence in government after the flamboyant excesses of President Warren Harding's administration. He devoted much time and effort to restore confidence in businesses to provide jobs and opportunities. He was quiet and had little to say because he was shy.

Calvin Coolidge was the son of John Calvin Coolidge and his wife, the former Victoria Josephine Moor. Calvin was born July 4, 1872, in Plymouth Notch, Vermont, where his father owned and operated a general store.

Young Calvin's mother became an invalid, probably from tuberculosis, when her son was only three years old. She died when he was twelve and also left a nine-year-old daughter named Abigail.

The children's paternal grandmother assumed the primary care of them, and she made it clear she preferred that they be seen and not heard. This attitude probably contributed to Calvin's reticence, as did her usual punishment of shutting him in a dark attic for misbehaving.

By this time John Coolidge had been elected to serve in the Vermont legislature and had inherited substantial property from his father. He built a new home for his family in 1876 and hired a man for outside chores and a girl to help with housework. He expected Calvin to do the work of a hired hand too. Calvin helped mend fences, planted crops and harvested them, piled up winter wood, and did any other farm jobs that needed doing.

There was still time, however, for Calvin to go fishing, bobsledding, and ice-skating, and he enjoyed playing roles assigned to him in school plays and minstrel shows.

Calvin was in frail health, suffering from allergies for years that caused his voice to have an odd quality because of chronic congestion and drainage from his nasal sinuses.

The boy attended a small local school as a child, one with a total of only twenty-three students. When he was fourteen, he went to Black River Academy in Ludlow, a Baptist-sponsored school which provided higher education for students whose parents could afford to pay the fees. There were no dormitories, and Calvin found a room and board in the town of Ludlow.

Calvin Coolidge. Reproduced from the collections of the Library of Congress.

In 1888, Calvin's young sister Abigail joined him at the school, but she died there two years later of appendicitis. Calvin was lonely without her cheerfulness to brighten his life, but he graduated a short time later and went on to St. Johnsbury Academy. After completing courses there, he entered Amherst College.

Calvin Coolidge studied willingly in college and made good marks, but he had difficulty making friends. Fraternities ignored him. He was neither athletic nor musical, and his school work required most of his time anyway. In his senior year, he became a member of the Alphi Chi chapter of Phi Gamma Delta.

Coolidge attended all the business meetings of the fraternity, but he took no part in the smoking, drinking, or gambling of his fellow "Fijis." The college professors tried to instill a moral sense and social responsibility in all the students, and they succeeded with Coolidge, at least.

In his senior year, Coolidge won a $150 gold medal for the best essay on "The Principles Fought for in the American Revolution" in a contest sponsored by Sons of the American Revolution. He graduated from college cum laude.

Coolidge went on to study law with John Hammond and Henry Fields, attorneys in Northampton, Massachusetts, and he was admitted to the bar in 1897. The next year he was elected to serve as a city councilman from his ward, and his political career began.

As Grace Anna Goodhue, a new teacher in Northampton, watered flowers outside her classroom in 1903, she looked up inadvertently toward an open window in a boardinghouse next door to the school. There she saw a man shaving before a mirror, wearing only a pair of long underwear and a hat.

Grace Goodhue was so surprised that she started laughing, and Calvin, the man who was shaving, heard her. He managed to find out that she was a lip-reading instructor on the faculty of the school, the Clarke Institute for the Deaf, and he asked a mutual acquaintance to introduce them. They began dating, and Calvin married Grace on October 4, 1905, at her parents' home in Burlington, Vermont.

Calvin and Grace were complete opposites in personality. He was dour and serious, while Grace was vivacious and friendly. He loved her with all his heart and felt he had finally found someone in whom he could confide. He pursued a political career with a new fervor.

Their first son, John, was born in 1906 and Calvin Jr. was born in 1908. Grace stayed home with the children while Calvin campaigned for a seat in the Massachusetts House of Representatives. He was elected and served two terms in 1907 and 1908.

In the legislature, Coolidge supported bills for women's suffrage, a six-day work week, and child labor laws. He helped formulate a code of laws for operation of state banks.

Coolidge served as mayor of Northampton in 1910 and 1911. During his term, he expanded the police and fire departments and improved conditions of the streets, even while voters got a tax-cut. He received a salary of only eight hundred dollars a year, and he and his family were forced to live frugally in a rented house.

From 1912 to 1915, Calvin Coolidge served in the Massachusetts Senate, the last two years as Senate president. He spent little time with his family, but he thought this was necessary and unavoidable. As he wrote in his *Autobiography*, "I thought a couple of terms in the Massachusetts Senate would be helpful to me, so when our senator retired, I sought his place."

When Coolidge was reelected as Senate president, he made the shortest speech of acceptance in that body's history, saying: "My sincerest thanks, I offer you. Conserve the firm foundations of our institutions. Do your work with the spirit of a soldier in the public service. Be loyal to the Commonwealth and to yourselves. And be brief; above all things, Be Brief."

Coolidge was popular with his fellow senators because of his open-mindedness and dry, witty remarks. One senator complained to Coolidge that another senator had told him to go to hell during a debate. Coolidge replied, "I've examined the Constitution and the Senate rules, and nothing in them compels you to go."

From 1916 to 1919, Coolidge served as lieutenant governor of Massachusetts, and later in 1919 he was elected governor of the state. When there was a police strike in Boston that year, he upheld the police commissioner's refusal to allow the strikers to return to their jobs, saying, "There is no right to strike against the public safety by anybody, anywhere, any time."

In 1920, Calvin Coolidge was nominated by the Republicans to be the vice presidential candidate with presidential candidate Warren G. Harding. They were elected and were inaugurated on March 4, 1921.

With his salary of vice president being only $12,000 a year, the Coolidges were unsure about a move to Washington. They decided to send their two sons to boarding school at Mercersburg Academy in Pennsylvania, and Calvin and Grace rented the suite of rooms in the New Willard Hotel being vacated by Vice President and Mrs. Thomas Marshall. The rent was two hundred fifty dollars a month. They had two bedrooms, a dining room, and a large room where they could hold receptions.

President Harding invited his vice president to attend cabinet meetings, which Coolidge did, but he made few suggestions or comments. He broke no tie votes in the Senate, and he earned the name Washingtonians gave him of "Silent Cal." He was, however, one of the most knowledgeable men in the capital city on the subject of national government. Nevertheless, President Harding rarely consulted him about anything.

In the evenings, the Coolidges made the social rounds to dinners and other gatherings, some of which etiquette required. While Grace Coolidge exerted herself to be charming and evinced an interest in the members of their social group, Vice President Coolidge said little and enjoyed the food.

Coolidge was not busy with official duties during adjournment of the Senate, so he and Grace decided to visit his father in Vermont in July and August of 1923, along with their sons.

On August 2, Coolidge had spent tiring hours in the hayfield helping his father, and he went to bed early that night. During the night, President Harding died in San Francisco, and Coolidge took the oath of office as president in his father's parlor at 2:47 A.M. on August 3, 1923. His father, who was a notary public, administered the oath. Then everyone went back to bed.

Before 6:00 A.M., the house was again astir as Calvin and Grace prepared to go back to Washington. Before he left, Calvin spent some minutes at his mother's grave, no doubt wishing she could have lived to see him become president of the United States.

Calvin and Grace moved into the White House on August 21, but his personality did not change as president. He remained cautious and heeded advice given him by cabinet members. He joined the Congregational church a few days after he became president, but he had never been a church member before.

Coolidge organized his work to be as efficient as possible, and he loved living in the White House. He considered its operation to be his concern rather than that of his wife. He tolerated no arguments from either Grace or the staff about how he wanted things done.

It was during 1924 that the Teapot Dome scandal hit newspaper headlines. During the Harding administration, Secretary of the Interior Albert B. Fall had managed to persuade President Harding to put him in charge of federal oil reserves in Wyoming. Fall then sold rights to the oil in the Teapot Dome reserve to the Mammoth Oil Company for over $300,000 and a herd of cattle. He also sold rights to oil in Elk Hills, California, to Pan-American Petroleum and Transport Company for $100,000.

When news of the scandal broke, Coolidge appointed a special counsel to investigate the Teapot Dome matter, and Fall was eventually sentenced to a prison term for his actions. In 1924 a grateful nation reelected President Coolidge with 54% of the popular vote, believing he would restore honesty to government.

Sadly, during the 1924 campaign, young Calvin Coolidge, Jr., died from blood poisoning when a blister on his heel became infected. His parents were devastated by grief, and President Coolidge said, "The power and glory of the Presidency went with him."

Three years later, the Coolidges staged the social event of the year when they hosted a reception for aviator Charles Lindbergh after he completed his trans-Atlantic airplane flight successfully.

The next year, 1928, President Coolidge announced he would not seek reelection. His statement even surprised Grace Coolidge, who did not know of his plans. He gave no reason for his decision.

After attending President Herbert Hoover's inauguration on March 4, 1929, the Coolidges returned to Northampton to live. The retired president filled his days writing his autobiography and articles for magazines such as *Colliers'*, *Good Housekeeping*, and the *Saturday Evening Post*.

Young John Coolidge graduated from Amherst College in 1928, and the next year he married Florence Trumbull, the daughter of the governor of Connecticut. John got a job as an executive with the New York, New Haven, and Hartford Railroad Company.

Coolidge campaigned for President Herbert Hoover's reelection in 1932, but President Franklin D. Roosevelt won.

Early in 1933, Coolidge complained of not feeling well, and a few days later on January 5, Grace Coolidge found him lying on their bedroom floor, where he had died. He had suffered a heart attack. He was buried beside his parents in Plymouth, Vermont.

Grace Coolidge survived her husband by twenty-four years, during which time she worked as a Red Cross volunteer and for causes which would benefit deaf persons.

She died in Northampton on July 8, 1957, and is buried beside her husband in Vermont.

Bibliography

McCoy, Donald F. *Calvin Coolidge: The Quiet President*. New York: Macmillan, 1967.
Ross, Ishbel. *Grace Coolidge and Her Era*. New York: Dodd, Meade, 1962.

30. Charles Gates Dawes

Charles Gates Dawes served as vice president for President Calvin Coolidge, received the Nobel Peace Prize for his work in 1924 on the Allied Reparation Commission, which arranged reduced payments by Germany following World War I and prevented the collapse of the German economy. He also wrote nine books, composed music, and played the flute and piano.

Charles was born August 27, 1865, in Marietta, Ohio. His father, Brigadier General Rufus R. Dawes, was an able commander of his Union troops in the Civil War. The baby's mother, the former Mary Gates, was the daughter of a local banker in Marietta.

As a child, Charles attended Miss Eells' private school in Marietta. He graduated from Marietta College in 1884 and from Cincinnati Law School two years later. In 1887 he set up his own law practice in Lincoln, Nebraska, heeding Horace Greeley's advice to "Go West, young man."

In Lincoln, Charles Dawes soon became embroiled in a legal battle with railroad officials, mostly on his own initiative, about higher freight rates charged in Nebraska and other states nearby.

Charles married Caro Blymer of Cincinnati in 1889. She was the daughter of W. H. Blymer, manufacturer of steam engines, ice machines, and other related items. They went to live in Lincoln, where his law practice was less than flourishing, but they were happy. Their two children, daughter Carolyn and son Rufus, were born during the next five years while they lived in Lincoln.

In 1894, Charles Dawes bought the Northwestern Gas, Light, and Coke Company, and they moved to Evanston, Illinois. He had been investing in small businesses in Lincoln, and finding he liked operating companies better than practicing law, he gave up his practice.

The Dawes family attended church regularly. They also attended theater performances, and Charles played the flute and piano at social functions. He enjoyed most sports, in particular, tennis, swimming, and golf.

The year of 1894 was a time of national economic depression, drought, and high winds on the Western plains; the temperature rose to 105 degrees some days. Landlords lost tenants in business buildings when occupants, including doctors and lawyers, left Evanston.

Charles G. Dawes. Reproduced from the collections of the Library of Congress.

Charles Dawes realized he too needed to move to a larger urban area with a more diversified economy. In January 1895, he went to Chicago and rented a room at the Union League Club until Caro and the children could join him. When they got to Chicago, they lived for a time in three rented rooms in the Auditorium Annex Hotel.

Just before moving to Chicago, Dawes had met Major William McKinley of Ohio and was impressed by him. He thought McKinley's ideas for improving the government were sound, and he hoped McKinley would be chosen by the Republicans to be their presidential candidate in 1896. Dawes decided to actively support McKinley's efforts to win the nomination, and he talked with leading politicians in Nebraska, North Dakota, and Wyoming about McKinley's qualifications. McKinley was in fact nominated.

Another campaign interesting to Dawes that same year concerned alleviating the human misery of Chicago's poor residents. He had never encountered such abject poverty before, and his heart ached for the people.

Within six months of his arrival in Chicago, Dawes had talked with editors of the *Times-Herald* and *Inter-Ocean*, asking them to write editorials recommending an increase in appropriations for charitable causes in Cook County from $100,000 to $200,000 a year. At his request, Dawes was not identified as the originator of the suggestion, but two months later he saw the appropriations doubled, as he had wanted.

William McKinley won the election and became president on March 4, 1897. He offered Charles Dawes a cabinet post, but Dawes declined with thanks. He hoped to be elected to the United States Senate from Illinois when he completed residence requirements.

Finally President McKinley convinced Dawes he should accept the position of comptroller of the currency. It was a high-ranking job in which Dawes would make annual reports to Congress directly. The salary was $5000 a year, and when he became comptroller officially on January 3, 1898, Dawes was on a payroll for the first time in his life.

Dawes rented a house for his family at 1337 K Street, which was within walking distance of the White House. President and First Lady McKinley often invited Charles and Caro Dawes to dine with them.

First Lady Ida McKinley was epileptic, and Caro Dawes visited her many afternoons also. Ida McKinley was dependent on visitors for company, and with her husband so busy as president, she was often lonely. Caro Dawes was one of her favorite friends. Ida McKinley crocheted bed slippers for the Dawes children. Crocheting slippers was her favorite hobby, and during her lifetime she made hundreds of pairs.

Charles and Caro Dawes also took Ida McKinley to the theater with them, as President McKinley was a workaholic and would not take time to go.

On June 23, 1901, Dawes decided to resign as comptroller and campaign for the United States Senate. President McKinley was unhappy about his decision and told Dawes both he and Ida would miss him and his family greatly. He begged Dawes to reconsider, but his decision was firm.

On September 5, 1901, President McKinley was shot in Buffalo, New York; Vice President Theodore Roosevelt became president a few days later when McKinley died of his wounds on September 14.

When Charles Dawes lost his bid to become a senator, he turned his attention back to business and organized the Central Trust Company of Illinois in Chicago. He was the company's president.

When banks failed all over Chicago in 1907, Dawes found himself again leading a drive for care of the poor people in Chicago. By 1911 he was operating a relief agency with his own money. In his journal he wrote: "Have run my bread wagon with Malcolm McDowell. The suffering is very great in the city. We will have fed between thirty to forty thousand during the winter. Thank God I am able to do it."

In 1909, Charles Dawes bought his family a house in Evanston that was situated on the shores of Lake Michigan. It was built of straw-colored bricks, had a tile roof, and corner towers. He had recently bought an automobile, and Caro had a horse so she could go riding with her friends.

Rufus Dawes was admitted to Princeton, and his sister became a student at Misses Masters School at Dobbs Ferry. Even though Dawes was not as active in politics during the period, he had a pleasant life and a beautiful home.

In 1911 he composed his first music, a piano score he entitled "Melody in A Major." Francis MacMillan, a friend and professional violinist, played the music and liked it. Dawes told him he could have the tune if he wanted it because he had composed it just to have something to do. A few months later Dawes passed a music store with a display of sheet music of his "Melody in A Major" and a large picture of Dawes with it.

The song had a life of its own. There was an arrangement for a pipe organ, one for both large orchestras and small groups, piano rolls for player pianos, with arrangements in waltz time and another for military bands. A phonograph record sold thirty thousand copies in one month. In 1951, the song was revived and retitled, "It's All in the Game."

No one was more surprised by his success than Dawes. He had never studied music formally, and he dreaded the teasing he thought he would get from his friends. Instead, they were impressed by his talent.

Sadly, young Rufus Dawes drowned in Lake Geneva in Wisconsin in 1912. He had contracted typhoid fever in 1908 and his heart was weakened, but he was unaware of the problem.

Both his parents were devastated with grief. Not many months later they adopted a little daughter they named Virginia and a little son they named Dana.

Charles Dawes also opened the Rufus F. Dawes Hotel for Men in Chicago on January 2, 1914, which contained 303 beds and was built to give shelter to unemployed homeless men. Dawes explained he had built the hotel "as a memorial to my son who had shown deep interest in the conditions which this hotel is designed to meet." There were soon Dawes Hotels in other cities.

On February 17, 1917, the Mary Dawes Hotel for Women, named in honor of his mother, was also opened in Chicago. Neither of the hotels had any difficulties with drunkenness or immortality of its guests, even though no attempt was made to invade their privacy. They kept one homeless man who had lost his legs, taking as payment two two-cent postage stamps, which was all he had. Beds usually rented for six cents per night.

Dawes turned the hotels over to trusts with endowments when the federal government assumed relief efforts.

In April 1917, the United States declared war on Germany, and in May of that year, Charles Dawes cleared his desk in his bank and donned a uniform. One of his best friends was General John J. Pershing, who allowed Dawes to join the Corps of Army Engineers as a major, even though he had a weak ankle and was now fifty-one years old.

When his contingent reached France, however, General Pershing assigned Dawes to work with the headquarters staff of the American Expeditionary Force and to serve as chairman of the purchasing board and supply procurement. Dawes soon had the departments whipped into shape with his usual efficient management.

Once when cross ties were desperately needed for a railroad at the front lines, an officer sent a telegram to Dawes saying, "Exigent we have cross-ties. Move heaven and earth to get them by Saturday."

Dawes replied the same day, "Raised hell and got them today."

Dawes stayed in the army until August 1919 and helped dispose of and sell all surplus war materials. He rose to the rank of brigadier general.

Charles Dawes received the United States Distinguished Service Medal, as well as similar decorations from the other Allied countries for his war work. He was thus astonished when he was asked to appear before a congressional committee in February 1921, which was investigating war purchases during World War I.

Republican Representative Oscar E. Bland from Indiana asked Dawes, "Is it not true that excessive prices were paid for mules?"

Dawes jumped out of his chair and strode angrily toward the congressman. "Hell and Maria," he thundered. "I would have paid horse prices for sheep, if the sheep could have pulled artillery to the front. . . . Sure, we paid. We didn't dicker. . . . We weren't trying to keep a set of books — we were trying to win a war!"

In June 1924, Republicans picked Charles Dawes to be their nominee for vice president to serve with presidential nominee Calvin Coolidge. They won the election, but they were never friends.

Vice President Dawes was impulsive and had a strong, forceful personality, while President Coolidge was quiet and had little to say. Dawes said exactly what he thought. When he expressed his views about his reluctance to attend cabinet meetings, Coolidge was horrified.

The president and his vice president were on opposite sides of farm policy, and eventually Dawes supported a farm bill the president had vetoed. When Dawes was absent from the Senate and did not return to break a tie vote on the president's nominee for attorney general, their rift was complete, especially when Coolidge learned his vice president had been taking a nap in his quarters at the Willard Hotel.

In 1925, Dawes won a Nobel Peace Prize, which he shared with Sir J. Austin Chamberlain, for the Dawes Plan he wrote to restore the collapsed German economy by means of reducing reparations payments and arranging a loan to Germany.

Dawes refused to change his belief in progressive farm policies, and the 1928 presidential candidate, Herbert Hoover, did not ask him to be his vice president. Many supporters urged Dawes to run for president, but he declined.

In April 1929, Dawes was surprised to receive a telegram from President Hoover telling him he had been named ambassador to the Court of St. James in England. His prime objective would be to reach an agreement with British officials concerning the size of naval forces each country would have.

On June 7 that year, Ambassador Dawes, accompanied by his wife, their children Dana and Virginia, and his nephew Henry, sailed for England. Henry Dawes would serve as his uncle's secretary.

An agreement between the governments was reached within a few weeks, and the Dawes family could begin to relax and enjoy their stay in England. They traveled and hosted dinner parties and other social gatherings, many of which were financed from Dawes's own resources, as the government allowance was inadequate for the purpose.

By the time Charles Dawes and his family returned to Chicago, the United States was in the depths of the Great Depression. He worked diligently to help some Chicago banks remain open and again used his own money to help impoverished citizens.

As he aged, Dawes slowed down, but he had many visitors during his last years, both American and foreign.

In the evening of April 27, 1951, Dawes was reading in his library. He had spent the day completing arrangements for a reception in honor of General Douglas MacArthur, who was leaving his command in the Far East.

Caro Dawes came into the library to tell her husband it was getting past his bedtime. He looked up at her, smiled, and fell back into his chair. His work on earth was complete.

Bibliography

McCoy, Donald R. *Calvin Coolidge: The Quiet President*. New York: Macmillan, 1967.
Ross, Ishbel. *Grace Coolidge and Her Era*. New York: Dodd, Mead, 1962.
Timmons, Bascom N. *Portrait of an American: Charles G. Dawes*. New York: Henry Holt, 1953.

31. Charles Curtis

Charles Curtis is the only American Indian to serve as one of the two top executives in the United States government. His ancestry was reportedly one sixteenth Kaw Indian tribe, one sixteenth Osage Indian tribe, three eighths French, and half Anglo American. Much was said about his ancestry during his campaign.

Charles Curtis was born on an Indian reservation in North Topeka, Kansas, on January 25, 1860, to Oren A. (Jack) and Ellen Pappan Curtis. The child's mother died when he was only three years old, and his father was away serving as a captain in the Union army for four years during the Civil War.

Little Charles and his younger sister, Elizabeth, divided their time between their paternal grandmother, who lived in Topeka, Kansas, and their maternal grandmother, who lived on the reservation. They attended mission schools at first and went to public school from 1869 until they graduated, when they went to live with their Grandmother Curtis full-time.

Captain Curtis remarried in 1866 to Lou Jay, and they had a daughter they named Dolly. Little Dolly was dearly loved by her older brother, and their lives were closely intertwined, even as adults.

Charles was slightly built when he was a child, and he worked as a jockey in horse races during summer months in Topeka from 1869 to 1875. He also peddled fresh fruit at train stations and clerked in stores to earn money so he could stay in school.

In September 1876, Charles entered high school because of his Grandmother Curtis's earnest entreaties. He had intended to drop out and become a full-time jockey, but fortunately for his future career, she persuaded him to finish his education.

Three years later Charles Curtis began reading law with a Topeka attorney, and in 1881 he was admitted to the bar. He had a horse-drawn hack he operated for hire to earn extra income while he studied law.

On November 27, 1884, Curtis married Anna E. Baird, a member of a family which had lived in Pennsylvania before moving to Kansas. Charles and Anna had three children born to them through the years—two daughters named Permelia and Leona and a son named Harry King Curtis.

Charles Curtis. Reproduced from the collections of the Library of Congress.

Curtis specialized in the practice of criminal law before he became Shawnee county attorney. He was determined to uphold the law, even if his friends were involved in misdeeds. Kansas was a dry state, but illegal saloons flourished in large numbers. In Topeka alone there were more than one hundred. County Attorney Curtis took aim at these illegal bars and had shut down all of them within a month after he took office, even though many of the saloon operators were his friends.

After serving four years as county attorney, Curtis was elected to the United States House of Representatives, where he served from 1892 to 1906. There he was named to be a member of the prestigious Ways and Means Committee.

On January 29, 1907, Representative Curtis became Senator Curtis. He served in the United States Senate until 1929, when he was elected vice president in President Herbert Hoover's administration.

Anna Curtis became a helpless invalid for several years before her death in 1924. Charles's sister Dolly had come to Washington earlier to serve as her brother's secretary, and now she took care of Anna. Charles always felt he owed her a large debt of gratitude.

Dolly married Edward Everett Gann while she lived in Washington, and after Anna died, Senator Curtis went to live with the Ganns. After he became vice president, the three of them moved to a ten-room apartment in the elegant Mayflower Hotel in Washington.

Dolly Gann was her brother's official hostess, but she was not his wife, and the matter of the protocol of seating Mrs. Gann (and at times Mr. Gann) at social functions occupied the minds of Washington hostesses for four years.

A number of circumstances caused difficulties for hostesses seeking to make a final decision at any social function. Vice President Curtis had influential friends, such as former president Theodore Roosevelt and his daughter Alice, with whom Curtis had traveled earlier to the Philippines. He played poker with Nicholas Longworth on the trip while Alice debated whether she should marry Nicholas. (They did marry later.)

Charlie Curtis had also been a poker-playing friend of President Warren G. Harding and served as a pallbearer at his funeral. He had friends in high places.

Another problem lay in Curtis's heritage as part-Indian. His sister had a different mother, so she did not have Indian heritage, but Charlie was sensitive about his background.

In spring of 1929, shortly after he became vice president, Charles Curtis took his sister to a luncheon hosted by the wealthy Ned McLeans in the capital. Charles led Dolly to a seat beside him, but someone else's name was on the place card, and she finally found her card on another table.

Vice President Curtis complained to Secretary of State Henry L. Stimson about his sister's lack of social acceptance by Washington hostesses. Since Stimson and other officials were preoccupied with the nation's growing financial problems, he did not reply to Curtis for several weeks.

Meantime, Mrs. Eugene Meyer, wife of the governor of the Federal Reserve Board, planned a dinner in honor of the vice president and invited other Washington socialites as guests. Alice Longworth asked Mrs. Meyer who would escort Dolly Gann into the dining room, and Mrs. Meyer told Alice Mr. Meyer would be her escort.

Alice said she doubted if she and Nicholas would attend because he was a stickler for protocol. They thought Dolly Gann should not be ranked above the wives of ambassadors.

The newspapers were delighted with the feud, and when reports of the controversy appeared in Washington papers, Dolly Gann decided she would not attend the Meyers' dinner party either. (The *Cleveland Plain Dealer* suggested the guests could play musical chairs.)

At last, Alice Longworth decided the matter had gone too far, and she apologized to the vice president and Mrs. Gann. They all attended the dinner as planned.

In his role as vice president, Curtis was not close friends with President Hoover, but he was invited to attend all cabinet meetings, and he usually did. He never got to break a tie vote in the senate or make a speech except to adjourn the sessions.

At the first New Year's reception that the Hoovers hosted at the White House, President Hoover offered his arm to Mrs. Gann to escort her to dinner, instead of properly escorting First Lady Lou Hoover, and he found out first-hand how easy it was to tangle with protocol.

In April 1931, the protocol problem surfaced again. At a reception for the king and queen of Siam held in the White House, dinner was scheduled to begin at 8 P.M. The Prince and Princess Svasti, parents of the queen, made a tour around the East Room, during which they were introduced to other guests. Then they took their places at the head of the line of guests to go into the dining room.

Vice President Curtis and Mrs. Gann had been asked to lead the guests to dinner, but Mr. Gann had accompanied them. He took his place beside his wife, and everyone waited. An aide whispered to him he should go to the back of the line, but after he had done so, another aide found his name listed with his wife's. He was then escorted back to rejoin Dolly but was told he would have to find his own place card on another table. Mr. Gann found his place card and dinner was served.

After dinner, the vice president insisted on following the king and queen out of the dining room, saying he wanted to say good-night to the royal couple. Despite some initial embarrassment, President and Mrs. Hoover allowed him to go ahead.

Despite all the difficulties, President Hoover asked Curtis to run with him for a second term in 1932. They were defeated by Democrat presidential candidate Franklin D. Roosevelt and his vice presidential candidate, John Nance Garner.

The depression had begun only seven months after President Hoover had started his first term, and despite all efforts to improve financial conditions, it grew worse. Voters believed Democratic statements that President Hoover had caused the depression, and they voted him out of office.

Alice Roosevelt Longworth had supported Hoover and Curtis during the campaign because she believed her brother, Theodore Roosevelt, Jr., should have been nominated by the Democrats instead of their cousin Franklin.

After leaving office as vice president, Charles Curtis returned to the practice of law, this time in Washington. He died there of heart disease on February 28, 1936, and was buried in Topeka Cemetery in Topeka, Kansas.

Bibliography

"Heap Big Chief." *American Mercury* (August 1929).

Merz, Charles. "Preconvention Portraits-I: Curtis of Kansas." *The Independent*, January 7, 1928.

Obituary of Charles Curtis. *Newsweek*, February 15, 1936.

Personal Glimpses Column. "Making Washington Safe for Diplomacy." *Literary Digest*, April 27, 1929.

Ross, Charles G. "Charles Curtis of Kansas." *Outlook*, May 16, 1928.

32. John Nance Garner

John Nance Garner must have heard many political discussions when he was a child. When he was two years old, his home state of Texas regained statehood after the Civil War, and from that time forward, politics was the leading subject in conversations between Texans.

John was born on November 22, 1868, in Red River County, Texas, to John Nance Garner II and his wife, the former Sarah Guest. The baby was the fourth male in the Garner family with the given name of John Nance. His father was a cotton farmer and had served as a soldier in the Confederate army in the Civil War.

The child began his education with his mother, who was proficient enough to teach him his ABCs and other beginning lessons. He moved on to learn from his Aunt Kitty Garner, his father's sister, who was not only well versed in history but also had a small library.

When John was seven, he attended the local school at Antioch, three miles from his home, which operated four months a year. He attended a local boarding school for a short time, and then at age fifteen, he went to Blossom, Texas, which was reputed to have the best schools anywhere in his part of Texas.

In Blossom there was a semiprofessional baseball team, and John Garner was taken on as a shortstop. He was by no means a star, but he enjoyed playing the game and had plenty of energy. He played for the Blossom team for about three years.

When he reached the age of eighteen, Garner decided he should go to college. He entered Vanderbilt University in Nashville, Tennessee, but his health began to fail and he had to return to his Texas home.

After the lung problems that forced him to leave college improved, Garner began studying law in the local law firm of Sims and Wright. At age twenty-one, he was admitted to the Texas bar, and he opened his own practice in Clarksville, Texas.

The new practice was not an immediate success, and Garner ran for the office of city attorney. He lost the election, and a few days later he learned he had tuberculosis and needed to move to a drier climate.

John Garner moved to Uvalde, Texas, located west of San Antonio, in

John Nance Garner. Reproduced from the collections of the Library of Congress.

December 1892 and joined the law firm of Clark and Fuller. He soon gained a reputation as a successful compromiser who worked out fair settlements for his clients.

When one client could not pay him for his services, Garner took the newspaper business the client owned for services rendered and became editor and publisher of the Uvalde *Leader*. His health improved steadily in the desertlike air.

When a vacancy arose for a county judge, Garner was appointed to complete the term of the previous judge and was then elected in his own right.

It was while he was serving as county judge that Garner married Mariette Rheiner, daughter of local rancher Peter Rheiner, a Swiss immigrant. They were married in the fall of 1895, and their only child, a son, was born September 24, 1896. They named the baby Tully for John's law partner, Tully Fuller.

Mariette had completed a secretarial course in a business school in San Antonio, and she began working as John's secretary. She would continue to work with him throughout his political career, both in Texas and in Washington, D.C.

In January 1899, John Garner began the first of two terms in the Texas House of Representatives. He began urging economy in government administration and moved on to reform insurance practices in the state. Then he took on the railroad tycoons and brought about reforms and regulations of those operating in Texas.

A new congressional district was formed in 1901, which included Uvalde, and John Garner was elected to represent the area in the United States House of Representatives in 1902. It was in Congress that he was dubbed "Cactus Jack."

In Washington he continued to promote government economy, but he also introduced a bill to construct a Gulf Intracoastal Waterway between the west coast of Florida and the Mexican border.

When the Garners first arrived in Washington, little Tully was seven years old. For three years they lived in a boardinghouse on K Street. They moved on to the Burlington Hotel in 1906, where they had eight rooms and could entertain their own guests as well as Tully's friends.

Garner continued to serve as a representative through World War I and the postwar period. Tully Garner joined the army in 1917 after his graduation from college. After Tully married, the Garners moved to a three-room suite in the Washington Hotel and ate their breakfasts and dinners in the hotel coffee shop. Mariette usually cooked their lunches on a hot plate in John's office.

One of Garner's best friends in Washington was a Republican representative from New York, Nicholas Longworth, who was married to Theodore Roosevelt's daughter Alice. Longworth was the Speaker of the House, and he and Garner were friendly rivals for the position in 1931. Unfortunately, Longworth died on April 9 that year. Garner then became Speaker.

Both men liked President Coolidge, and he returned their respect and often invited them to eat breakfast with him. As Garner said, "I liked to have breakfast with him. He would invite me and Longworth down. I was never late and Nicholas was never on time. I had nice visits with him while waiting for Nick to arrive. . . . He seemed to have an unerring judgment of people."

In 1932, John Garner entered the California primary election as a candidate for president. There he defeated both Alfred E. Smith, former governor of New York, and Franklin D. Roosevelt, then current New York governor. Garner also had the support of Texas delegates at the Democratic National Convention.

When none of the three men could break the balloting deadlock at the convention, William Randolph Hearst, Garner's financial backer, asked him to relinquish his delegates' votes in favor of Franklin D. Roosevelt. Roosevelt thus became the Democratic nominee for president, and Garner was nominated vice president. They were elected in 1932 by a comfortable majority.

The depression was gripping the country, and no one appeared to have a solution in mind when Roosevelt and Garner took their oaths of office on March 4, 1933. President Roosevelt was granted sweeping powers by Congress to cope with the financial problems in the nation, and Vice President Garner was one of the most valuable supporters for the New Deal programs President Roosevelt submitted to Congress.

As the wife of the new vice president, Mariette was unsure if she should continue to work as a secretary in her husband's office, and she asked First Lady Eleanor Roosevelt for her opinion. Mrs. Roosevelt assured Mariette it would be proper for her to continue her secretarial job if she so desired.

The Garners never participated in the social scene in Washington in any great extent. Mariette did go to lunch occasionally with another Washington wife, and she and John attended obligatory dinners, such as the dinner given by the president for the vice president. Mariette and John found the emphasis placed on protocol and the social feuds in the capital to be amusing.

The Garners did host a dinner annually for the president and first lady. They went back to Texas every chance they got so John could go hunting and fishing.

Vice President Garner's relationship with President Roosevelt was friendly, and the president consulted him frequently concerning problems caused by the depression.

By 1934, Vice President Garner was becoming dissatisfied with his job and complained in a magazine interview that the office of vice president was obscure and unimportant. His real friends and interests were in the legislative branch of government, not the executive.

President Roosevelt began to suspect Garner was repeating details of programs proposed during cabinet meetings, and thus no matters of importance were discussed until after Garner left the meetings.

Later that year Garner was asked by the president to go to the Philippines, Japan, and China as an official representative of the United States. He participated in the initiation of a new government in the Philippines by attending the inauguration of Manuel Quezon as the Philippine president. Then he traveled to Japan, where he was the highest-ranking United States official ever to visit that country. The trip ended in China, where he and Mariette were warmly welcomed.

Both the president and vice president were renominated in 1936 by acclamation. After their reelection, Garner became concerned about the increasing liberality of spending in President Roosevelt's New Deal proposals. When congressmen also protested, the Supreme Court ruled some of the proposals were illegal. It was at this time that President Roosevelt determined he would "pack the court" with justices who would support his plans.

Garner went back to Texas for a rest when the Supreme Court bill was scheduled to be brought to the Senate floor. He was adamantly opposed to it, and he did not want to have to vote in the event of a tie vote in the Senate. The bill was defeated.

In 1937, Garner and Roosevelt quarreled about the proper action to take in dealing with sit-down strikers in the automobile industry. Garner believed the workers had no right to seize or control property belonging to someone else. President Roosevelt refused to intercede, fearing bloodshed.

The Garners went back to Texas in June of that year to visit their son and his family. Tully had gone into the banking industry in Amarillo. For the past several years, John Garner had also been investing in both banks and real estate.

President Roosevelt became angry when his Supreme Court proposal was defeated, and in the 1938 election, he campaigned against the representatives and senators who had opposed him. He was only partially successful, but some of the men with whom Garner had been friendly were defeated.

In January 1939, the president was still defending his New Deal policies to the voters, despite advice from Vice President Garner and his other "antediluvian friends," as he termed them.

Garner told President Roosevelt during a cabinet meeting that a group of senators from the opposition planned to investigate some of the New Deal programs, including the Works Progress Administration (WPA) and others. President Roosevelt exuded his usual confidence. "Jack," he said, "you are talking about eleven people who can't do anything about it."

When he learned President Roosevelt planned to run for a third term, Garner lost his temper because he believed no president should serve three consecutive terms. He allowed his own name to be placed in consideration for nomination to show his acute disapproval, but President Roosevelt was renominated and elected.

Garner had come to believe the president was trying to increase the authority of the presidency and lessen that of the legislative and judicial branches of government. He described Roosevelt as "the most destructive man in all American history."

After officiating at the swearing in of the new vice president, Henry Wallace, Garner and Mariette went back to Uvalde. He had become a wealthy man, owning forty-six thousand acres of Texas land and more than one hundred houses and business buildings.

Mrs. Garner's health began to fail after they left Washington, so they did not get to take the trips they had anticipated when he left office.

On November 7, 1967, John Garner died in Uvalde at the age of ninety-nine. He was buried beside Mariette, who had preceded him in death. He had devoted forty-six years to service in public office.

Garner was a true statesman — one of a dying breed. He said, "I astounded people in Washington once by saying I was for the welfare of the country first and that of the Democratic party second."

Bibliography

Adams, Henry H. *Harry Hopkins: A Biography.* New York: G. P. Putnam's Sons, 1977.
Burns, James MacGregor. *Roosevelt: The Lion and the Fox.* New York: Harcourt, Brace and World, 1956.
James, Marquis. *Mr. Garner of Texas.* Indianapolis: Bobbs-Merrill, 1939.
Timmons, Bascom N. *Garner of Texas: A Personal History.* New York: Harper and Brothers, 1948.

33. Henry Agard Wallace

Henry Wallace was one of the most unusual men to hold office as vice president in our nation's history. President Franklin D. Roosevelt selected Wallace to be on the ticket with him as he sought a third term. He admired Wallace for his previous work in the Department of Agriculture from 1933 to 1940 during Roosevelt's first two administrations.

When convention members balked at nominating Wallace because they considered him a liberal radical, President Roosevelt threatened to withdraw his own name from the ticket if Wallace did not get nominated. At least nobody asked, "Who's Wallace?" when his name was mentioned, as had happened in prior conventions when less well-known candidates were proposed.

If First Lady Eleanor Roosevelt had not gone to the convention to ask the delegates personally to give President Roosevelt the "strong right hand" he needed to help him in troubled days ahead, Wallace would probably not have been nominated.

Henry Agard Wallace was born on October 7, 1888, in Adair County in Iowa. His father was Henry Cantwell Wallace, a newspaper editor and secretary of agriculture during both President Harding's and President Coolidge's administrations. The baby's mother was Carrie May Brodhead Wallace.

When Henry was four years old, his father went back to college at Iowa State. In 1893 the elder Wallace became an assistant professor in the agriculture department there.

In 1895 the Wallace family moved to Des Moines, where Mr. Wallace and his father began publication of a farm magazine/newspaper.

By the time Henry himself entered college at Iowa State, he was a serious young man. He had few close friends, did not participate in any sports or social events on campus, and spent most of his time studying.

Wallace became interested in economic theories propounded by Thorstein Veblen in his *The Theory of Business Enterprise*, in which he advocated an international economy which would enhance the lives of all people. Veblen believed such a worldwide common market would ensure peace between nations.

In 1912 Henry Wallace went to Europe for several weeks. Shortly after his return home, he met a young lady named Ilo Browne in Indianola, Iowa, and

Henry A. Wallace. Reproduced from the collections of the Library of Congress.

they began dating. Ilo was intelligent and was interested in Henry's crop experiments and the other facets of his agricultural work.

They were married on May 20, 1914, and went to live in a house they bought in Des Moines. Henry Browne Wallace was born on September 18, 1915, followed in a few years by a brother Robert and a sister Jean. The family lived in Des Moines continuously until 1933, when Henry was asked to join President Roosevelt's cabinet as secretary of agriculture and they moved to Washington, D.C.

Henry Wallace was much more than the liberal radical the convention delegates believed him to be. He was a well-known authority on agriculture, and he had a record of successful experiments in developing new strains of strawberries, chickens, and hybrid corn. In fact, he started his own company to sell the new corn — the Hi-Bred Corn Company.

Wallace's biggest flaw lay in his idealism. He really believed the "common man," as he referred to the general public, was destined for ever greater scientific achievements and brotherhood. He had most recently been editor of the family publication called *Wallaces' Farmer*, on which he had been employed since 1921.

In 1928, Henry Wallace left the Republican party, which he had joined when he registered to vote, because he wanted to support Al Smith, the Democratic candidate for president in 1928, and Franklin D. Roosevelt the Democratic candidate in 1932. Wallace had become disillusioned with the farm policies of the Republicans.

When President Roosevelt asked Wallace to join his cabinet, he, Ilo, and their three children moved to Washington to live in the Wardman Park Hotel. All their children were of school age, and they attended local schools.

When farm prices hit rock-bottom in 1933 during the depression, Secretary of Agriculture Wallace decided to use economics based on scarcity to raise prices paid to farmers. He told farmers that if they would plow under ten million acres of cotton and kill six million hogs, the prices they received for their farm products would be higher.

By the next year, pork prices were fifty percent higher, but Henry Wallace was criticized by welfare officials for not giving the meat from the slaughtered animals to poor, hungry people in the nation. In Syracuse, New York, dairy farmers had dumped thousands of gallons of milk in the open streets and fields that could have fed destitute children.

In 1934 it appeared even nature was criticizing the appalling waste of food when a severe drought hit mid-Western states and cattle began dying from a lack of water. This time Wallace arranged for the government to buy the cattle, had them slaughtered, and distributed the beef to the poor.

President Roosevelt was in favor of Henry Wallace's work in the Department of Agriculture, and when Vice President Garner joined in a movement to keep Roosevelt from being nominated to run for a third term, the president insisted he wanted Henry Wallace as his running mate.

Roosevelt explained to Frances Perkins, secretary of labor: "Henry is the kind of man I like to have around. He is good to work with and he knows a lot — you can trust his information. . . . He is as honest as the day is long. . . . He can help people with their political thinking."

Opposition to Henry Wallace continued as he worked in the Department of Agriculture because he had also become a disciple of a White Russian named Nicholas K. Roerich. Roerich claimed that in his travels he had found evidence that Jesus Christ had been in Asia at one time, and he thought the place would be the location of the Second Coming.

Wallace commissioned Roerich, through the Department of Agriculture, to go to Asia and search officially for drought-resistant grasses, but his real mission was to find evidence of the Second Coming. Letters written by the two men were released about the time of the election.

When the United States Treasury Department charged Roerich with tax evasion, Wallace fired him.

With closer exposure to the viewpoints of New Deal programs, Vice President Wallace became an ardent advocate of public service. He envisioned a New Frontier, where men's hearts would be free of hatred, prejudice, greed, and other undesirable traits, and all would work together for the common good. He believed religion, science, and nature could combine to achieve the Kingdom of God on earth.

Wallace's book *The American Choice*, published in 1940, espoused his beliefs, and he urged cooperation with other nations.

Neither Vice President Wallace nor his wife drank alcoholic beverages or smoked. He did not gamble or swap dirty jokes with other government officials. He and Ilo entertained very little and seldom attended any of the cocktail parties so in vogue in Washington as World War II started. They enjoyed listening to classical and Latin-American music, and Henry was an avid reader of books on a wide variety of subjects.

In 1943, Jean Wallace attended the University of Mexico for the summer and worked on projects of the Friends Service Committee. Their sons, Henry B. and Robert, joined the navy and army respectively.

President Roosevelt appointed his vice president to serve on the Board of Economic Warfare, where Wallace was in charge of procuring military supplies for the armed services. It was a responsible position, and he did his job well.

Wallace's idealism began to intrude, however. He decided to send free food to workers on rubber plantations in South America because he believed the workers there were being unfairly exploited by their employers. He urged the United States government to stop trading with Latin American countries until wages improved.

At that point, President Roosevelt returned Wallace to his vice presidential duties. They remained friends, and Wallace attended cabinet meetings, where he spoke out on issues he considered important. When President Roosevelt needed a touring diplomat, the vice president made trips for him to China and the Soviet Union.

Wallace became the darling of the liberals in the United States with his proposals of massive aid to foreign nations and his insistence that Premier Stalin of the USSR was reforming Soviet society and government in a desirable way. He said it was "because Stalin pushed educational democracy with all the power he could command that Russia today is able to resist Germany."

While Henry Wallace was traveling, President Roosevelt made plans to replace him with another candidate for vice president when he sought his own fourth term as president in 1944. The president's Democratic supporters insisted Wallace had to be dropped from the ticket because of his affection for the Communistic form of government in the Soviet Union.

Henry was disappointed when he was not renominated, but he worked hard to get President Roosevelt reelected in 1944. When the election was over, Roosevelt had won, Senator Harry Truman was vice president, and Henry Wallace was named to be the new secretary of commerce.

Just after his fourth term began, President Roosevelt went on an exhausting trip to a conference at Yalta in Crimea with Stalin, the Soviet leader, and Winston Churchill, the prime minister of Great Britain. When he returned, the president went on to his retreat at Warm Springs, Georgia, to rest. While there, he suffered a stroke, and he died on April 12, 1945. Vice President Harry Truman was the new chief executive.

Henry Wallace felt obliged to continue with the plans President Roosevelt had commissioned him to formulate for full employment in the country. He wrote a book that year entitled *Sixty Million Jobs*, in which he outlined what he believed was the government's responsibility to provide employment for returning servicemen and women. He also believed the government had a duty to promote the hiring of minorities. The Full Employment Bill passed, in modified form, as the Employment Act of 1946.

President Truman complimented his secretary of commerce for bringing his ideas for improved employment to his attention. Truman did not agree that full employment was carrying out "social ideas of the Sermon on the Mount," as Henry Wallace thought, but he agreed his ideas deserved examining.

Wallace insisted the United States and the Soviet Union must continue their collaboration, even though World War II was ending, while George Kennan, who was a counselor at the American Embassy in Russia, disagreed.

Henry Wallace thought the United States should give the Soviet Union all the scientific knowledge it had about atomic energy in its various forms because he maintained the Soviet Union wanted peace, not war, with the United States.

In the meantime, Secretary of State James Byrnes was at a conference in Paris trying to work out a bipartisan foreign policy agreement, and Byrnes told President Truman that he would resign if Wallace continued with his interference and criticism of his efforts. As a result, President Truman requested and received Wallace's resignation on September 20, 1946.

Later that year, Henry Wallace accepted an editorial job at *The New Republic*. He and his wife moved to New York State, where he bought a country estate at South Salem, near the Connecticut state line. He bought a small garden tractor from Sears Roebuck with which to help him farm part of his one hundred and fifteen acres. He wrote his friend, Dr. Henry Taylor, "I am looking ahead to having a good time of it this summer."

Henry Wallace decided to join a political party formed to oppose both Democrats and Republicans in 1947. The Progressive party was started on December 30, 1946, and Wallace was nominated as its presidential candidate in the 1948 election. He received only 2% of the popular vote and no electoral votes. American Communists had endorsed him, and that was like waving a red flag to most American voters.

Finally, when North Korea invaded South Korea, Wallace realized Communist threats toward the United States really existed, and he withdrew from the Progressives in 1951.

Wallace returned to his farm and his research into plant and animal science. He grew exotic plants such as Yugoslav lettuce, different varieties of grapes, and odd flowers and plants from other regions of the world. His main focus continued to be on corn, however, and in 1956 he wrote a history of corn entitled *Corn and Its Early Fathers*.

Henry Wallace remained physically strong and mentally capable until 1964. During a trip to Guatemala, he noticed a numbness in one of his legs while he was climbing a pyramid. After he returned home, it was determined he was suffering from amyotrophic lateral sclerosis, more commonly known as Lou Gehrig's disease.

In this incurable disease, the muscles slowly stiffen. Wallace was confined to a wheelchair and later lost most of his ability to speak. He died on November 18, 1965, in a Danbury, Connecticut, hospital with his beloved wife at his side.

Bibliography

Schapsmeier, Edward L. and Frederick H. *Henry A. Wallace of Iowa: The Agrarian Years 1910–1940*. Ames: Iowa State University Press, 1968.
———. *Prophet in Politics: Henry Wallace and the War Years 1940–1945*. Ames: Iowa State University Press, 1970.

34. Harry S Truman

Harry Truman served two eventful terms as president of the United States after having served only eighty-two days as vice president for Franklin Roosevelt. During Truman's first term, he ordered that the atomic bomb should be used against Japan, which finally brought an end to the four-year war between the United States and that country in 1945. A few months later he recommended that the new nation of Israel be recognized by the United States government. The Palestinians and Israelis are still at odds on the matter.

During his second term, Truman sent Congress the first civil rights message and desegregated the United States Army, Navy, Marines, and Air Force. The Korean War began in 1950 and was still in progress when he left office. His tenure was never boring, to say the least.

Harry Truman was born May 8, 1884, in Lamar, Missouri, to John Anderson Truman and his wife, the former Martha Ellen Young. John Truman was a farmer and mule trader at the time of Harry's birth. Later the family moved to the Young family farm, and John Truman joined his father-in-law in farming there.

Young Harry loved their new home and being with his Grandfather Young, who loved him greatly. They attended county fairs, hunted birds' nests, and picked wild strawberries from the fields. When his grandfather died, Harry was only nine years old, but for the rest of his life he talked loving of the "great big man" who gave him a strong sense that he was somebody important.

In 1890, Harry got his first pair of eyeglasses, and he felt as if he were in a new world. He was extremely farsighted, and he had been learning more by sound than by sight.

The Trumans moved to Independence, Missouri, in 1890, so that their children, now four in number, could receive a better education than Lamar offered. The children also found plenty of playmates and had many more interests to pursue.

John Truman resumed his livestock trading and became an inventor of a fence staple puller and an automatic railroad switch. He prospered in Independence, and at last his family could afford to indulge in a few luxuries such as a piano.

Harry S Truman. Reproduced from the collections of the Library of Congress.

Young Harry evinced such intense interest in the instrument that his mother arranged for him to take music lessons from a neighbor. Later he traveled to Kansas City twice a week for more advanced training.

Harry was painfully shy with girls in his younger years. His romantic attention was fastened on a pretty, blue-eyed, blonde girl named Elizabeth Wallace, who was in his fourth grade class in school. She also attended the Presbyterian church where he went to church, but it took him five years to start talking to her.

Elizabeth was called "Bess" by her family and friends, and Harry discovered she was especially interested in sports. She played baseball better than her brothers, played tennis very well, and enjoyed both ice-skating and dancing.

Truman was entranced by her, but he was not athletic, his family was not on the same social level as hers, and the Trumans were really Baptists. Her father was a wealthy partner in a large milling company, which had a large interstate trade. To a teenage boy, all these obstacles appeared to be insurmountable.

Harry Truman devoted himself to getting an education, and he read many books from the local library. History interested him most, and his heroes were the famous generals in all parts of the world. He enjoyed reading James Fenimore Cooper's historical novels, but he complained, "His sentences are too long."

In the summer of 1900, Truman attended his first Democratic Convention in Kansas City with his father, where the delegates nominated William Jennings Bryan as their candidate to oppose incumbent President William H. McKinley in the upcoming election. Truman was exhilarated by the large convention center, the enormous crowd of seventeen thousand people, and the excitement generated by the nomination.

Harry Truman had graduated from high school earlier that year and applied for admission to West Point Academy. He was rejected because of his poor eyesight, however. At about this same time, John Truman went bankrupt, losing the family farm, his business, and all the family's assets. There was no money to pay for Harry to attend any college.

The Trumans moved to Kansas City, where Harry's father got a job as a night watchman for a grain elevator company. Harry got a job working in the mailroom of the *Kansas City Star.*

After working about two months for the newspaper, Harry Truman got a better job as a timekeeper for the construction company building more tracks for the Santa Fe Railroad into Kansas City. He earned thirty dollars a month, plus his bed and board, for ten-hour workdays, six days a week.

Six months later the job was finished, and Truman found he was sorry to leave it. He had enjoyed the rough camaraderie of the laborers and being involved in a large work project.

Truman's next job was as a vault clerk in the National Bank of Commerce in Kansas City, where he worked from 1903 to 1905, finally reaching a salary of forty dollars a month.

While Truman was working in the bank, Elizabeth Wallace suffered a terrible personal tragedy when her father committed suicide after he went bankrupt also.

Elizabeth went with her mother and sister to Colorado Springs, Colorado, to live for a year to assuage their grief. When they returned to Independence, they moved in with Elizabeth's grandparents, Mr. and Mrs. George Porterfield Gates.

Harry's parents moved to a farm in October 1905 that was so large John Truman could not farm it by himself. When his father said he was needed to help work on the Blue Ridge Farm, Harry left the bank and returned to live with his parents.

For the next five years, the hard labor was unending. There were so many chores to do, so much responsibility, that Harry's full attention had to be focused on the farm.

The farmhouse in which they lived was not wired for electric power, had no running water or indoor plumbing, and was heated by the coal stove on which Harry's mother cooked.

Fortunately, there were seven rooms in the house, and the family managed to get by with what it had. Harry's muscles developed with all his hard work. This was an unexpected pleasure for him, as he had always been slight in stature.

Harry Truman was visiting old friends in Independence in 1910 when someone mentioned a cake plate needed to be returned to Mrs. Wallace. Truman volunteered quickly to run the errand, and when he reached the Wallace home, Bess answered the door. He took two hours to finish his errand.

After their reunion, Truman came to visit Bess as often as he could, and he wrote her hundreds of letters. They were not love letters in the usual sense, but rather journal-like accounts of his daily life on the farm and his opinions about books he had read and various events. Their friendship and knowledge of each other increased steadily through the correspondence.

In June 1911, after much thought, Truman wrote a letter in which he asked Bess to marry him. She did not reply for the next three weeks, while he suffered. He wrote her again on July 12: "I couldn't help telling you how I felt. . . . I never had any desire to make love to a girl just for the fun of it, and you have always been the reason." He promised he would not mention the subject again if she would continue seeing him.

In November 1913, Bess finally told Harry that if she married anyone, he would be the one. He was deliriously happy to learn she cared for him.

Before they could even plan their wedding, however, both of Truman's parents died, and he had to operate the farm and help his younger siblings get an education.

Truman joined the National Guard when World War I started in Europe, and he was sent overseas as part of the American Expeditionary Force, landing in France on April 13, 1918.

All the time he was in Europe, Truman longed for home and Bess. They had decided to marry when he got back, and the waiting grew more difficult each day. At last, he returned on May 3, 1919.

Harry married his beloved Bess on June 28, 1919, in the Trinity Episcopal Church in Independence with a large group of friends and family present. Harry was now thirty-five, and Bess was thirty-four.

The couple toured eastern cities in the United States on their honeymoon. After they returned, they moved in with Bess's mother, Madge Wallace.

Truman and a longtime friend, Eddie Jacobson, opened a men's clothing store in Independence that carried top-line merchandise. It was called "Truman and Jacobson" and was initially successful.

As the depression began and continued, however, their business went bankrupt, and Truman spent years paying off their creditors. He lost a total of twenty-eight thousand dollars on the venture.

Truman first entered the political arena in 1922, when he ran for eastern judge of Jackson County in Kansas on the Democratic ticket. He was elected but only served one two-year term before he was defeated in his bid for reelection. In 1926 he was elected a presiding judge in the county, and he continued in that post for the next eight years.

Bess suffered two miscarriages in the early years of their marriage, and the birth of their daughter, Mary Margaret, on February 17, 1924, was thrilling indeed. Truman adored his baby daughter and spent time with her whenever he could, but he was extremely busy with official duties which kept him away from his family more than he liked.

In 1934, Truman was elected to serve in the United States Senate, and Bess and Margaret spent several months in Washington with him each year, where they rented small apartments in various sections of the city for their temporary home. Margaret attended Gunston Hall, a private school for girls.

Senator Truman supported President Franklin Roosevelt in his New Deal programs, including his plan to "pack" the Supreme Court. Truman was not really a liberal, but rather a loyal Democrat. He angered liberals when he became President by replacing New Dealers in government positions, and he did not advocate civil rights or integration in public transportation in the capital city.

As time passed and the New Deal programs did not end depression woes, Truman became more and more convinced some other way out was needed. He also feared Adolf Hitler, the German dictator, would cause serious trouble for the United States sometime in the future.

Truman could not have been more accurate if he had consulted a crystal ball. Hitler destroyed much of Europe during his military campaigns between September 1939 and the end of World War II in Europe in May 1945. The United States became an active participant in the war after Japan attacked Pearl Harbor in Hawaii on December 7, 1941.

Before the war with Germany and Japan had ended, Truman was elected as President Roosevelt's third vice president in 1944. After serving as vice president for only eighty-two days, he became president when President Roosevelt died on April 12, 1945. Truman must have felt his own world had spun out of control with events moving so rapidly.

Shortly after becoming president, Harry Truman ordered the use of the newly developed atomic bomb on Japanese targets. Even though Germany had surrendered, Japan continued with the war. If allied forces had to invade Japan, there would be a massive loss of life on both sides.

Truman saw no other solution. Even though he was not sure what the total effect of the A-bombs would be, he ordered them dropped on Hiroshima on August 6, 1945, and on Nagasaki three days later. Japan began negotiating a surrender on August 10, and the formal surrender was signed on September 2, 1945, bringing the bloodiest conflict in world history to an end.

President Truman has been criticized by later generations for using the bombs, but to the Americans then living, the end of the war came as a total relief because they had seen no indication that it would surrender.

President Truman was a leader in the formation of the United Nations, which it was hoped would help maintain peace in the world. He also promoted the recognition of the nation of Israel as an independent nation.

Communist leaders in Russia and other countries began spreading their doctrine of government throughout the free world after World War II ended. It was the invasion of the democratic country of South Korea by Communistic North Korea that led to the Korean War, which began in June 1950. Many Americans questioned United States involvement in what was essentially a civil war in Korea, but it was ostensibly a United Nations effort led by United States forces.

President Truman brought the wrath of many American citizens down on himself during the Korean conflict when he removed General Douglas MacArthur from his Far East command. General MacArthur had publicly questioned President Truman's decisions about the war, and Truman dismissed him for insubordination.

The war continued until President Truman had completed his second term in office and General Dwight D. Eisenhower had been elected president. The final armistice was signed in July 1953, in South Korea.

After leaving office, Harry Truman continued to live an interesting and fulfilling life. He returned with Bess to Kansas City to live. His mind was full of plans for the public library to be built in Grandview to house his papers and official documents. He said, "There never is and never can be anything like coming back home!"

At the end of March 1953, he, Bess, and Margaret took a trip to Hawaii to spend a dream vacation. They stayed for a month, during which they toured the islands, flew over Mauna Kea and Mauna Loa volcanoes, and relaxed on the beach. Truman received an honorary degree from the University of Hawaii.

In June 1954, Truman had gallbladder surgery and recovered uneventfully. He received over one hundred thousand get-well cards and letters during his illness.

Truman's next project was to complete the book he had begun to write about his experiences, which he entitled *Memoirs*. The book enjoyed good sales after its publication by Doubleday.

In March 1956, Margaret Truman announced her engagement to Elbert

Clifton Daniel, Jr., who worked for the *New York Times* as a foreign news editor. Harry Truman wrote his friend Dean Acheson, "As every old man who had a daughter feels, I'm worried and hope things will work out all right."

The couple's wedding was held on April 21, 1956, in the little Trinity Episcopal Church where Margaret's parents had been married thirty-seven years earlier. The marriage was a success, and in time the Daniels had two sons they named Clifton Truman and William Wallace. Harry had the two boys he had always wished for, and he and Bess doted on them.

Margaret and Clifton went to Key West for vacations, and Harry and Bess often joined them here. Later Margaret had two more sons they named Harrison and Thomas.

Margaret gave up her singing career after her marriage and became a successful author of murder mysteries, most of them with a setting in Washington, D.C.

Harry Truman lived to see the Truman Library completed, and he spent many happy hours there. His health began to fail, however, and he developed congestive heart failure. He died on December 26, 1972, in Kansas City's Research Hospital.

Harry had told Bess and Margaret earlier that he did not want to lie in state in Washington and preferred a simple funeral. They tried to respect his wishes, but several thousand soldiers came to Independence for the funeral of their former commander in chief. He was buried in the courtyard of the Truman Library.

Bess Truman survived him by ten years and continued to live in their home, where she died on October 18, 1982. She was buried beside Harry.

Bibliography

Hamby, Alonzo. *Beyond the New Deal: Harry S Truman and American Liberalism*. New York: Columbia University Press, 1973.

McCoy, Donald R. *The Presidency of Harry S Truman*. Lawrence: University Press of Kansas, 1984.

McCullough, David. *Truman*. New York: Simon and Schuster, 1992.

35. Alben William Barkley

Vice President Alben William Barkley, with the assistance of President Harry Truman, brought new duties to the office of the vice presidency and new respect for it. Barkley had served many years in government service before he was elected vice president, and he was valuable to President Truman in helping formulate policies of his administration.

Alben Barkley was born near Lowes, in Graves County, Kentucky, on November 24, 1877, to John Wilson and Ellen A. Smith Barkley, who were tenant farmers. The baby was named Willie Alben at birth, but he changed his name to Alben William when he reached adulthood, believing it was more dignified.

As a child, Alben helped his father and brothers with farm chores, but he did not like farm life, and he decided education would provide a way out. He attended Marvin College at first and worked to pay his own expenses. He went on to Emory College in Georgia, and later to the University of Virginia Law School. He was admitted to the Kentucky bar in 1901.

Alben was an effective lawyer, and he served as prosecuting attorney of McCracken County, Kentucky, from 1905 to 1909, and as a judge in the county court there from 1909 to 1913.

Barkley had married Dorothy Anne Brower on June 23, 1903, before his political career began, and he remained active in politics for forty-two of their forty-four years of marriage. They had one son, David Murrell, and two daughters, Laura Louise and Marian.

In 1912, Barkley was elected to the United States House of Representatives, and he served seven consecutive terms there, until 1927. He supported President Woodrow Wilson in his attempt to get the United States to join the League of Nations after World War I.

Barkley got his father a job as doorkeeper for the House of Representatives, his son David worked as his father's secretary from 1927 to 1929, and Laura Louise was a member of his staff from 1933 to 1935.

In 1926, Barkley was elected to the United States Senate, and he served there continuously until 1949. In 1937, he was named Senate majority leader. His wife, Dorothy, was in Paducah, Kentucky, at the time, and he sent her a telegram to give her the good news that said, "Won by one. Alben."

Alben Wm. Barkley. Reproduced from the collections of the Library of Congress.

The Barkleys bought a house in Paducah that same year, and Dorothy was there supervising the repairs and remodeling done on the old mansion, which had been built before the Civil War. They called the house "Angles."

As Senate majority leader, it was Senator Barkley's obligation to work for the passage of administration-sponsored bills in the Senate and to oppose those presented by Republicans or rebel Democrats. Barkley liked President Franklin Roosevelt and gladly supported most of his New Deal proposals.

When Barkley ran for the Senate in 1938, his opponent, Governor Albert B. ("Happy") Chandler accused him of being away from both Kentucky and the United States too often. Barkley denied the charge, saying: "I have been criticized because I went to Europe twice. The first time I went on a mission of peace. . . . On the second occasion I went to visit my grandchild in Paris, France. My daughter [Laura] was there with her husband [Douglas MacArthur II, a career diplomat]. They were making $2,700 a year, and I had to send them money once in awhile so they could make out. I went over to see my grandchild on his second birthday."

When the primary election was held, Senator Barkley was reelected with 56% of the votes cast for him. In the general election of 1938, he received 62% of the popular votes to 38% for his Republican challenger.

Senator Barkley took office for his third term as war clouds gathered over Europe. After Hitler's army invaded Poland on September 1, 1939, the focus of the United States government turned to events occurring in the war in Europe. President Roosevelt's decision to seek a third term as president had Senator Barkley's approval because, as he said, "I felt that Roosevelt was the best available leader, and that we should not be bound by an ancient tradition."

In 1942, Dorothy Barkley became ill with a heart condition she had developed in childhood. She never recovered her health, and from 1944 to 1947 she had to have trained nurses caring for her continuously. Senator Barkley's salary was not sufficient to pay all her expenses, and he added to the family income by giving speeches or lectures to various organizations.

When Dorothy became unable to climb steps, Alben sold their home in Washington and rented an apartment for them. He continued to perform his duties faithfully in the Senate and often studied the Senate calendar while sitting by his wife's bedside.

Young David Barkley joined the air force and became a pilot. Their daughter, Marian, married a Washington attorney, Max O'Rell Truitt. In time, they had a son named Stephen, and Senator Barkley doted on the child.

When the 1944 Democratic Convention started, President Roosevelt had four different men convinced that each was his choice to be nominated as his vice president for his fourth term. They were incumbent Vice President Henry Wallace, Senator Barkley, Senator Harry Truman, and Director of War Mobilization James Byrnes.

Senator Barkley was scheduled to deliver the nominating speech for Roosevelt, and James Byrnes told Barkley he would advise him not to be too complimentary about Roosevelt.

Barkley had already guessed the president was enjoying playing the possible nominees against each other, and he told a news reporter he was tired of trying to find which shell covered the pea. He said he was tempted to leave the convention and go home, but he did not do so.

Senator Harry Truman was selected to be vice president to run with Roosevelt, and after they were elected and Truman had served only eighty-two days as vice president, he became president when Roosevelt died unexpectedly. The other men must have reflected on how altered their lives would have been if they had been nominated as vice president at the convention.

When Barkley returned to the Senate in 1947, Republicans were now the majority party, so he was elected leader of the minority party.

Dorothy Barkley died in Washington on March 10, 1947, and was buried in Mount Kenton Cemetery in Paducah. Despite her long illness, Alben was deeply grieved by her death.

About a month later, Barkley went to Cairo, Egypt, as president of the American group attending the first Inter-parliamentary Union Conference. He made a speech there in support of the United Nations organization. Following the conference, he and his group went on to visit Bethlehem, Jerusalem, and Jericho. From there, they traveled to Greece, Turkey, and Italy. Barkley then went on to Paris to visit his daughter and her family again. He stayed with the MacArthurs for a week.

At the 1948 Democrat Convention in Philadelphia, Barkley was nominated to run for vice president with incumbent President Harry Truman. They were elected despite a November 3 headline that year in the *Chicago Daily Tribune* which read, "Dewey Defeats Truman."

When Barkley got back to Washington, he and President Truman greeted well-wishers on the steps of the White House. Barkley had a wide grin on his face when he said, "Mr. President, in the language of Minnie Pearl of the Grand Ole Opry 'I'm just so proud to be here!'"

On January 20, 1949, Barkley took the oath of office as vice president on the platform built on the east front of the capitol building. His salary was increased to $30,000 a year, and he had a tax-free expense account of $10,000 each year. He was named a member of the National Security Council.

Gossip columnists watched the vice president closely for any hint of romantic attachments. "They have been marrying me off with monotonous regularity to almost every eligible widow in the country," he complained.

In fact, Barkley did remarry later. His bride was Jane Rucker Hadley from St. Louis. He had met her for the first time in July 1949, when she visited friends in Washington, the Clark Cliffords.

Vice President Barkley had to endure some ribbing in the press, and cartoons appeared showing him asking the Honorable Dan Cupid in the Senate, "For what purpose does the gentleman wish to be recognized?"

Barkley married Jane on November 18, 1949, in St. John's Methodist Church in St. Louis, and they went back to Washington to live.

By now, Barkley was known familiarly as "the Veep," a title his grandson Stephen Truitt gave him when his grandfather complained "Mr. Vice President" was too long.

Barkley and President Truman were on friendly terms. They came from similar backgrounds, had seen the administrations of Franklin Roosevelt come and go, and had a sincere interest in seeing the new nation of Israel succeed. Barkley had believed for years that a part of Palestine should be given to the Jews for a homeland.

President Truman did not consult with his vice president about foreign policy, but instead consulted with various senators.

Vice President Barkley said he sometimes felt like a catcher in a night baseball game — he never knew what was coming across the plate and every time the ball was thrown, the lights went out.

On March 1, 1951, President Truman came to the Senate chamber to present Barkley with a gavel made from wood from the White House that had been removed during remodeling. The vice president was touched by President Truman's thoughtfulness, and he assured Truman he would treasure the little mallet for the rest of his life.

In November of that year, Alben and Jane Barkley took a trip to Korea and Japan. They visited with servicemen at the air base in Korea, and Barkley visited the front lines and the men fighting there. The Korean War had begun a short time before.

When President Truman decided he would not run for president again in 1952, Barkley made up his mind he would try for the office, even though he was now seventy-four years old. Labor leaders and other Democrat groups felt he was too old, however, and would not nominate him as their candidate.

In 1954, Barkley was elected to serve as a senator again. He was happy to be able to return to old haunts as the "junior senator from Kentucky."

On April 30, 1956, Senator Barkley made a speech to the students at Washington and Lee University in Lexington, Virginia. He explained differences between Democrats and Republicans in their political philosophies, and he ended his speech by saying: "And I am willing to be a junior. I'm glad to sit in the back row, for I would rather be a servant in the House of the Lord, than to sit in the seats of the mighty!"

An unbelieving student body watched as former president Barkley collapsed while still in the rostrum; he died a few minutes later from a heart attack. He was buried in Kentucky.

Bibliography

Davis, Polly Ann. *Alben W. Barkley: Senate Majority Leader and Vice President.* New York: Garland, 1979.

36. Richard Milhous Nixon

Richard Nixon has been the only president in the history of the United States government to resign from office. Rather than undergo impeachment proceedings and have a verdict rendered by Congress as to his guilt or innocence in the Watergate affair, he chose to leave office.

The only other president who was impeached was Andrew Johnson in 1868, and he was found not guilty. He was not renominated by the Democrats for a second term, however.

Richard Milhous Nixon was born in Yorba Linda, California, on January 9, 1913, to Francis (Frank) Anthony and Hannah Milhous Nixon, the second of their five sons.

Frank Nixon operated a grocery store and butcher shop when Richard was a child, and when he was older, Richard had to go get fresh produce for the store from Los Angeles. He went early in the mornings, so no one would see him bringing in the produce. He also had to wash the fruits and vegetables and arrange them in a display at the store.

Richard's father was described as good-hearted by neighbors and friends. Richard had his Quaker mother's reticent personality, and his father's loquacious tendencies and loud voice must have embarrassed him.

Richard attended Yorba Linda school until 1922 and moved on to Whittier that year. After starting high school in Fullerton, he transferred to Whittier High School in his junior year. In 1930 he graduated from Whittier at the top of his class, receiving the California Interscholastic Gold Seal Award for his efforts and the Harvard Award as best all-around student.

Richard Nixon attended Whittier College from 1930 to 1934, where he played football, was elected captain of the debating team, and majored in history. He was a student at Duke University Law School in Durham, North Carolina, from 1934 to 1937 and was admitted to the California bar later that year.

Nixon first met Thelma Catherine Ryan, called "Pat," at the Whittier Little Theater, where both had gone for an audition in 1937. They both got a part in *The Dark Tower,* and that same night Nixon proposed to her.

To say Pat was startled would be an understatement. She refused his proposal then, but they continued to date for the next two years.

Richard M. Nixon.
Courtesy of The Richard Nixon Library & Birthplace, Yorba Linda, California.

Pat's life had been difficult — her mother died when Pat was only thirteen and her father died when she was seventeen. Mr. Ryan was a copper miner and had developed silicosis from his years in the mines.

Pat Ryan worked as a bank clerk, as a secretary, as an X-ray technician, and in any other jobs she could find to pay for her college expenses at the University of Southern California, from which she graduated cum laude in 1937. She had been working for only a few weeks at Whittier High School teaching business subjects when she met Richard for the first time.

On June 21, 1940, Pat married Richard in the Mission Inn in Riverside, California. They went on a two-week auto trip through Mexico for their honeymoon and came home to live in an apartment over a garage.

Pat continued teaching until Richard joined the navy in June 1942 as a lieutenant, junior grade. He stayed in the navy throughout World War II.

While he was in military service, Pat worked in San Francisco as a secretary, and she got a job later with the Office of Price Administration as an economist. Richard had worked there in the tire-rationing division before he joined the navy.

Nixon was discharged from the navy in March 1946, with the rank of lieutenant commander. He was involved in military action in the South Pacific during the war and received a citation for "meritorious and efficient performance."

Later that same year, Nixon was elected by California voters to represent them in Congress, where he served from 1947 to 1950.

In 1946, Richard and Pat Nixon's first child, a daughter, was born. They named her Patricia, but her family and friends call her "Tricia." Two years later Julie Nixon was born.

Richard Nixon had been elected a United States representative because the Committee of One Hundred in Whittier wanted to replace their liberal congressman, Jerry Voorhis. The committee's advertisement, which appeared in all the district newspapers, said they were seeking a candidate "with no previous political experience to defeat a man who had represented the District in the House for ten years. Any young man, resident of the District, preferably a veteran, fair education, no political strings or obligations . . . may apply for the job. Applicants will be reviewed by one hundred interested citizens, who will guarantee support, but will not obligate the candidate in any way."

When they reached Washington, the Nixons had to live in a two-bedroom apartment in Park Fairfax, Virginia, twenty minutes from the capital, because housing was in short supply in Washington.

Representative Nixon was named a member of the education and labor committees, as well as the House Committee on Un-American Activities. He was reelected to the House in 1948 for a second term, but he thought the arduous campaigning every two years might hurt his marriage because he had to be gone from home so often. It seemed more logical to him to run for a seat in the Senate next time, where the terms were six years in length.

In 1950, Richard Nixon was elected to the Senate. During the campaign, he accused his opponent, Democrat Helen Gahagan Douglas, of being a Communist, and charges and countercharges flew between the two political camps.

Nixon won by a larger plurality of votes than did any other Republican candidate that year.

The next year, a month after Richard was sworn into office, he and Pat bought a two-story white brick home in a Washington development called Spring Valley. It was their first real home.

In 1952, rumors began to circulate that Richard Nixon would be nominated at the Republican Convention to run as vice president, with the probable nomination of General Dwight D. Eisenhower as the presidential candidate. The rumors proved to be accurate, and both men were nominated.

On September 18, following the convention, newspaper headlines told of a so-called slush fund established for Nixon when he defeated Helen Gahagan Douglas three years before. Nixon feared Eisenhower might drop him from the ticket before the election if he believed the story.

Nixon went on television to deny that there was anything unusual or illegal about his campaign finances, and he meticulously listed all of his and Pat's assets. He admitted a Texan had sent little Tricia Nixon a cocker spaniel, which she named Checkers, "and we plan to keep him," Nixon told the television audience.

Eisenhower was elected president and Nixon vice president in 1952 with 55.1% of the popular vote; they received a majority popular vote in each of thirty-nine states and were officially inaugurated on January 20, 1953.

Vice President Nixon was a useful member of President Eisenhower's administration. He presided over cabinet meetings when the president was absent from Washington and following Eisenhower's heart attack in 1955. He also had the usual assigned duty of presiding over the Senate.

Richard and Pat Nixon traveled extensively as goodwill ambassadors for the United States government. Their first trip was a ten-week, forty-five-thousand-mile journey to the Far East. They visited New Zealand, Vietnam, Korea, India, Pakistan, and Afghanistan. They were both exhausted by the time they returned to Washington.

When President Eisenhower announced he would seek a second term in 1956, he did not announce that Vice President Nixon was his choice as a running mate. Weeks passed during which the president did not mention Nixon's place on the ticket, but in April 1956, he said his vice president had not given him his decision about staying on the ticket. When Nixon assured him he did hope to win a second term, President Eisenhower said, "I'm delighted by the news."

In the 1956 campaign, the Nixons had to do most of the traveling and speaking because President Eisenhower's health was not robust, and he feared a vigorous campaign might cause a second heart attack.

The Nixons visited thirty-two states in sixteen days. Pat Nixon said later, "We killed ourselves," but their efforts were rewarded. President Eisenhower and Vice President Nixon were reelected, receiving 57% of the popular vote and carrying forty-one states. During this term in office, Richard and Pat went to Latin America and Russia.

Vice President Nixon was nominated to run for president in 1960 by the Republicans, but he was defeated by the Democratic candidate, John F. Kennedy. In 1962, Nixon was also defeated in his bid to unseat the incumbent California governor, Edmund "Pat" Brown.

The Nixons returned to California in 1961 and decided they would build a home in Beverly Hills, since they were unable to find a house they liked. Nixon rented a house from movie producer Walter Lang while their house was under construction, and he began writing his memoirs, *Six Crises.* They moved into their new home in 1962.

Richard Nixon could not give up his dream of becoming president, but from 1963 to 1968 he practiced law in New York City with the Nixon, Mudge, Rose, Guthrie, and Alexander law firm.

The Nixon family moved into an apartment at 810 Fifth Avenue, where one of their neighbors was Governor Nelson Rockefeller. Tricia and Julia Nixon entered the Chapin School, a private school for girls in New York. When the time came for Tricia to go to college in 1964, she chose to attend Finch College in Manhattan so she could live at home.

When the 1964 election neared, Richard Nixon had to swallow his disappointment when the Republican Convention chose Barry Goldwater to be its candidate for president. Nixon campaigned diligently for Goldwater's election, but President Lyndon Johnson was elected to serve in his own right, after having become president when Kennedy was shot in Dallas.

By 1968, frustration had been building steadily among American voters because of the escalation of the war in Vietnam. On August 8 of that year, the Republicans nominated Richard Nixon to be their candidate for president and Spiro T. Agnew of Maryland as vice president.

The Democrats chose Hubert Humphrey as their presidential nominee, with Senator Edmund Muskie of Maine as his running partner.

Richard Nixon was elected president with 43.4% of the popular vote and he carried thirty-two states.

In 1968, Julie Nixon married David Eisenhower II, former president Eisenhower's grandson. They lived in southern California for several years, but they moved to Pennsylvania in 1980.

President Nixon had promised to bring an end to the war in Vietnam with honor, if elected, and he ordered the training of South Vietnamese men to defend their own country with armaments provided by the United States when its own armed forces returned home.

In August 1972, the last ground combat soldiers came home to the United States, and a peace agreement was signed between the Vietnamese factions in Paris in January 1973. North Vietnam did not bargain in good faith, however, and its forces began fighting again as soon as United States forces had been withdrawn. In time South Vietnam was conquered by its northern neighbors.

On July 20, 1969, Astronaut Neil Armstrong became the first man in history to walk on the moon. Astronauts Eugene Cernan and Harrison Schmitt spent seventy-five hours on the moon's surface in December 1972. President Nixon was a strong supporter of space exploration.

Young Tricia Nixon married attorney Edward F. Cox in a ceremony in the White House Rose Garden in 1971, and they went to live in New York City.

President Richard Nixon was a forceful, decisive chief executive who never hesitated to take appropriate action in foreign policy matters. In his travels as vice president, he had become personally acquainted with some leaders of nations who were on their way up in power as he was. He enjoyed the secrecy involved with diplomacy in arranging agreements with other nations, such as the SALT agreement with Russia.

Nixon's foreign policy successes often overshadowed the successes of his domestic reforms. He led an effort to complete desegregation of public schools in the South. Integration had been moving forward in a halting fashion before he became president, and in 1968, 68% of black students were still attending all black schools. By 1970 that figure had dropped to 18.4%.

President Nixon was the leader in the establishment of the Environmental Protection Agency to control the quality of air and water in the nation, as well as to regulate the use of pesticides and other hazards perceived to be potentially harmful to American citizens. He promoted the establishment of the Occupational Safety and Health Administration, which implemented safer working conditions for blue-collar workers and reduced the number of job-related illnesses and injuries in the workplace.

In 1969, Democrat Thomas S. Foley, Speaker of the House of Representatives in Washington, D.C., gave President Nixon credit for alleviating hunger among Americans. Foley said, "The Nixon administration was most important in advancing the anti-hunger fight in America. You get in trouble if you say a good word about Richard Nixon in Democrat circles, but that's the truth." This remark followed President Nixon's successful efforts to have a uniform application of the Food Stamp program in each of the fifty states and to enable more people to qualify for the assistance.

The latter part of the Nixon presidency was marred by financial scandal involving Vice President Agnew and by the allegations that President Nixon had encouraged some of his political supporters to commit a burglary at the Democratic National Headquarters in the Watergate complex in Washington to obtain the names of campaign contributors. The burglary occurred in June 1972, and White House involvement did not become clear until after the voters had already reelected Nixon and Agnew in November 1972.

Newsmen insisted President Nixon lied when he said he knew nothing about the burglary. John Dean, the former White House counsel, testified at a Congressional hearing in 1973 that Nixon did cover up evidence about the burglary, and the event occupied television and newspaper reports for years.

President Richard Nixon resigned on August 9, 1974, rather than undergo an impeachment hearing. He pointed out that if he continued to resist the efforts of his opponents, the entire time and attention of both Congress and the presidency would be absorbed in impeachment rather than focusing on national affairs.

Vice President Agnew had resigned earlier in October 1973, and Congressman Gerald Ford had been appointed vice president under the provisions of the Twenty-Fifth Amendment. Ford then became president when President Nixon resigned.

President Nixon was disbarred from practicing law, and he and Pat returned to San Clemente, California. He was severely depressed for a time, according to news reports, and to add to his problems, on September 8, 1974, he developed a blood clot in his left leg and was hospitalized for four weeks. A month later he developed a second clot, for which he had to have surgery, and he was hospitalized for another month.

Richard Nixon received a full pardon from President Gerald Ford in September 1974. President Ford's action set off another firestorm of criticism, but he believed the pardon was needed to end all the controversy.

Patricia Nixon had a stroke on July 7, 1976, which curtailed many of her activities, and she suffered another one in 1983. All of her husband's problems had a negative effect on her general health.

Richard Nixon wrote six books: *Memoirs of Richard Nixon* (1978), *The Real War* (1980), *Leaders* (1982), *Real Peace: Strategy for the West* (1984), *No More Vietnams* (1985), and *1999: Victory Without War* (1988).

On February 9, 1980, the Nixons moved back East to live in New York City in a four-story Eastside Manhattan townhouse. Eighteen months later they moved to a house in Saddle River, New Jersey. Both of their daughters and their families now lived in the East, and they could visit often.

Pat Nixon died on June 22, 1993, of lung cancer in their New Jersey home, and she was buried on the grounds of the Nixon Library in Yorba Linda, California. She had restricted all public appearances since her husband left the White House.

Richard Nixon lived quietly after his wife's death. He died on April 22, 1994, after suffering a stroke. He was eighty-one years old. He was buried beside Pat in California at the Nixon Library.

Bibliography

Bailey, Thomas A. *Presidential Saints and Sinners*. New York: Free Press, 1981.
Eisenhower, Julie Nixon. *Pat Nixon: The Untold Story*. New York: Simon and Schuster, 1986.
Wicker, Tom. *One of Us: Richard Nixon and the American Dream*. New York: Random House, 1991.

37. Lyndon Baines Johnson

Lyndon Baines Johnson served as both vice president and president during one of our nation's most turbulent eras, when popular President Kennedy was assassinated and the controversial Vietnam War was waged. President Johnson was often the object of criticism, but many of the events were beyond his control.

Lyndon was born on August 27, 1908, in Gillespie County, Texas. His father, Sam Ealy Johnson, Jr., was a farmer on a small scale and a member of the Texas legislature from 1904 to 1908, the year Lyndon was born.

Lyndon's mother, the former Rebekah Baines, was the daughter of lawyer Joseph Wilson Baines. In her younger years, she had attended Baylor University, where she majored in literature and hoped to become a great novelist. Her father lost everything he owned in a business deal and died while she was in college. She never graduated because of a lack of money, and she married Sam Johnson eight months later on August 20, 1907.

When Lyndon was five years old, his family moved from the farm on the Pedernales River to Johnson City, Texas. There his father started selling real estate, and his mother taught public speaking. In 1918, Sam Johnson was once again elected to serve in the Texas legislature, and he continued in office there until 1924.

Lyndon's sister, also named Rebekah, was born in 1910, a second sister, Josepha, was born in 1912, his brother Sam was born in 1914, and his youngest sister, Lucia, was born in 1916.

Young Lyndon attended public school in Johnson City, where he was frequently reprimanded for misbehaving. He took violin lessons and dancing lessons, neither of which lasted long. In Johnson City High School, he was a member of the debate team, and the class prophecy said he would be governor of Texas one day.

Lyndon's mother was a gloomy, tearful woman who ruled her children by making them feel guilty. When Lyndon told her he did not plan to go on to college after graduating from high school in 1924, Rebekah Johnson refused to either look at him or speak to him for a week.

In July that year, he and five friends went to California in a Model T Ford to

Lyndon B. Johnson. Reproduced from the collections of the Library of Congress.

seek their fortunes. There Lyndon worked as a fruit picker and elevator operator, and he even washed dishes for a time in a restaurant.

Two years later he arrived back in Texas with no money. He got a job working as a laborer on the road repair and maintenance crew, but he hated the hard work. He believed college might be a wise choice after all.

Lyndon Johnson enrolled in Southwest Texas State Teachers' College in 1927 and graduated in 1930. To pay his college expenses, he worked as a garbage collector, a janitor, and finally as an assistant secretary to the president of the college. In 1928–29 he taught school part-time at the State College Extension.

In college, Johnson was also on the debate team and a member of the student council. He decided he would study law and entered Georgetown University in 1934, but he left the next year before completing all his courses.

On November 17, 1934, Johnson married Claudia Alta "Lady Bird" Taylor, with the hearty approval of her father. The newlyweds honeymooned for a week in Mexico and then went to live in a duplex apartment in Austin. As a new husband, Lyndon believed he had to find a good job to support his wife. Her father was wealthy, and she had never had to scramble for her education at the University of Texas, as Lyndon had to do for years. She had graduated only a few months before their wedding with a degree in journalism.

In 1935, Johnson was hired to be the director of the state National Youth Administration, one of President Franklin Roosevelt's training programs to provide job skills and public works jobs for needy young people. Johnson worked with the NYA for two years.

Lyndon Johnson had a habit of inviting his political friends to go home with him unexpectedly, and Lady Bird would often have less than an hour to prepare dinner for as many as eight to ten extra people.

Johnson was elected to the House of Representatives in 1937, and he and Lady Bird moved to Washington, D.C., where they lived in a one-bedroom apartment. There Lyndon served on the Naval Affairs Committee and supported President Roosevelt's programs.

Johnson joined the Naval Reserve in January 1940 and was called to active duty in December 1941. He served as a lieutenant commander in the navy until July 1942, when President Roosevelt ordered all congressmen to resign their commissions and return to their duties in Congress.

While Lyndon was away, Lady Bird kept his congressional office operating efficiently. He was awarded a Silver Star for his war exploits.

When Johnson returned to Texas on a visit in 1943, he learned that a radio station in Austin, KTBC, was for sale. Lady Bird had inherited some money from her father, and Lyndon persuaded her to invest $17,500 in the station. She was overseer of operations at the station because Lyndon was so busy with politics.

Lyndon Johnson now had a forum where he could express his political views, as well as a profitable business in the family. The Federal Communications Commission granted the Johnsons permission to increase the station's power to one thousand watts to give its signal wider coverage. By 1964 the Johnsons had made more than $500,000 profit from KTBC.

On March 19, 1944, Lynda Bird Johnson was born, and both her parents were ecstatic. Lady Bird had suffered three miscarriages previously, and they had begun to fear they would never have children. On July 2, 1947, Lucy Baines Johnson was born, and their family was complete.

In November 1948, Johnson was elected to the United States Senate by a margin of only eighty-seven votes out of almost one million votes cast. Charges of ballot-box stuffing raged throughout Texas, but nothing was ever proved.

On January 3, 1953, Johnson was elected Senate Minority Leader after he had waged an intensive campaign to get the position. No other senator particularly wanted the post, but Johnson thought his new position made him the Democratic party leader.

To give him credit, Senator Johnson worked long, hard hours in the job, so much so that on July 2, 1955, he suffered his first heart attack. He was a demanding and difficult patient, but he improved, and when the Eighty-Fourth Congress convened on January 2, 1956, Johnson was present to begin serving as Senate majority leader.

Senator Johnson was at home on his Texas ranch when the news of the Russian space rocket, Sputnik, was broadcast on October 4, 1957. The event caught Johnson's imagination; his efforts to bring the United States into the Space Age led to the creation of the National Aeronautics and Space Administration (NASA), the Apollo program, and eventually the first man landing on the moon in 1969.

Under Senator Johnson's leadership, the Civil Rights Act was approved by the Senate on August 7, 1957, the most comprehensive legislation to be enacted in the field. It gave black citizens full protection by the government to attend schools and churches of their choice and the right to vote freely and without hindrance in national elections.

When Senator John F. Kennedy was chosen as the presidential nominee at the 1960 Democratic Convention, he was expected to name a liberal choice for vice president. No one thought about Senator Lyndon Johnson, and if they had, it would have been considered unlikely that he would accept. His senate seat had brought him both power and prestige, and being vice president would offer him neither.

Lyndon Johnson knew a young, active president would have ideas and successes of his own, however, and he decided to accept the vice presidential nomination as a stepping stone to the presidency.

President Kennedy was very popular with the American public, and the Peace Corps he established and his success in having Soviet missiles withdrawn from Cuba in 1962 only added to his stature. He made a major mistake, however, by steadily increasing the number of United States advisers on duty in South Vietnam to more than 16,000 after a United States–sponsored military coup there failed early in November 1963. Earlier there had been less than 1,000.

About two weeks later, President Kennedy was assassinated in Dallas,

Texas, and Vice President Johnson was now the president. The burden of Vietnam would prove his own undoing in politics.

What was the national interest for the United States in South Vietnam? That question is still being asked by citizens all over America, and the deaths of the fifty-eight thousand American military men there continue to nag the public conscience. Recently, Robert McNamara, one of the top advisers in the United States government, admitted the reasoning in the conflict was flawed on his own part and that of other advisers, Dean Rusk and McGeorge Bundy.

To give President Johnson credit, he often questioned the advisability of increasing the number of soldiers sent and the expenditures needed to continue the war, but his advisers always assured him it was right to continue the struggle. They said they were convinced Communist forces would overrun all of southeast Asia if United States troops left the region.

President Johnson had grown up in relative poverty, and his greatest interest lay in improving the lives of poor people in America. His War on Poverty made more sense to him than war on the North Vietnamese. He was conscious of a lack of knowledge in foreign policy, however, and he thought McNamara, Rusk, and Bundy were more informed than he.

During the Johnson presidency, discrimination became illegal in employment and in the sale and rental of housing. Voting rights of all citizens were assured by the elimination of poll taxes and literacy tests.

President Johnson led the way in the establishment of Medicare and Medicaid programs in 1965. Medicare, which would pay medical costs for elderly citizens and was funded through Social Security deductions, later was broadened to include disabled persons as well. The Medicaid program paid for all medical bills of needy people, based on income.

President Johnson was a promoter for the Job Corps, which offered technical training to disadvantaged young men and women, the Head Start program which allowed poor children to get a year of kindergarten experience before entering school, the Work-Study program which helped provide jobs for young people to pay their college expenses, and Legal Aid to pay lawyers to defend the rights of poor people who could not afford to pay legal fees.

As can be seen from the above list, President Johnson's real interest in his Great Society was to improve the everyday lives of the poor, but all the programs cost a lot of money and the Vietnam War did too.

Some congressmen warned Johnson flatly that the American economy could not provide "guns and butter" at the same time. Johnson remembered that President Roosevelt had both during his administrations, but he failed to realize that President Roosevelt's welfare programs and World War II did not occur simultaneously.

First Lady "Lady Bird" Johnson loved flowers, and she promoted cleaning and beautifying the highways and planting flower-beds at public facilities. The trees and shrubs along public highways today remind Americans of her efforts.

All the criticism about the Vietnam War, the student protests, which became violent, and the general resentment of Americans who had to send their sons to fight in Southeast Asia caused President Johnson to announce on March 31, 1968, that he would neither seek nor accept another term as president.

In actual fact, Congress could have ended the war in Asia at any time without President Johnson's approval by refusing to appropriate money for Defense Department requests, but it was easier and more popular to blame the president.

After attending the inauguration of the Republican president, Richard Nixon, on January 20, 1969, Lyndon and Lady Bird went back to the hill country of Texas, where, he said, "The people know when you're sick and care when you die. . . . I was glad to see it end."

By this time, both of the Johnson daughters had married, and the Johnsons had several lively grandchildren to visit and entertain. Lyndon threw all his energies into operating the family ranch.

President Nixon did not value Johnson's Great Society programs, and Johnson worried about their future. President Nixon was inaugurated for a second term on January 20, 1973, and the next day he announced plans for eliminating some of the Great Society projects and also announced a cease-fire in Vietnam.

Two days later, on January 22, Lyndon Johnson lay down to take an afternoon nap while Lady Bird went into Austin on a business and shopping trip. No one knew he was feeling ill until he called his Secret Service guards to come at once to his bedroom. He had died from a heart attack before the guards reached him.

Funeral services were held in the National City Christian Church in Washington after Johnson's body had lain in state in the Capitol rotunda. He was buried in the Johnson family cemetery near Johnson City, Texas, and graveside rites were conducted by the Reverend Billy Graham, a personal friend.

Lady Bird Johnson is still living in Texas, but her health is declining.

Bibliography

Califano, Joseph A., Jr. *The Triumph and Tragedy of Lyndon Johnson*. New York: Simon and Schuster, 1991.

Caro, Robert A. *The Years of Lyndon Johnson*. Vol. 1, *The Path to Power*. New York: Vintage Books, 1982.

———. *The Years of Lyndon Johnson*. Vol. 2, *Means of Ascent*. New York: Alfred A. Knopf, 1990.

Kearns, Doris. *Lyndon Johnson and the American Dream*. New York: Harper and Row, 1976.

Miller, Merle. *Lyndon: An Oral Biography*. New York: Ballantine Books, 1981.

Van DeMark, Brian. *Into the Quagmire*. New York: Oxford University Press, 1991.

38. Hubert Horatio Humphrey

Hubert H. Humphrey was a member of the United States Senate for most of his political life. There he was regarded as a friend of labor, a civil rights advocate, and a New Deal liberal with his sponsorship of welfare and farm programs. All his political activities were undertaken with a view of helping him realize his dream of becoming president of the United States one day — a dream that never came true.

Hubert Humphrey was born in Wallace, South Dakota, on May 27, 1911. His father, also named Hubert Horatio Humphrey, was a small-town druggist. Hubert's mother, the former Christine Sannes, was of Norwegian ancestry. She was a college graduate and taught school for several years before she married.

The family moved to the little village of Doland, a few miles from Wallace, when Hubert was about six years old. He attended the public school there and eventually graduated from the Doland high school.

Hubert and his brother Ralph enjoyed playing baseball, hopping freight trains as they slowed down coming into the depot area, and skinny-dipping in a nearby creek.

The family had little money, and Hubert sold newspapers from the time he went to live in Doland, carrying the *Chicago Herald and Examiner* in his little wagon. By the time he was nine, Hubert began helping his father in the drugstore by running errands and making sodas for customers. He had to stand on a small platform his father built for him in order to reach the fountain spigots.

Hubert enjoyed debating more than any other school activity, and his debating team won a place in the statewide tournament on two different occasions. He was valedictorian of his graduating class, and he delivered an address at the commencement exercises entitled "I Am Responsible for My Own Life."

The depression started early in South Dakota, and Hubert's father was forced to sell their family home. They rented a small house at the edge of town, and Mr. Humphrey started selling paint, lawn tools, toys, and candy in his drugstore, as well as medicine, in an effort to stay in business. Unfortunately, most of his sales were on credit.

Hubert attended the University of Minnesota in 1929 and 1930, but was forced to leave college when his father's business failed. The family moved on to

Hubert H. Humphrey. Reproduced from the collections of the Library of Congress.

Huron, where Mr. Humphrey opened another store. Hubert had to work in the store, as did the other family members. Mrs. Humphrey and her daughters cooked the meals they served at the lunch counter they had installed in the new store.

Hubert became the leader of a Boy Scout troop sponsored by the Huron Methodist Church, where the Humphreys were all members. About this time,

Hubert developed a stomach problem and suffered from intermittent fainting episodes. He felt trapped in his life, but he knew he had to keep working to help support his parents and the other children in the family.

Hubert Humphrey qualified as a pharmacist himself after completing a course at the Capital College of Pharmacy in Denver, Colorado. His hours of work and his health problems both increased. He consulted doctors, but they could not find any reason for his symptoms.

In the summer of 1933, Humphrey met Muriel Fay Buck, a sophomore student at Huron College. They fell in love, but they could not even consider marriage. Her mother was critically ill, and Hubert's father planned to open some branch drugstores, one of which would be Hubert's responsibility.

It was in his role as a Boy Scout leader that Hubert Humphrey found the courage to change his life to fulfill his own dreams for his future. He took his scout troop to Washington, D.C., and they visited the Senate gallery, the Jefferson Memorial, and other historical places Humphrey had only read about. He decided politics might be a way out, but he would need more education. He wrote Muriel about his decision.

Muriel was supportive of his aims, and they married in September 1936. Hubert's father began paying him a salary for his pharmacy work for the first time, and Muriel got a job at a local power company as a bookkeeper.

Humphrey's fainting spells continued, even while the couple accumulated money to enable him to return to college. At last one night he summoned his courage and told his father he did not like working in a drugstore, and his father did not argue with him.

In the fall of 1937, Hubert and Muriel moved to Minneapolis, where he reentered the University of Minnesota. He took a part-time job as a pharmacist to help pay their bills, and Muriel got another bookkeeping job, which paid fifty cents an hour.

When Humphrey enrolled in a course in American constitutional government, it changed his life. As the instructor lectured the class, all the political views and beliefs of Hubert's father came back to Hubert, and he found he was fascinated by the topics.

What was even more enjoyable, Humphrey could make speeches when he answered questions asked by the instructor. The other students answered, but Humphrey gave orations. He was a natural for the debate team, and he traveled to other college campuses, where he received high marks for content, but low marks for his delivery.

The Humphreys' first child, a daughter named Nancy, was born in 1939, the same year Hubert graduated. He got a teaching fellowship at Louisiana State University, and he began working toward a Ph.D. in Baton Rouge. They lived in a run-down area of the city, where Muriel typed papers for students and made jelly and butter sandwiches for Hubert to sell to fellow students at lunchtime.

After the Humphreys had lived there for several months, World War II started when Hitler's army invaded Poland. Hubert and Muriel returned to Minneapolis in 1940, where he got a job as instructor of adult education teachers working for the Works Progress Administration, a New Deal program. His job was only for the summer, but he got a full-time job later as director of the program. His salary was $150 a month, and he made speeches at club meetings for extra income.

Hubert H. Humphrey III, called "Skip," was born June 26, 1942, just about the time Muriel's sick father moved in with them. Humphrey had considered trying to get a job in wartime Washington, D.C., but he knew it would be difficult, if not impossible, to find housing for his large family.

In July 1943, Humphrey got a job teaching political science courses at MacAlester College in St. Paul, and at last their lives seemed to be entering a more settled phase.

The Democratic party in Minnesota had been split into two factions for several years, and at the Democratic Convention that year, Humphrey worked to reunite the factions into one group.

The war kept intruding into the Humphreys' lives, however, as it did into everyone else's life. Humphrey had been classified 1-A in the draft, which meant he was subject to be called into service at any time. He passed his pre-induction examination in January 1945 and hoped to get a commission in the navy. When he reported for duty in February, however, a doctor found a scrotal hernia, which disqualified him.

In June 1945, Humphrey was elected mayor of Minneapolis by a margin of more than 31,000 votes, the largest plurality in the history of the city. As mayor, he dealt with strikes by telephone company employees, he ordered policemen to enforce laws more stringently, and he worked to improve community relations.

While Humphrey was engrossed in politics, Muriel was required to assume the role as head of the family. When her father died, she and the children attended his funeral without Hubert. They spent summers in a rented cottage on a lake, and Hubert was never there. Later he would regret his lack of involvement in the lives of his children.

As he moved up the political ladder and became better known to Democratic party leaders, Humphrey hoped he might be asked to be President Harry Truman's vice president in the 1948 election. Instead, Representative Alben Barkley of Kentucky was nominated. Humphrey was elected to serve in the United States Senate that year.

When the Humphrey family went to Washington, they had to borrow money to pay movers to unload the truck carrying their furniture. They had bought a house in nearby Chevy Chase, which had four bedrooms, a den, and a recreation room, in addition to the living room, dining room, and kitchen. They needed all the living space they could get to house them and their four children, Nancy, Skip, five-year old Robert, and twenty-two-month-old Dougie.

Humphrey was an active, vocal senator, and his family usually saw him only on Sundays when he went with them to Sunday school and church at the Chevy Chase Methodist Church. He was busy on weekdays urging civil rights improvements, to the dismay of southern senators, and a repeal of the Taft-Hartley Act, to the dismay of some northern senators. Only Senator Lyndon Johnson from Texas befriended him.

In 1956, Humphrey announced he was willing to be the vice presidential candidate for the Democratic presidential nominee, Adlai Stevenson. Estes Kefauver was nominated, however, and Humphrey felt betrayed. The Republicans, Eisenhower and Nixon, won the election anyway, and Humphrey had been reelected to the Senate two years earlier, so he still had a job. He was also reelected in 1960 to the Senate.

In 1964, Senator Humphrey saw the Civil Rights Act he had sponsored win passage; the bill changed life for everyone in the United States. No longer would public restrooms, water fountains, and restaurants be segregated by race. Housing would be open to everyone, as would all schools and jobs.

When Lyndon Johnson, now President Johnson since 1963, was certain to be a candidate for president in the 1964 election, news reporters besieged Humphrey with questions about his own plans for 1964. Humphrey had not given it much thought at that time, but he began to wonder if his good friend might ask him to be his running mate.

Humphrey knew Bobby Kennedy was a Democratic favorite and that Senator Eugene McCarthy, Minnesota's other senator, was being considered. Humphrey also knew President Johnson disliked Kennedy and would never choose him on his own, and Senator McCarthy withdrew his name from consideration.

Humphrey won the nomination for vice president, and he and President Johnson were elected.

President Johnson was a complex man. He had been helpful and friendly to his vice president when they were fellow senators, but now he humiliated Humphrey in subtle ways. He chose Chief Justice Earl Warren to attend Winston Churchill's funeral in England, instead of designating his vice president to be his representative. He ordered Humphrey to stop sending him memorandum notes, and he stopped asking him to attend top-level meetings.

Vice President Humphrey was loyal by nature, and he used his considerable influence in the Senate to get many of President Johnson's Great Society bills passed. He supported President Johnson's policy on Vietnam, even after almost every American voter had decided the United States forces should leave Vietnam.

Protestors of the war staged demonstrations all around the nation; riots were frequent and some demonstrators were killed. President Johnson became afraid to leave the White House, but his vice president kept urging support for Johnson's policies in his speeches.

Finally, conditions were so bad that President Johnson decided he would not seek reelection in 1968. Vice President Humphrey and Robert F. Kennedy, the brother of the former president, were front-runners for the Democrat nomination for president, along with others, and they entered primary elections in various states. Robert Kennedy was campaigning in San Diego in May 1968 when he was also assassinated.

Hubert Humphrey was the nominee in 1968 for president, but he lost the election to Republican Richard Nixon.

Hubert and Muriel went back to Minnesota after the election, and Hubert was more discouraged about his future than he had ever been before.

In 1968, Humphrey had written a book entitled *Beyond Civil Rights* and had signed a contract for another look on foreign affairs. After returning to Minnesota, he wrote political articles for *Encyclopædia Britannica*, which paid substantial sums, and a book contract for his memoirs gave him a handsome advance payment of $70,000. He also received a Federal pension for his years in Congress.

For the first time in their married life, the Humphreys were more than financially solvent. They were almost wealthy, but Hubert felt he had to get back into politics.

Humphrey was reelected to the Senate in 1970, and his world was filled again with sunshine. He was named to his first chairmanship — it was on the Joint Economic Committee.

Skip Humphrey was elected to serve in the Minnesota Senate in 1972, and his father campaigned for him.

In 1973, Senator Humphrey was told he had bladder cancer. He endured eight painful weeks of X-ray therapy, and his condition improved.

Humphrey traveled to China in April 1974 to investigate economic conditions there, and he wrote a 756-page report on his findings for his committee.

A few months later, Humphrey took Skip with him to the World Food Conference in Rome. They went on to visit Vienna, Israel, and England before returning home.

Senator Humphrey was reelected in 1976. He had been urged to seek the Democratic nomination for president, but he declined to do so because of his health.

In September, Humphrey learned his cancer was active again and had metastasized. His bladder was removed, and he had a series of chemotherapy treatments.

After President Jimmy Carter was elected in 1976, Senator Humphrey peppered his office with memos, but in February 1977, he had to have intestinal surgery and a colostomy.

After Humphrey had recovered from surgery, President Carter invited him to come to Camp David to spend a few days. Humphrey had never been there before, and he enjoyed talking with the president about world affairs.

On January 13, 1978, Senator Hubert Humphrey lost his battle with cancer. Many famous people attended his funeral at the Presbyterian Church in St. Paul, including former presidents Nixon and Ford. Humphrey was buried in the Minneapolis Lakewood Cemetery.

Bibliography

Kearns, Doris. *Lyndon Johnson and the American Dream.* New York: Harper and Row, 1976.
Solberg, Carl. *Hubert Humphrey: A Biography.* New York: W. W. Norton, 1984.

39. Spiro Theodore (Ted) Agnew

At least some of Vice President Spiro Agnew's public troubles arose because of the militant opposition to the Vietnam War, which was still in progress when Agnew and President Richard Nixon took office. It was a time to challenge authority, as young people saw it, and they represented authority.

Spiro Agnew was born on November 9, 1918, in Baltimore, Maryland, the only son of Theodore Spiro Anagnostopoulas, a Greek immigrant. Mr. Anagnostopoulas had his name shortened legally to Agnew not long after his arrival in the United States in 1897.

Theodore Agnew first arrived in Boston, where he operated a vegetable cart while he learned English. Later he went to Baltimore and opened a restaurant, the Piccadilly, which prospered.

It was in his restaurant that Theodore met his future wife, Margaret Akers Pollard, from Bristol, Virginia. She and her husband, Dr. William P. Pollard, ate at the restaurant frequently and became Mr. Agnew's friends.

After Dr. Pollard died, Mr. Agnew and Mrs. Pollard continued their friendship, and eventually they married. She and Dr. Pollard had a son named Roy, and Spiro (called Ted) was born of her second marriage to Theodore Agnew. The two boys were always close.

Roy Pollard said his stepfather was a reader of philosophical books, and he had received his college education in Greece before he came to the United States. Theodore Agnew became interested in politics through his association with the Greek fraternal order of Ahepa (American Hellenic Educational Progressive Association), in which he was a national leader.

Young Ted attended Baltimore public schools, where he made average grades. He worked after school delivering groceries from local supermarkets and distributing advertisements for a hardware store.

Ted was not husky enough to play football on the high school team, but he gained recognition and popularity with his ability to play a piano. He played mostly by ear, but he had some lessons while he was in grammar school.

Ted was accepted at Johns Hopkins University after he graduated from high school. He studied chemistry there and meant to major in it, but when his father suffered financial reverses, Ted left college.

Spiro Ted Agnew. Reproduced from the collections of the Library of Congress.

Ted Agnew went to work at Maryland Casualty Insurance Company in Baltimore, starting as a clerk in 1939, and by 1942 he progressed to an assistant underwriter. He began studying law at Baltimore Law School at night after he left his insurance job, but he was not licensed to practice law until 1947 after he had earned a law degree from the University of Maryland.

Ted Agnew met Elinor "Judy" Judefind at Maryland Casualty, where she worked in general records. They married on May 27, 1942, after he had been commissioned a second lieutenant in Officers Candidate School at Fort Knox, Kentucky.

The newlyweds lived in an apartment off-base near Fort Knox. When he was moved to Fort Campbell, Kentucky, they had to find another apartment.

In March 1944, Agnew was sent overseas to become a member of the Tenth Armored Division of the United States Army. Later that year he joined the Fifty-fourth Armored Infantry Battalion in France.

Agnew and his fellow soldiers were involved in combat and supply mainte-nance in northern France in the Battle of the Bulge. They crossed the Siegfried Line and went on through Germany under enemy fire or in imminent danger of attack most of the time. He received a Bronze Star and four battle stars after the war was over.

When he returned home, Agnew was determined to settle down and finish his law training, which he did in night classes at the University of Maryland, with financial aid from the G.I. Bill of Rights. He worked during the daytime at the law firm of Smith and Barrett as a law-clerk trainee.

Ted and Judy Agnew's first child, a daughter named Pamela, was born be-fore he went to Europe. Over time, they had three more children — daughters Susan and Kim and son Randy. With his increasing responsibilities, Ted Agnew knew he had to be dedicated to his career training.

The Agnews bought a small house in Lutherville, Maryland, in 1947, and after his job ended at Smith and Barrett, he got a job as an insurance investigator and claims adjuster with Lumbermens Mutual Casualty Company. The job only paid $3,600 a year, and soon he moved on to work as assistant personnel man-ager of a large supermarket chain.

Agnew was still struggling to get started in his new life and career when the Korean War started in 1950, and he was recalled to active duty with the army. He was somewhat bitter about being recalled, feeling he had done more during World War II than many other American men. He finished his retraining, but was soon released to go home.

In 1955, Agnew entered into a law partnership with attorneys Samuel Kimmel and George W. White, Jr., in Towson, Maryland. He and Judy bought a row-house in the Loch Raven Village development and became involved in com-munity affairs. They joined the country club, and Ted was appointed a member of the zoning commission, where he gained respect for his fair-minded work with the commission.

In 1962, Agnew was elected county executive of Baltimore County on the Republican ticket, and in 1966 he was elected the governor of Maryland.

Agnew was an able and effective governor. He managed to get laws passed to combat water pollution and to improve law enforcement, roads, and schools. He won praise nationwide for sponsoring the first law enacted by a border state to prohibit racial discrimination in housing.

Agnew decided in 1967 that Nelson Rockefeller would be a good choice for

president of the United States, and he began campaigning for his election. Rockefeller insisted he did not want to be president, however, and Agnew switched his
loyalty and efforts toward electing Richard Nixon in 1968.

When Nixon was nominated to be the Republican candidate for president,
he chose Ted Agnew to be his vice president. They won the election, receiving
43.4% of the popular vote and 301 electoral votes out of a 538 total.

Agnew's friends and relatives of Greek descent had supported the Republican campaign vigorously with both money and hard work. Agnew felt his contributions to the winning were substantial, but President Nixon ignored his vice
president and never included him in significant meetings. Vice President Agnew
got the message that Nixon did not value his efforts. "I first began to feel isolated
from the really important Nixon decisions after our 1968 victory," he said. They
never became friends.

Ted and Judy lived in the Sheraton Park Apartments in Washington while
he was vice president.

Vice President Agnew became irate every time he saw young people demon-
strating in protest against the Vietnam War. He had gone willingly to serve his
country, and the sight of wildly dressed, unkempt demonstrators carrying a Viet
Cong flag down Pennsylvania Avenue in Washington dismayed and shocked him.

"Suppose this had been World War II, and the demonstrators had been
marching with a Nazi swastika banner," he said. "They would not have evoked
sympathy for their compassion, but would have been justly condemned for being
traitors to their country."

Although Agnew heard rumors that President Nixon planned to drop him
from the ticket in 1972, it did not happen and they were reelected by 60.7% of
the popular vote.

The future for Vice President Agnew had never looked brighter. President
Nixon allowed him to attend some policy meetings, and the vice president was
put in charge of arranging the bicentennial celebration of the nation's beginning.
He appeared to be the logical successor to President Nixon in the 1976 election.

Ted and Judy Agnew moved to a new home in Kenwood, Maryland, in June
1973, just after his second term as vice president began.

In August that year, the Justice Department made public an investigation it
had been conducting into the business affairs of Lester Matz, a professional con-
sulting engineer from Baltimore County, Maryland, and Jerome Wolff, chairman
of the State Roads Commission in Baltimore. Both men had been charged with
paying kickbacks to local government officials in return for being awarded lucrative contracts to do work for the state government.

Matz and John C. Childs, a member of the Matz Engineering firm, had also
been accused of paying fake bonuses to their employees. Both men claimed Vice
President Ted Agnew was the highest-ranking official who had received kickbacks for his aid and silence during the time he was county executive and later
when he was governor of Maryland.

Agnew denied all their claims vehemently. He said Matz and Wolff had approached him earlier to ask him to get the United States attorney to drop the charges against them. He said he told them he could not do such a thing, and they threatened to ruin his reputation if he did not do as they asked. He admitted all three men charged had made financial contributions to his various political campaigns, but he insisted he had never been paid kickbacks by anyone.

Actually no proof was ever presented that Agnew had received kickbacks, but the damage to his reputation was done. Between the Watergate controversy involving President Nixon and the financial wrongdoing allegations against Vice President Agnew, the Democrats were ready to dance in the streets.

Vice President Agnew was frantic to have his reputation restored. He asked for an appointment with President Nixon, but was refused. Chief of Staff Alexander Haig and Attorney General Elliot Richardson began urging Agnew to resign. At last he got in to talk with President Nixon, but Nixon gave him no help or encouragement.

Haig and Richardson kept insisting Agnew should resign as vice president. Finally, he agreed to plead nolo contendere to a tax evasion charge, and he did resign on October 10, 1973. Matz and Wolff never received any sort of punishment.

News reporters had harassed Agnew unmercifully during the entire period of investigation. When his half-brother, Roy Pollard, died and Agnew attended his funeral, reporters yelled questions at him as he entered the church.

On October 18, 1973, Attorney General Richardson also resigned, after refusing to fire Special Prosecutor Archibald Cox, who was in charge of the Watergate investigation.

President Nixon chose Senator Gerald Ford to replace Vice President Agnew, and Ford was subsequently confirmed by both houses of Congress.

Ted Agnew was convicted of tax evasion, for which he was fined $10,000 and given a three-year probationary sentence. In 1974 he was disbarred from the practice of law.

In 1976, Agnew wrote a novel entitled *The Canfield Decision*. In October 1977, Ted and Judy Agnew moved to California to live in Rancho Mirage, only a few miles from Palm Springs. Ted Agnew works as an international business consultant.

Bibliography

Agnew, Spiro T. *Go Quietly or Else*. New York: William Morrow, 1980.
Marsh, Robert. *Agnew: The Unexamined Man*. New York: M. Evans, 1971.
Witcover, Jules. *White Knight: The Rise of Spiro Agnew*. New York: Random House, 1972.

40. Gerald Rudolph Ford, Jr.

Early in 1973, with the Democrats in firm control of the U.S. House of Representatives, Gerald Ford, Jr., was discouraged about his chance for reelection to the House. Before the year ended, Ford became vice president of the United States when Vice President Ted Agnew resigned. Even more incredible, eight months later Gerald Ford became president when President Richard Nixon resigned. Ford's meteoric advancement was unprecedented in the history of the United States.

Gerald Ford was named Leslie Lynch King, Jr., when he was born in Omaha, Nebraska, on July 14, 1913. He was named for his father, who divorced his wife a short time after his son was born and severed contact with the two of them.

When Gerald's mother, Mrs. Dorothy Gardner King, remarried, her new husband, Gerald Rudolf Ford, took the child as his own and adopted him. The little boy wanted to be named for his stepfather, and his name was changed legally, but Gerald Jr. changed the spelling of his new middle name.

In time three little Ford brothers named Tom, Dick, and Jim joined Gerald in the family. Gerald was now called Jerry, and he still loved his stepfather.

Mr. Ford was a kind father, but he expected and got obedience from his sons. He led a Boy Scout troop, played ball and golf with the boys, and took them hiking and fishing.

Life was pleasant for the Ford family, and when Mr. Ford started a new paint and varnish company in 1929, there was no reason to doubt it would be successful. The family moved to a fine new home in East Grand Rapids, Michigan, and Jerry was the star of the South High School football team.

Then came the stock market crash later that year, and the Ford family lost their new home and all their savings and almost lost the paint and varnish company.

Jerry was sixteen, and he got permission from the South High School board to finish high school there, even though he and his family had been forced to move out of the area. They granted him permission to continue in school, but it meant commuting fifty minutes by bus each way every day.

Jerry Ford made good, but not outstanding, grades in school, but they were

Gerald R. Ford. Reproduced from the collections of the Library of Congress.

high enough to qualify him to enter the University of Michigan, where he got a football scholarship.

Because Ford was an outstanding football player, he was offered a job with the Green Bay Packers and the Detroit Lions to play professional football after his graduation from college, but he turned down the offers.

To get spending money in college, Ford had to work as a dishwasher in the fraternity house of Delta Kappa Epsilon, where he was a member. He also worked as a waiter in the dining room for interns at the university hospital.

When Jerry graduated from the University of Michigan, he decided he wanted to enter Yale Law School. As a first step toward his goal, he got a job as assistant coach of the Yale football team and as coach of the boxing team; he stayed with both teams from 1935 to 1940.

Law school officials feared Jerry would not be able to manage to study law sufficiently while working full-time, but in 1938 they agreed to let him take two courses, which he passed. In the spring of 1939, he entered law school on a full-time basis.

On December 7, 1941, Jerry and his good friend, Philip Buchen, opened their own law office in Grand Rapids. They survived on client referrals from other firms and court-assigned clients, who were unable to pay for a lawyer.

After the attack on Pearl Harbor by the Japanese, Jerry joined the navy on April 20, 1942, where he was commissioned an ensign. He worked at first as a physical trainer for aviation cadets, but soon he was assigned to the *Monterey*, an aircraft carrier, and was involved in heavy naval action in the South Pacific theater of operations.

After forty-seven months of active duty, Jerry returned home to his family in December 1945. When he was formally discharged from the navy, he joined the Grand Rapids law firm of Butterfield, Keeney, and Amberg.

Late in 1947, Jerry Ford met and started dating Betty Bloomer Warren, recently divorced. Jerry did not tell Betty he was planning to run for a seat in the United States House of Representatives when he proposed marriage to her in February 1948. She accepted his proposal, and they planned their wedding for October 15 that year. Soon they were both heavily involved in campaign activities, so much so that Betty wondered if Jerry would even have time to get married.

Their wedding took place as planned, but Jerry did forget to change his dusty shoes he had worn that morning while campaigning, and his mother was appalled by his appearance as he walked down the aisle.

On November 2, Jerry Ford won the election, and as Betty wrote in her book, *The Times of My Life*, "We came to Washington for two years and stayed for twenty-eight." Plainly, her new husband had voter appeal.

As a representative, Ford supported President Harry Truman and gained a high regard for him. He voted for Truman's Point Four program to aid underdeveloped nations and his requests for increases in defense spending. World War II was still on everyone's mind.

In 1954 the Fords had a new home built in Alexandria, Virginia, near Washington. Betty did not want their children shifted back and forth between schools in the Washington area and Michigan, so they decided to make Alexandria their permanent home while Jerry served in Congress.

As time went on, there were four Ford children to go to school. Michael was born on March 15, 1950; John, called Jack, was born on March 16, 1952; Steven on May 19, 1956, and daughter Susan on July 6, 1957.

When President John F. Kennedy took office, Representative Ford found himself defending the military disaster at the Bay of Pigs in Cuba on April 17, 1961, during which invading American-backed Cuban forces were soundly defeated. President Eisenhower had conceived and developed the invasion with the Central Intelligence Agency before his term ended, and since the invasion originally was a Republican plan, Jerry Ford did not feel he could criticize President Kennedy when the operation was a failure.

Ford also supported President Kennedy in September 1961, when a proposal was made to make major cuts in the president's foreign aid program. Representative Ford openly and actively opposed the proposal.

In 1965, Ford was named House minority leader, and he served in that position until 1973. He became known for his special abilities in budgetary matters, which he utilized fully before and during the Korean War and the required rapid expanse of defense in the years following.

When Lyndon Johnson became president after Kennedy's assassination, House Minority Leader Ford found the flood of bills President Johnson sent to the House to be overwhelming. Ford and his fellow Republicans barely had time to read and absorb their meaning, and they had no opportunity to prepare alternative proposals.

Ford became increasingly vocal about his unhappiness with the growing United States involvement in Vietnam. He was humiliated by the passage of President Johnson's Appalachian Development program after his own frantic attempts to get it amended seventeen times. Ford decided to focus on replacing House Democrats with Republicans.

In the 1966 election, he got results; the Republicans won three seats in the Senate and forty-seven in the House. There were now a total of 187 Republican House members.

By 1968, Republicans were hopeful the growing resentment of the voters about the Vietnam War would increase their numbers in Congress. President Johnson had recently requested a ten percent income tax surcharge to pay the costs of the war and had announced 45,000 more servicemen would be going to the Asian theater, bringing the total there to 525,000 military personnel.

Jerry Ford made a major speech to his fellow House members on the proposals, in which he asked: "Why are we pulling our best punches in Vietnam? . . . Vietnam . . . has become an American war. . . . Recent surveys show that more than half our people are not satisfied with the way the war in Vietnam is being conducted. . . . Why are we talking about money when we should be talking about men? I believe ending the war must have the highest of national priorities — now."

Ford's critics said that if United States troops were withdrawn, China and the Soviet Union would enter the war to help the North Vietnamese.

President Johnson announced he would not seek reelection in 1968, and at the Republican Convention at Miami Beach in August, Ford accused Johnson of having "blundered into a war in Vietnam."

Former vice president Richard Nixon was chosen the Republican candidate for the presidency on the first ballot, and many people thought Gerald Ford would be named the candidate for vice president. Nixon wanted Maryland governor Spiro Ted Agnew, however.

If Representative Ford expected an immediate improvement in government policy and activities when Nixon and Agnew were elected, he was disappointed. Not only did the Vietnam War continue on and on until July 1976, when South Vietnam was overrun by North Vietnam, both Vice President Agnew and President Nixon became involved in scandals questioning their honesty and integrity.

By the time Agnew had resigned in October 1973 and President Nixon continued to protest his innocence in the Watergate affair, Jerry Ford was discouraged about Republican chances to win more offices anywhere.

Ford was pleased when President Nixon asked him to become vice president to replace Agnew. He became Vice President Ford in December 1973. A scant eight months later he became president when Richard Nixon resigned on August 9, 1974.

Between the angry protests about the Vietnam War and all the political turmoil in Washington, President Ford decided it was time to heal the country. Before that could be achieved, President Nixon's problems had to be settled, as did the question of amnesty for young men who had fled the United States rather than serve in the war.

Therefore, on September 8, 1974, President Ford granted a full pardon to President Nixon and offered clemency to all the draft evaders if they would agree to do two years of public service work and swear their allegiance to the United States. Some exiles refused the offer, but most accepted.

President Ford went to Pinehurst, North Carolina, the next day to play golf. He admitted the adverse public reaction to his pardon for Nixon had surprised him and said ruefully: "I spent much of today trying to get a hole in one. Tomorrow I'll be back in Washington trying to get out of one!"

In 1975 the leaders of the United States and the Soviet Union signed agreements in Helsinki designed to ease tensions between their two countries. The Soviets agreed to relax travel restrictions to their country, and the United States agreed not to interfere in internal affairs of Communist-bloc nations.

When Democrat Jimmy Carter defeated incumbent President Ford in the 1976 election, Jerry was disappointed, but Betty was philosophical. She said, "I'd been through many elections with Jerry, I knew someone had to win and someone had to lose, and we lost."

After his inauguration on January 30, 1977, President Carter said, "I want to thank my predecessor for all he has done to heal our land." Ford appreciated that statement.

After they attended Carter's inauguration, Air Force One took Betty and Jerry to Pebble Beach, California, where Jerry played in the Bing Crosby Golf Tournament. They went to live in a fifteen-room hacienda in Rancho Mirage, eleven miles from Palm Springs.

Ford worked as a consultant for various companies and served on the board of trustees for others. He wrote his memoirs, *A Time to Heal*, and became co-chairman of People for the American Way, which seeks to counterbalance the influence of the Moral Majority.

Young Michael Ford studied for the ministry and later became director of student affairs at Wake Forest University in Winston Salem, North Carolina.

Jack Ford has worked as a journalist and in public relations. He has always been interested in politics.

Steven Ford is an actor and has appeared in both television and movies. He was a regular performer on the daytime serial "The Young and the Restless" in the 1980s.

Susan Ford has worked as a photographer and was a partner for a time in a private security company with her husband, Charles Vance, in Washington, D.C.

Betty Ford had a mastectomy for cancer in 1974 when she was first lady, and she later battled drug addiction that led her to establish in September 1982 the Betty Ford Center for the treatment of patients with alcohol or drug addition. Her business venture is in better health than its founder. On November 20, 1987, Betty had to have quadruple bypass heart surgery, described as a "preventive measure."

Jerry Ford continues to play golf and enjoy life. With his pleasant, affable approach to living, he always will. The Gerald R. Ford Museum in Grand Rapids, Michigan, was dedicated on September 18, 1981.

Bibliography

Ford, Betty, with Chris Chase. *The Times of My Life.* New York: Ballantine Books, 1978.
― ― ― . *Betty: A Glad Awakening.* New York: Jove Books, 1988.
terHorst, Jerald F. *Gerald Ford and the Future of the Presidency.* New York: Third Press of Joseph Okpaku, 1974.

41. Nelson Aldrich Rockefeller

Although Nelson Rockefeller had many more of life's rewards than most people will ever see, one prize eluded him — the presidency of the United States. It wasn't because he did not try to get elected to the country's highest position. He just never seemed to choose the right time to enter the race.

Nelson was the second son of Abigail Aldrich and John D. Rockefeller, Jr. He was born on July 8, 1908, at their summer home in Bar Harbor, Maine. His father was rich from the moment of his own birth, and Nelson was also. The Rockefeller wealth came from ownership of Standard Oil Company and other business interests.

Mrs. Rockefeller was the daughter of a United States senator, Nelson Aldrich, for whom she named her new baby. She was both an artist and art patron and was known as "Abby" to her friends and relatives.

Nelson was the one of her children who shared her love of art, and they were always close. Nelson's father was a stern, distant parent who always demanded correct behavior from his children, while Abby was vivacious and loving. Nelson respected his father and adored his mother.

Nelson grew up in a loving family with three brothers, John, Laurance, and Winthrop, and one sister, Abby, or "Babs." They had a family musical group in which Nelson played cello, his father and John played violins, and Babs or Laurance played the piano. During these years Winthrop was still a toddler.

Sundays were observed strictly, reserved for rest and attending Sunday school and church. The children attended Lincoln School for their education. It was sponsored by Columbia University Teachers' College. The teachers there used an approach of democratic discipline, with students formulating a code of conduct. The students had diverse backgrounds.

All the Rockefeller children did well in school except Nelson, who could never learn to read well. He complained the letters "danced around." He was dyslexic, but he studied more and worked harder than his classmates, and he managed to earn passing grades.

When he reached the age of fourteen, Nelson discovered girls. He was a handsome young man and a good dancer, so he had no trouble acquiring girlfriends. He attended six parties at Christmas that year.

Nelson A. Rockefeller. Reproduced from the collections of the Library of Congress.

Abby Rockefeller was worried about Nelson, and she asked the headmaster at the Lincoln School if he thought Nelson should be sent to a boarding school. Instead, the headmaster put Nelson in a higher grade so he would have to do more work.

As he worked his way through high school, Nelson decided he would like to go to college at Princeton, but his grades were too low. He was so serious he even cut back on dating, a great sacrifice for him, to give himself more time to study and improve his grades.

Nelson Rockefeller's efforts were successful. He was admitted to Dartmouth, which had become his choice by the time he finished high school.

When he was still in college, Rockefeller's romantic attention turned to Mary ("Tod") Todhunter Clark, the daughter of a wealthy Philadelphia lawyer. They had been friends since childhood, and both of Nelson's parents were fond of her.

On June 23, 1930, a few days after his graduation from Dartmouth, Nelson and Tod were married in Bala, with a reception in Cynwyd, the fashionable Philadelphia suburb that was the home of the bride. They took a nine months' long honeymoon cruise around the world, with Nelson making some business calls for his father as they traveled.

Nelson and Tod's first son, Rodman, was born April 30, 1931, followed by Ann and Steven; their twins, Michael and Mary, were born in 1938.

Rockefeller went to work first in the family business office, but he was extremely bored there. After he got a real estate broker's license in 1933, he went to work getting tenants for the Rockefeller Center. He had all the zeal of a used car salesman, and in 1938 his father named Nelson the president of Rockefeller Center.

Nelson Rockefeller invested in Creole Oil Company, a subsidiary of Standard Oil, in Venezuela, where he and Tod lived for a few months.

Rockefeller was involved also in the Art and Architecture Committee of Rockefeller Center. In 1933 he commissioned Mexican artist Diego Rivera to paint a large mural on the wall opposite the main entrance to the lobby. Rivera's fee was $21,500. The artist painted a portrait of the Russian leader Lenin in the mural, as well as other propaganda objects. Rockefeller paid Rivera his commission, and then he had the mural painted over, despite the protests of art lovers who made an effort to save it.

Abby Rockefeller died in 1948, and Nelson was deeply grieved by his mother's death. His father remarried three years later to Martha Baird Allen, the widow of one of his schoolmates at Brown University.

Nelson Rockefeller first entered politics when President Franklin Roosevelt appointed him co-ordinator of interAmerican affairs; later he became assistant secretary of state for Latin America, a post he kept until 1944.

Rockefeller served in President Truman's administration on a committee advising on the Point Four program, which was designed to bring technological advances to underdeveloped countries. In President Eisenhower's administration, Rockefeller became the first undersecretary of the Department of Health, Education, and Welfare.

Nelson Rockefeller was elected governor of New York in 1958, and by this time his marriage to Tod was showing signs of strains.

In 1961 their son Michael died in New Guinea, where he had gone to study Stone Age tribesmen in the Asmat. He was an avid student of anthropology, and his untimely death was a severe blow to the whole family.

In November of that year, Nelson and Tod Rockefeller separated. Nelson had fallen in love with a neighbor's wife. The neighbor, Dr. James "Robin" Murphy, was a microbiologist in medical research at the Rockefeller Institute. Dr. Murphy and his wife, the former Margaretta Fitler, had four children, and when they separated, he demanded and got custody of them.

Nelson and Margaretta, called "Happy," were married on May 4, 1963. They had two sons named Mark and Nelson Jr.

Rockefeller wanted the Republican nomination for president in the 1960 election, but the best offer he got was from nominee Richard Nixon to be a candidate with him for vice president. He refused the offer.

In 1964, Rockefeller was again offered the vice presidential nomination, with Barry Goldwater as the presidential candidate, and in 1968 Democrat Hubert Humphrey asked Rockefeller to run with him for vice president. Again he refused. During all these years, he was serving as New York's governor.

Nelson Rockefeller was one of New York's best governors. He loved solving problems, and New york was a fertile area for his talents. He built up the educational system from a group of small teachers colleges to the State University of New York with an enrolled total of 235,000 full-time students occupying seventy-two college campuses.

Rockefeller also enjoyed having buildings constructed, and the Nelson A. Rockefeller Empire State Plaza was one of his projects. It is known locally as the South Mall, and it contains state offices, the largest museum and the largest state library in the United States, and many other occupants.

During his years as governor, Rockefeller was instrumental in the building of hundreds of water treatment plants. He worked to prevent the collapse of public transportation, added more than fifty state parks, and kept an active Department of Environmental Conservation. His Urban Development Corporation built a record number of homes for New York's poor and disadvantaged citizens.

In September 1971, Governor Rockefeller came under criticism for his handling of a riot in the Attica State Prison. When negotiations failed to end the uprising, he sent one thousand policemen to regain control. More than forty inmates were killed, but it seemed a logical move. His critics could offer no better suggestion to end the takeover of the prison.

After trying to get the Republican nomination for president for so many years, Rockefeller decided he would accept an appointment as President Nixon's vice president when Ted Agnew resigned. It was not offered to him, however, and Senator Gerald Ford became vice president instead.

After President Nixon resigned, President Ford did ask Rockefeller to serve with him as vice president, and he accepted. His nomination was confirmed by Congress on December 19, 1974.

Vice President Rockefeller had no authority to remake the government or solve its many problems, and he was not content. "I go to funerals. I go to earthquakes," he said scornfully.

That was not really all he did. He led an investigation of the Central Intelligence Agency, and he served on the Water Quality Commission, the Committee on the Right to Privacy, and other committees. He planned and worked out ideas for government projects that never materialized.

Nelson and Happy were the first to live in the vice president's official residence in Washington. They hosted nine housewarming parties for more than three thousand guests during the first month. They spent only one night in the house, however, preferring to live in a house they already owned on Foxhall Road. Happy spent most of her time in New York while Nelson was vice president.

President Gerald Ford decided to drop Rockefeller from the ticket in the 1976 presidential race. Before he could do so, Rockefeller learned of his plans and wrote President Ford a letter in which he said, "After much thought, I have decided further I do not wish to enter into your consideration for the upcoming Republican Vice Presidential nominee."

Democrat Jimmy Carter defeated President Ford anyway, and Rockefeller would not have been vice president again.

Nelson Rockefeller returned to his private life and art interests after his term as vice president ended. He compiled pictures of the art treasures owned by family members and planned to have them published. He planned to offer reproductions of art objects for sale to the public through exhibits and catalogs.

Rockefeller was working on a book about his art treasures when he suffered a sudden fatal heart attack on January 27, 1979.

Funeral services were held in Riverside Interdenominational Church in New York, whose construction had been financed by Nelson's father, John D. Rockefeller, Jr., many years before. Former President Ford and President Jimmy Carter attended the services in addition to hundreds of relatives and friends.

Bibliography

Kert, Bernice. *Abby Aldrich Rockefeller*. New York: Random House, 1993.

Persico, Joseph E. *The Imperial Rockefeller: A Biography of Nelson A. Rockefeller*. New York: Simon & Schuster, 1982.

Rodgers, William. *Rockefeller's Follies*. New York: Stein and Day, 1966.

42. Walter "Fritz" Mondale

Walter Mondale, called "Fritz" from birth, will be remembered more for his legislative efforts in the Senate to extend civil rights and aid senior citizens and migrant workers than for his service as vice president in the administration of President Jimmy Carter. Mondale was a hard-working, dedicated vice president, but the administration he served was plagued with record-breaking inflation, hostages held captive in Iran for months, and other national problems which eclipsed his efforts.

On January 5, 1928, Fritz Mondale was born in Ceylon, Minnesota, to the Reverend Theodore Mondale and his second wife, the former Claribel Cowan. The Reverend Mondale was a Methodist minister, and the family was very poor. They ate well because the congregation at their church gave them garden produce and meat from their farms, but they had little money.

Fritz had four brothers who supplemented family income by delivering newspapers, working in grocery stores, and helping harvest crops of neighboring farmers. Claribel Mondale gave music lessons to children living nearby.

Fritz spent most of his childhood years in Elmore, Minnesota, where the Reverend Mondale was assigned a church in 1937. Fritz graduated from the local high school in 1946. His father suffered a serious heart attack that same year, so Fritz knew any further education would have to depend on his own efforts.

Fritz Mondale chose to attend Macalester College in St. Paul, a Presbyterian-founded college. In 1946, veterans of World War II were entering colleges in record numbers because their expenses were paid under the G.I. Bill passed in 1944. In fact, in 1946, 70% of the students at Macalester were veterans.

Macalester had a new president, Dr. Charles Turck, who emphasized study of the larger world and its problems. A United Nations flag flew on campus, and important public figures such as Vice President Henry Wallace and Mayor Hubert Humphrey of Minneapolis made speeches to the students.

Mondale was intrigued by these well-known politicians, and when Hubert Humphrey ran for a Senate seat in 1948, Mondale organized a local Students for Democratic Action group on campus to aid him in his campaign. Mondale was not as enthusiastic about the campaigns of incumbent President Harry Truman and Vice President Wallace.

Walter "Fritz" Mondale. Reproduced from the collections of the Library of Congress.

All the Democratic candidates Mondale supported won, and he decided politics would be his choice for a job. His father died in 1949, and Mondale did not have money to continue in college anyway, so he knew he would have to go to work.

Bill Shore, a fellow campaign worker, told Mondale about an opening as secretary in the national office of Students for Democratic Action in Washington, D.C. Mondale was hired, and he and Shore rented a basement apartment located near the White House for $50 a month. They soon joined a student group living in a large house in Georgetown.

As funds dried up and workers drifted away to other jobs, Mondale found his new job disappointing. He had believed President Truman could bring about needed changes in government, but one by one Truman's proposals were defeated by the Republicans and Southern Democrats in Congress.

Mondale saved money so he could return to college, and he reentered in 1950, this time at the University of Minnesota. He graduated cum laude the next year with a degree in political science.

The Korean War had started in 1950, and Mondale decided he would volunteer for army service; the government would then pay his way in law school after he was discharged. He was inducted a few weeks after his graduation from college. His assignment was to serve as an information officer for inductees in basic training.

In 1953, Corporal Mondale returned to the University of Minnesota to enroll in law school. His mother had moved to St. Paul following her husband's death, and she and Fritz lived together. On weekends he worked as a recruiter for the Democratic-Farmer-Labor party.

In 1955, Fritz Mondale met Joan Adams, daughter of the chaplain at Macalester College. Even though they had been students at the same time years earlier, their paths had never before crossed. Joan was interested in art instead of politics, even though she had chosen history as her college major.

Fritz and Joan began a whirlwind romance during which he visited her workplace at the Minneapolis Institute of Arts, and she taught him to ski. Skiing became their favorite recreational activity.

The two were married on December 27, 1955, eight weeks after they met. Her father, the Reverend John Maxwell Adams, officiated at the wedding in the Macalester College Chapel. Fritz was twenty-seven, and Joan was twenty-five.

The newlyweds went to live in an apartment in southeast Minneapolis while Fritz completed his last year of law and Joan continued to work at the Institute of Arts. He completed his course work in May 1956 and was admitted to the bar later that summer. He joined the law firm which included Governor Orville Freeman of Minnesota as one of its partners.

Mondale was assigned to handle lesser legal chores as a newer attorney, and he became dissatisfied. After eighteen months there, he and a classmate, Harry MacLaughlin, started their own practice.

Joan Mondale left her job when she became pregnant, and their first child, Teddy, was born in 1958. The couple had two more children — Eleanor Jane, born in 1960, and William, born in 1963.

In November 1959, the Mondales bought their first house on Park Avenue in Minneapolis. A few months later, Mondale entered politics seriously when he was elected attorney general of Minnesota with the endorsement of his former law associate, Governor Freeman. The governor had appointed him to complete the unexpired term of Attorney General Miles Lord when Lord retired, but Mondale was elected to the position in his own right in 1960.

Attorney General Mondale zeroed in on consumer fraud as one of his top priorities. He successfully prosecuted a furnace company that sent phony repairmen to homes, where they told the homeowner the furnace was a "deathtrap" and should be replaced by a high-priced model.

In another case Mondale forced Family Publications Service to change their telephone solicitation technique in which they claimed to be offering a buyer two magazines for the price of one, which was untrue.

Mondale became a favorite with voters, who perceived him as a protector of their rights and interests, and he won reelection easily.

In 1964, Mondale was named to complete the unexpired term of Senator Hubert Humphrey when Humphrey left to campaign for vice president with President Lyndon Johnson. Mondale was elected to the Senate in his own right in 1966 and was reelected in 1972.

Senator Mondale worked diligently to improve working conditions for migrant farm workers and to eliminate discrimination in housing, and he voted for bills to aid older people and children. The one Democratic-endorsed activity he did not condone was the war in Vietnam. He thought it was impossible for the United States forces to win, and he urged a unilateral unconditional halt to the bombing on September 17, 1968.

Mondale was uncomfortable with the liberal factions in the Democratic party that approved of gay rights, abortion, and the legalization of marijuana. He believed these issues were divisive to the party.

Unlike many of his fellow senators, Mondale had no savings or family wealth, and his annual salary of $44,500 for his Senate duties was his family's main income, except for fees he received for speeches.

Fritz and Joan sacrificed to send Ted and Eleanor to Georgetown Day School and William to St. Albans when they learned the public schools were of poor quality and contained some violent students.

Joan Mondale joined local civic groups, served as a tour guide at the National Gallery of Art, and wrote an art book for children entitled *Politics in Art*, which was published in 1972.

While events occurring during President Nixon's administration led Senator Mondale to believe the Democrats could win back the presidency in 1976, citizen confidence in government was eroding and many social programs had not proved as effective as their promoters had promised.

Jimmy Carter, governor of Georgia, made an excellent race in primaries around the country, and most Democrats believed he would be the nominee for president in 1976. They were correct, and Carter interviewed several possible vice presidential candidates before deciding to choose Senator Mondale.

Carter and Mondale were the victors in an extremely close race, winning 297 electoral votes over incumbent President Gerald Ford's 241 votes.

President Carter, determined he would give his vice president an active role in his administration, made Mondale second in command for nuclear weapons deployment and control. He was assigned an office in the White House, instead of in the Executive Office Building where other vice presidents had been assigned offices, and Mondale and Carter began making joint decisions on cabinet appointments.

On January 20, 1977, Fritz Mondale took the oath of office as vice president, and Jimmy Carter was inaugurated as president.

Joan Mondale was known as "Joan of Art" in Washington because of her success in reactivating the Federal Council on the Arts and Humanities in 1977, for which she served as an honorary chairperson. She managed to persuade the General Service Administration to increase money spent on art in federal buildings, and she worked to stimulate public interest in art at museums and exhibits all over the United States.

As vice president, Mondale was a strong and vocal supporter of human rights in all countries, especially those involved in United States affairs, whether by receiving direct aid or in peace negotiations. He disagreed with President Carter's decision to return the control of the Panama Canal to the government of Panama, his insistence that the Jews were the cause of continuing disruption of the peace process in the middle East, and his indiscriminate firings of many of his cabinet members in 1979.

President Carter faced difficult problems in his reelection bid in 1980 because sixty-three Americans were being held hostage by the Iranian government, there was record-breaking inflation of almost 20% per year, and a cut of $13 billion in social programs such as food stamps and child health had been proposed.

Ronald Reagan, the Republican nominee for president, beat President Carter decisively in the 1980 election, winning 489 electoral votes to Carter's 49.

Before leaving office as the vice president, Mondale told his friends and family he planned to run for president in 1984, and he was nominated that year.

In the 1984 election, however, incumbent President Reagan received 525 electoral votes, the most received by any candidate in United States history, while Mondale only received 13. Mondale only carried his home state of Minnesota and the District of Columbia. His campaign was notable for having the first woman to be nominated as vice president — Representative Geraldine Ferraro of New York.

In September 1987, Fritz and Joan Mondale moved back to Minneapolis, where he went to work for the law firm of Dorsey and Whitney. The former vice president questioned himself and others about what mistakes the Democrats had made in recent elections to cause such overwhelming Republican victories.

Mondale has been serving as ambassador to Japan during President Bill Clinton's administration.

Bibliography

Gillon, Steven M. *The Democrats' Dilemma: Walter F. Mondale and the Liberal Legacy.*
  New York: Columbia University Press, 1992.
Lewis, Finlay. *Mondale: Portrait of an American Politician.* New York: Harper Brothers,
  1980.

43. George Herbert Walker Bush

George H. W. Bush had always felt a compulsion to serve his country from his days as a navy pilot in World War II, when he served in the Pacific theater of operations, to his eventual service as president of the United States. In between, he served as United States ambassador to China, director of the Central Intelligence Agency, a representative from Texas in the United States House of Representatives, ambassador to the United Nations, and vice president during the two administrations of President Ronald Reagan.

This distinguished, accomplished statesman was reared in a home where his parents emphasized duty, self-denial, and respect for elders and governmental authority.

George Bush was born on June 12, 1924, in Milton, Massachusetts, to businessman Prescott Bush and his wife, the former Dorothy Walker. The baby was named for his maternal grandfather, who was president of the Brown Brothers, Harriman Company, a highly successful investment business.

Prescott Bush served as an excellent role model for all his sons, being a devoted family man as well as a prosperous partner in his father-in-law's company in New York City.

Prescott had served in the United States Army in the First World War, where he held the rank of captain, and his children enjoyed hearing stories of his wartime experiences. During World War II, he led the campaign for the organization of the USO, which provided entertainment for men in uniform. In later years he was elected to represent Connecticut in the United States Senate, where he held office from 1952 to 1962.

Dorothy Walker Bush was an avid tennis player, who emphasized sportsmanship to her children, which included fair play, decency, and courtesy. Her children adored her.

Young George grew up in Greenwich, Connecticut, where he attended school first at Greenwich Country Day School. Summers were spent in Kennebunkport, Maine, in the Walker family ten-room vacation home. In later years an unpretentious cottage was built nearby for Dorothy and Prescott and their five children, Prescott Jr., George, Jonathan, William, and Nancy.

In 1936, when George was twelve, he entered Phillips Academy, a college-

George H. Bush. Reproduced from the collections of the Library of Congress.

preparatory school in Andover, Massachusetts. Here stress was placed on learning the classics, mathematics, and physical fitness. Culture was promoted by studies of art and music.

It was in Andover, as the school is called familiarly, that George Bush developed his interest in serving humanity. Graduates of such schools both in England and the United States usually assume leadership roles in adult life.

George graduated in 1942 from Andover, a year late, as a result of a serious staphylococcus infection he got in his arm, which resulted in a long-term hospitalization. There were no antibiotics available to fight such infections at the time. World War II had begun for the United States a few months earlier, and when George heard of the Japanese attack on Pearl Harbor on December 7, 1941, he made up his mind to join in the war effort as soon as he graduated.

It was at a Christmas dance at the Greenwich Country Club, a few days later, that he met Barbara Pierce, and he fell in love. Barbara was a student at Ashley Hall, a small preparatory school in Charleston, South Carolina. She had come home for the holidays also. She was just sixteen and in her junior year at Ashley Hall.

Their romance began then and never flagged, although much of it was conducted through letters to each other. Barbara did attend his senior prom with George.

George Bush enlisted in the United States Navy in June 1942, and when he qualified as a navy pilot in June 1943, at age nineteen, he was the youngest man ever to get his wings. Barbara visited him once while he was in preflight training in Chapel Hill, North Carolina.

Barbara graduated in 1943 and entered Smith College in Northampton, Massachusetts, that September. Future first lady Nancy Davis (later Reagan) happened to be in the senior class at Smith, but she and Barbara never met there.

With the true optimism of youth, Barbara and George had plans to marry on December 19, 1944, but he had the misfortune of having his plane shot down by Japanese gunners on Chichi Jima. He was rescued from his dip in the ocean by a submarine crew from the United States, but he did not get home until Christmas Eve, 1944. He had taken part in a total of fifty-eight combat missions by this time and received the Distinguished Flying Cross for his contributions.

George and Barbara were married at last on January 6, 1945, in the First Presbyterian Church in Rye, New York, and honeymooned on Sea Island, Georgia. For the next nine months, they moved from military bases in Michigan to Maine and to Virginia. They learned of the Japanese surrender in Virginia in August 1945.

Later that year, in September, Bush enrolled in Yale University, and their first child, George Walker Bush, was born in New Haven on July 6, 1946. George was busy with his studies in economics, and Barbara kept house and took care of their baby son.

After George's graduation in June 1948, the Bushes went to Odessa, Texas, where he started a new job with International Derrick and Equipment Company. They had not been in Texas a year, however, before George was transferred to California to work as a salesman of drilling bits. Their daughter Robin was born in December 1949 in Compton, California. She died at age four from leukemia. A second son, John, called Jeb, was born only a few days before little Robin's illness was diagnosed.

In 1950 the Bush family returned to Midland, Texas, where George and his uncle, G. Herbert Walker, Jr., and a partner, John Overbey, formed an oil development company. Three years later Bush-Overbey merged with the Liedtke Company to form the Zapata Petroleum Corporation.

During this period, Bush became active in politics with the Republican party. He campaigned for General Dwight D. Eisenhower in 1952 and 1956.

Ten years later, in 1966, Bush was elected to serve in the United States House of Representatives and he stayed there until 1971, at which time he was appointed ambassador to the United Nations by President Nixon.

George Bush had hoped to be nominated as vice president with both President Nixon and President Ford, but they found other jobs for him. President Ford sent him to China in October 1974 to serve as the chief United States liaison officer there.

In 1975 four of the Bush children were able to visit their parents in China after their schools got out for summer vacation. George Jr. had just graduated from Harvard Business School. Neil, born in 1955, was a student at Tulane University in Louisiana. Marvin, born in 1956, was scheduled to enter the University of Virginia when he returned home, and Dorothy, called Doro and born in 1959, was sixteen and still in high school. Only Jeb Bush did not get to visit his parents in China. He had recently married, and his job with the Texas Commerce Bank required him to stay home and work.

George and Barbara returned home on December 7, 1975, and in January 1976 he was named to be director of the Central Intelligency Agency. He served almost a year until President Jimmy Carter appointed someone else to the post. Bush received high praise for his work with that secret, sensitive agency from the Senate Intelligence Committee, now controlled by Democrats.

After he left the CIA, the Bushes went back to Texas to live in Houston. In 1980 he ran in some state primaries for the presidential nomination, but Ronald Reagan was chosen at the Republican National Convention. Reagan saw Bush was popular with voters, and he asked George to be his vice president on the Republican ticket.

Reagan and Bush were elected by 51% to 41% of the popular vote over incumbents President Carter and Vice President Mondale. They were inaugurated on January 20, 1981.

Two months later, President Reagan was shot in an attempted assassination in Washington, D.C., and Vice President Bush presided over cabinet meetings in his absence. He deferred all important decisions on policy matters until the president could return to his duties.

As vice president, George Bush served on task forces to revise or eliminate burdensome government regulations on businesses, on a task force to combat terrorism, and on one to stem the flow of illegal narcotic drugs into the country.

Bush traveled extensively in his eight years as vice president. He went to Russia, several European countries, China, and Beirut, for more than a million miles total. He attended cabinet meetings and meetings of the National Security Council, but he offered few comments and no suggestions. He viewed his role as being completely supportive of President Reagan.

Reagan and Bush were reelected in 1984 by the largest Electoral College vote ever received by any president in United States history — 525 votes to 13 for the Democratic challenger, Walter Mondale.

In 1988, Bush was seen as the heir apparent to the office of president, and he was nominated by the Republicans. His opponent was Democrat Michael Dukakis, governor of Massachusetts. George was elected with 54% of the popular vote and 426 Electoral College votes to defeat Governor Dukakis, who received 46% of the popular vote and 111 Electoral College votes.

During President Bush's administration, the Sandinista rebels were defeated at the polls in a free election in Nicaragua, and a woman president, Violeta Chamorro, was elected in that country.

Believing that Panama's leader, General Manuel Antonio Noriega, was a major drug trafficker who sent narcotics to the United States for sale, President Bush ordered an invasion of Panama by the United States armed forces. Noriega was captured and is still being held in a prison in Florida.

Annual inflation rates were low at about 3% while Bush was president, and interest rates were the lowest in twenty years.

The Communist government in Russia collapsed, and shaky democracies rose in many of the Eastern European countries. A civil war began in Yugoslavia between opposing parties, and it was still raging in 1995.

The Persian Gulf War erupted on August 2, 1990, when Iraqi forces invaded the emirate of Kuwait. President Bush told Iraq's President Saddam Hussein that if he did not withdraw his soldiers from Kuwait by February 23, 1991, a major offensive ground war would be added to the intensive aerial bombardment of Iraq already in progress.

President Hussein ignored all deadlines, and in one hundred hours United Nations soldiers from the United States, Saudi Arabia, Great Britain, Egypt, France, Syria, Pakistan, Morocco, Bangladesh, Canada, Italy, Senagal, Niger, and Argentina drove the Iraqis from Kuwait.

During their occupation, the Iraqis had set 732 oil wells on fire, burning six million barrels of oil each day, and they destroyed many homes, buildings, roads, bridges, and other facilities. Kuwait has a long, slow process to rebuild its country.

First Lady Barbara Bush was immensely popular with the American public, who responded to her grandmotherly image. She sponsored programs to aid children with disabilities to learn more easily to read and write, and she volunteered in helping homeless people. Her son Neil suffered from dyslexia in his childhood, and Barbara Bush knew the frustrations children with disabilities and their parents feel.

When Democratic challenger Bill Clinton, governor of Arkansas, defeated

President Bush in the 1992 election, the Bushes attended his inauguration before returning to Houston, Texas, to make their home. They make frequent vacation trips to Kennebunkport.

George Bush still owns interests in oil companies, and there are many grandchildren in the family to occupy George and Barbara's time and attention.

Bibliography

Bush, Barbara. *Barbara Bush: A Memoir.* New York: Charles Scribner's Sons, 1994.
Green, Fitzhugh. *George Bush: An Intimate Portrait.* New York: Hippocrene Books, 1989.
Radcliffe, Donnie. *Simply Barbara Bush: A Portrait of America's Candid First Lady.* New York: Warner Books, 1989.

44. James Danforth Quayle

Vice President Dan Quayle was the subject of many media jokes that verged on insults while he served his country. He had never lost an election before he became vice president and had served in both the United States House of Representatives and the United States Senate. Yet if one believed accounts of his career by news reporters, he was totally inept and incapable of serving in public office. Were potential voters so eager to vote for the handsome young man from Indiana that they ignored flaws evident to the reporters?

James Danforth Quayle was born in an Indianapolis hospital on February 4, 1947, to James C. Quayle and his wife, the former Corinne Pulliam. James C. Quayle was the advertising manager and sports editor of the *Reporter*, a Lebanon, Indiana, newspaper owned by Mrs. Quayle's father.

When the little boy was about twenty months old, he and his parents moved to Huntington in northern Indiana, where his father got a job with the *Herald-Press* and eventually moved up to become its publisher.

Dan attended the local public schools, made average grades, and was well liked by his classmates. His parents and grandparents were dedicated members of the Republican party. They discussed politics frequently, attended political meetings, and contributed to the campaigns of various candidates.

As a boy, Dan devoted his time to playing football and Little League baseball. He discovered golf when he was nine, and after that he spent most of his athletic efforts in improving his golf score.

In 1955, Dan and his family moved to Phoenix, Arizona, where they lived for the next eight years. In Phoenix, Dan had access to some of the finest golf courses in the nation.

When Dan was a junior in high school in Scottsdale, Arizona, his father decided to return to Huntington, Indiana, where he was named publisher of the *Herald-Press*.

Dan had not been eager to make the move, but he renewed old friends at Huntington High School and became a member of the varsity golf team. His friends were in the college preparatory group, and they attended ball games and dances for recreation.

Dan was good-natured and did not mind working at the newspaper during

J. Danforth Quayle. Reproduced from the collections of the Library of Congress.

his summer vacations. All the jobs available required lifting, sweating, and getting ink-stained.

Although Dan was not the top student in his class, his grades were good enough for him to gain admission to DePauw University, in Greencastle, Indiana. There he joined the "Dekes" (Delta Kappa Epsilon) fraternity.

Dan Quayle attracted more attention for his golfing ability at DePauw than for any other facet of his college career. He was a member of the college varsity team, and his coach, Ted Katula, said he became very competitive on the golf course, in contrast to his usual easy-going personality.

The Vietnam War raged during Quayle's college years, and antiwar demonstrators voiced their opinions vociferously, but Quayle never took any part in their protests. He graduated in 1969 with a major in political science. He had adopted the conservative political views of his parents and grandparents.

Six days before he graduated from college, Dan Quayle joined the National Guard. He was assigned to work in the information detachment, where he and others published a quarterly newspaper about National Guard activities.

A few months later, Quayle decided to go to law school, and he entered the Indiana University/Purdue University Law School at Indianapolis. He attended afternoon and evening classes, and during the day he worked in the office of the Indiana attorney general.

Quayle met Marilyn Tucker in law school. She was the daughter of Warren and Mary Tucker of Indianapolis. In 1972 they were married in a small family wedding. Marilyn held conservative views like Dan's, and she planned to practice law also.

Their first child, a son they named Tucker, was born in 1974 while Marilyn was studying for the bar examination. Both Marilyn and Dan were admitted to the bar that year, and they returned to Huntington, where they opened a law practice together.

They had only been working in their practice for a few months when Dan's father offered Dan a good-paying job with the *Herald-Press*, which he accepted. Marilyn stayed home to care for their baby son, who was joined by a brother Benjamin in 1977 and a sister Corinne in 1979.

Dan Quayle progressed in his job to being general manager and associate publisher of the newspaper. He and Marilyn were active on the social scene, which included sports events such as golf tournaments, in which Dan competed, Sunday school and church activities, and involvement in local civic organizations and projects.

Quayle was a member of the board of directors of the Press Club in Fort Wayne, and Orvas Beers, Republican chairman of the county which included Fort Wayne, asked Dan if he would consider accepting nomination for a seat in the United States House of Representatives in 1976. The incumbent representative, Democrat J. Edward Roush, had been in office for sixteen years, and the Republicans yearned to replace him with one of their own party.

When Dan asked his father's opinion, Mr. Quayle told Dan to run if he chose, but said he had no chance of winning. In this instance Father did not know best, and Dan won. Quayle's opponent had shared the senior Quayle's opinion; he had underestimated his rival's appeal and had done little campaigning.

Quayle served two terms in the House, and he continued to criticize congressional activities to voters back home as if he were not a member himself. He did not enjoy being a representative, and in May 1979, he decided to run for a seat in the United States Senate against incumbent Senator Birch Bayh, another long-term office holder.

To the surprise of many, Quayle won that election also by appealing to voters who viewed Senator Bayh as too liberal. He tied Bayh's record in the Senate to President Jimmy Carter's record in the White House, blaming the president for the widespread unemployment and raging inflation then plaguing the nation. Bayh did campaign, but the fact that Jim Quayle supported Dan's campaign in his newspaper also helped the young man.

As a senator, Quayle supported President Reagan's tax cuts, but he was distressed when youth training money was reduced. He enlisted the aid of Democratic Senator Ted Kennedy to help him get a jobs training bill passed that would help pay for training disadvantaged young people so they could get and hold jobs.

The Quayle-Kennedy Job Training Partnership Act was passed in 1982; President Reagan took credit for it in his 1983 State of the Union address.

For years Senator Quayle had been an advocate of term limits for government officials, and he tried unsuccessfully to rally support for such legislation in the Senate.

Quayle was chairperson of a task force of the Senate Armed Services Committee, which handled procurement for defense, and his fellow committee members considered him to be well informed. He remained skeptical about the wisdom of signing arms control agreements with officials in the Soviet Union.

In 1986, Senator Quayle was reelected by 61% of the popular vote in Indiana. Democrats regained control of the Senate, however, and he found himself a member of the minority party. For the next eighteen months, he did not present or promote any new legislation.

On August 16, 1988, George Bush called Quayle to ask him if he would accept a nomination for vice president to run with him on the Republican ticket that year. Quayle accepted in stunned surprise.

Quayle had barely begun campaigning when media reporters began relentlessly pointing out every mistake he made in his speeches. Michael Barone, who wrote for *U.S. News and World Report*, told Dan the reporters "could not stand the fact that the first baby-boomer in national political limelight wasn't a Doonesbury generation figure." In other words, Quayle was not perceived as politically correct.

Dan Quayle had a rough campaign — so much so that he finally began to see the endless attacks in a humorous light, and he quoted Winston Churchill of Great Britain, "There is nothing more exhilarating in life than to be shot at without result."

The verbal shots continued to fly until the 1988 election, when vice presidential candidate Dan Quayle and presidential candidate George Bush took the ultimate revenge on their critics by winning the election. On January 20, 1989, Justice Sandra Day O'Connor administered the oath of office to Dan Quayle, making him our forty-fourth vice president.

The Quayles moved into the official residence for vice presidents located on the grounds of the Naval Conservatory. It was originally built in 1893 for the admiral in charge of the conservatory. The Quayles had the third floor of the house remodeled to include bedrooms for their children; the work was done with money furnished by private donors.

Vice President Quayle's office was in the White House, and he spent most of his time there for the next four years. Marilyn Quayle assumed an active role in cancer awareness and prevention programs, as well as in disaster preparedness.

Dan Quayle wrote in his autobiography that he and President Bush had an excellent relationship. "I developed a true affection for George Bush," he wrote. "He was a completely genuine, decent man. As Vice President I was proud to have George Bush's confidence and was honored to serve him."

President Bush and his vice president always lunched together on Thursdays in the Oval Office or out by the White House pool, unless one of them had travel plans. Dan Quayle often did, as he and Marilyn traveled extensively in Asia and Latin America while he was in office.

The Constitution only assigns one definite duty to the vice president— presiding over the Senate and breaking tie votes on bills presented, if necessary. Quayle never got to break a tie vote during his four-year term. If President Bush had not sent him on foreign fact-finding missions, he would have had little impact on the government.

By 1993 the Quayles had made a total of seven trips to Latin American countries, each usually involving visits to several different countries.

They traveled to Bulgaria in 1991, accompanied by their children, Ben and Corinne. Vice President Quayle's mission was to sign an agreement with the Bulgarian president to send two hundred thousand tons of corn to that country to aid its faltering economy.

In February, 1992, the Quayles went to the European countries of Estonia, Lithuania, and Latvia, where the vice president congratulated the citizens on their newfound freedom from Soviet domination and promised medical aid from the United States government while they rebuilt their governments.

Dan Quayle believed it was President Bush's decision to vote for a tax increase in 1990 that led to their defeat in the 1992 election. He knew Bush had been elected on the promise he would not increase taxes, and Quayle thought voters believed they had been betrayed.

The success of the Desert Storm operation in Kuwait and Iraq did restore some of the public trust in the president, and Quayle supported the Bush decision to send American troops to defend Kuwait against the Iraqi invaders. Quayle went to Saudi Arabia and Kuwait to visit the troops during the rising conflict. He said he felt a special kinship with them since many of the defenders were National Guardsmen.

Quayle was ridiculed in 1992 when he protested about an episode on the "Murphy Brown" television program that depicted an unmarried pregnant Murphy choosing to have her baby without marrying the father, who offered marriage.

Dan Quayle said the scenario indicated an approval of such behavior and glamorized the situation, whereas in reality such children usually grow up in poverty and have more behavioral and emotional problems than children who live with both of their parents in a settled home environment.

Dan and Marilyn Quayle are both Christian church members who are not afraid or ashamed to talk about their religious beliefs. The media attention focused on their moral stand was critical, however, and jokes on the subject abounded.

Quayle's son Ben told his father that he and President Bush would lose the election in 1992. When the vice president asked why he thought so, Ben said, "Because you raised taxes." He said all his friends at school said the same thing.

When Dan Quayle debated the Democratic vice presidential nominee, Al Gore, Jr., Quayle stated that the presidential nominee, Bill Clinton, would raise taxes on everyone who made more than $36,000 a year and that he was not qualified to deal effectively with foreign crises. In response to these charges, newsmen Tom Brokaw and Jeff Greenfield both accused the vice president of misleading voters. Less than a month after President Clinton took office, however, his budget plans called for increasing taxes on all incomes of more than $30,000 a year.

After the inauguration of President Clinton, the Quayle family returned home to Indiana. Marilyn joined the law firm of Krieg, DeVault, Alexander, and Capehart in Indianapolis, where she worked only part-time and commuted. The Quayles built a new home, and Dan began writing a syndicated column for newspapers.

Dan Quayle mentioned he might be a candidate for president in 1996, but he was hospitalized on November 28, 1994, in Indianapolis for treatment of blood clots in his lungs, followed shortly thereafter by an appendectomy. He withdrew his name from consideration as a nominee for president in February 1995.

Bibliography

Fenno, Richard F., Jr. "The Making of a Senator: Dan Quayle." *Congressional Quarterly Press* (1989).
Quayle, Dan. *Standing Firm: A Vice President's Memoir.* New York: Zondervan, Harper Collins, 1994.

45. Albert Gore, Jr.

Albert Gore, Jr., was an environmentalist long before the movement became popular. He began holding hearings in 1981 about the greenhouse effect of global warming. Gore proposed methods that the United States could use to solve the problem, but President Reagan and his administration officials ignored him.

Albert Gore was born in Carthage, Tennessee, on March 31, 1948, to a United States congressional representative, Albert Gore, Sr., and his wife, the former Pauline LaFon. The couple already had a ten-year-old daughter Nancy.

Both of Albert's parents were well educated. His father had worked as a county school superintendent and studied law at night before he was elected to serve as one of Tennessee's representatives in the United States Congress. Pauline Gore was a graduate of Vanderbilt University, where she also received a law degree. She practiced law in Texarkana, Arkansas, for a year before she married Mr. Gore.

Al Jr. divided his time as he grew up between the apartment his parents kept in the Fairfax Hotel in Washington, D.C., and the Gore family farm of 250 acres in Carthage, Tennessee. He started school in Carthage and later attended St. Albans for Boys, a private school in Washington, D.C.

Alota and William Thompson were tenant farmers for the Gores, and they kept young Al when he was in Carthage. He considered Alota his "second" mother. Their son Gordon seemed like a brother to Al, and on hot days they swam in the cow trough, which was filled with the sulphur water so common in Tennessee. Alota worked as a nurse, and the two boys would either make their own breakfast, or William Thompson would cook for them.

Al attended school in Carthage through the third grade, and he always made good grades. At St. Albans he played football, basketball, and was a track runner. He received school letters in each sport his last three years in high school. His scholastic achievements qualified him for a National Merit Scholarship Award, which he decided to use to attend Harvard University.

At his graduation party at St. Albans in May 1965, Al met Mary Elizabeth Atchison, whom everyone called "Tipper." She had one year left at St. Agnes' Episcopal School for Girls in Alexandria, Virginia.

Albert Gore, Jr. Reproduced from the collections of the Library of Congress.

Both Al and Tipper went with other dates that night, but something clicked when they met. The next day Al called her and invited her to go to the movies, and she accepted. Tipper had heard of Al before she met him, and she was pleased to learn he was as attractive in person as she had been told. Their courtship continued for the next five years while they went to college and Al went to war.

Al entered Harvard University in September 1965, as the Vietnam War intensified. He was elected president of the freshman class at Harvard, and he graduated in 1969 cum laude with a bachelor of arts degree in government.

Tipper entered Garland Junior College in Boston in September 1966, so she could be near Al. She graduated with honors in 1968 and went on to Boston University, from which she received a bachelor of science degree in child psychology in 1970. By that time Al had been drafted and was serving as a journalist for the army base newspaper in Fort Rucker, Alabama.

Al and Tipper were married in the Washington, D.C., Cathedral on May 19, 1970, and went back to Alabama immediately after their honeymoon to find an apartment. The found a mobile home they liked in Horseley's Trailer Park, which had the Expando feature to enlarge the living room.

That same year, Senator Albert Gore, Al's father, lost his bid for reelection, even though his wife, his daughter Nancy, and Tipper had made political speeches for him all across the state of Tennessee.

Just after the election, young Al received orders to report to the 20th Engineer Brigade, stationed near Saigon in Vietnam. He reported for duty as ordered, but he and his father both believed United States' involvement in the war was wrong.

Al Gore was so profoundly shocked by the horrors he witnessed during the war, such as American gunners strafing civilians, that after he returned home in May 1971, he enrolled in the School of Divinity at Vanderbilt University to try to make peace with what he had seen.

Gore got a job as a night reporter with *The Tennessean* to pay his and Tipper's living expenses, and he worked there for the next three years. Tipper worked as a photographer for the newspaper after completing a night study course in the art of photography at Nashville Tech.

The Gores' first child, a daughter they named Karenna, was born on August 6, 1973, in Nashville. Shortly after her birth, Al and Tipper bought a farm near Nashville which had a nice brick house on it for their family's home.

In 1974, Al transferred to the law school at Vanderbilt, from which his mother had graduated in 1936. He left before graduating to campaign for a seat in the United States House of Representatives. Tipper quit her job to help him campaign, and he won the election at age twenty-eight, one of the youngest Tennessee congressmen ever elected. He was sworn into office on January 20, 1977. Tipper and their daughter moved to Washington with him, but he kept in close touch with Nashville, returning each weekend.

On June 5 that year, their second daughter, Kristin, was born, and Sarah, their third daughter, was born on January 7, 1979.

Representative Gore was honored for his effective work in the House on the issue of organ transplants and his interest in small business successes. He served on science and technology committees in the House, investigated illegal toxic waste disposal, and introduced legislation on environmental, health, and energy issues during his eight years in Congress.

In 1984, Al Gore ran for a seat in the United States Senate after Tennessee Senator Howard Baker announced his retirement. During the campaign Al's beloved sister Nancy was diagnosed with terminal lung cancer, and she died in Vanderbilt Hospital in July 1984.

Al won the election, receiving 61% of the popular votes. In the Senate, he was named to serve on the Governmental Affairs, Commerce, Science, Transportation, and Rules committees.

In 1987, Senator Gore decided to seek election in 1988 as president of the United States, and he campaigned vigorously. His hopes began to fade, however, as he failed to win primaries in Connecticut, Wisconsin, and New York. He withdrew from the race on April 21, 1988, and announced he would concentrate on his Senate duties in the remainder of his term.

Al and Tipper's son, Albert Gore III, was born on October 1982, while his father was still serving in the House. On April 3, 1989, the little boy was struck by a car in Baltimore, Maryland, as he and his parents were leaving a baseball game. He was seriously injured and required surgery and months of therapy to regain his health.

In 1990, Al Gore began writing a book on ecology, which was published by Houghton-Mifflin in January 1992. In *Earth in the Balance: Ecology and the Human Spirit*, Gore describes potential disasters to our planet if global warming occurs, if world populations continue to grow unrestrained, and if we continue destruction of our national resources such as wetlands and rain forests. Sales of the book were brisk; more than 100,000 copies were sold in 1992.

In May 1992, the question of Senator Gore running for president resurfaced, but he insisted he did not want the office of either president or vice president. Presidential nominee Bill Clinton, governor of Arkansas, had other ideas, and Al Gore was his first choice to be his running mate. They won the election, receiving 43% of the popular votes and defeating the incumbent president, George Bush, who got 37% of the votes, and the independent candidate, Ross Perot, who received 19%.

As vice president, Al Gore believes that he and President Clinton are close personal friends and that their administration is a true partnership. Gore stated firmly in an interview with James Brady in *Parade* magazine that he would be beside President Clinton in 1996, helping to reelect him.

Gore said in the same interview that his relationship with Speaker of the House Newt Gingrich is friendly, although he believes some of the policies included in the Contract with America would mean hardship for many American citizens. He hopes the Republicans will moderate their drives for reforming some programs and eliminating others.

Vice President Gore also said he has more time to spend with his family now than he had as a senator. They have weekend outings, and he attends most of their school and sports events.

Tipper Gore has most famously devoted her attention to a campaign to clean up profane and sexually explicit music lyrics, urging that the objectionable words in them be eliminated. She is a participant in child welfare projects and is a proponent of government efforts to eliminate homelessness in America.

Will the Gore family be future residents in the White House? Time will tell.

Bibliography

Brady, James. "In Step with Al Gore." *Parade*, April 16, 1995.
Hillin, Hank. *Al Gore, Jr.: His Life and Career*. New York: Carol, 1992.
McKnight, Gail. "Tipper Gore: The Vice President's First Lady." *Saturday Evening Post* (March–April 1993).

General Bibliography

DeGregorio, William A. *The Complete Book of United States Presidents.* Avenel, N.J.: Wings Books, 1993.

Foner, Eric. *Reconstruction 1863–1877.* New York: Harper and Row, 1988.

Gray, Ralph D., ed. *Gentleman from Indiana: National Party Candidates, 1836–1940.* Indianapolis: Indiana Historical Bureau, 1977.

Harwood, Michael. *In the Shadow of Presidents.* Philadelphia and New York, J. B. Lippincott, 1966.

Hoover, Irwin Hood (Ike). *Forty-Two Years in the White House.* Westport, Conn.: Greenwood, 1974.

Johnson, Gerald W. *America's Silver Age.* New York: Harper and Brothers, 1939.

Mintzer, Richard. *The Faking of the Vice President.* New York: Putnam Publishing Group, 1992.

Rugoff, Milton. *America's Gilded Age.* New York: Henry Holt, 1989.

Tally, Steve. *Bland Ambition.* New York: Harcourt, Brace, Jovanovich, 1992.

Witcover, Jules. *Crap Shoot: Rolling the Dice on the Vice Presidency.* New York: Crown, 1992.

Young, Donald. *American Roulette: The History and Dilemma of the Vice Presidency.* New York: Viking, 1974.

Index